Bloom's Literary Themes

Bloom's Literary Themes

THE LABYRINTH

Bloom's Literary Themes

THE LABYRINTH

Edited and with an introduction by
Harold Bloom
Sterling Professor of the Humanities
Yale University

Volume Editor
Blake Hobby

BLOOM'S
LITERARY CRITICISM
An imprint of Infobase Publishing

Bloom's Literary Themes: The Labyrinth

Copyright © 2009 by Infobase Publishing
Introduction © 2009 by Harold Bloom

All rights reserved. No part of this book may be reproduced or utilized in any form or by any means, electronic or mechanical, including photocopying, recording, or by any information storage or retrieval systems, without permission in writing from the publisher. For information contact:

Bloom's Literary Criticism
An imprint of Infobase Publishing
132 West 31st Street
New York NY 10001

Library of Congress Cataloging-in-Publication Data
The labyrinth / edited and with an introduction by Harold Bloom ; volume editor, Blake Hobby.
    p. cm. — (Bloom's literary themes)
  Includes bibliographical references and index.
  ISBN 978-0-7910-9804-2 (hc : alk. paper) 1. Labyrinths in literature. I. Bloom, Harold. II. Hobby, Blake.
  PN56.L223L325 2009
  809'.93364—dc22   2008042991

Bloom's Literary Criticism books are available at special discounts when purchased in bulk quantities for businesses, associations, institutions, or sales promotions. Please call our Special Sales Department in New York at (212) 967-8800 or (800) 322-8755.

You can find Bloom's Literary Criticism on the World Wide Web at
http://www.chelseahouse.com

Text design by Kerry Casey
Cover design by Takeshi Takahashi

Printed in the United States of America

IBT EJB 10 9 8 7 6 5 4 3 2 1

This book is printed on acid-free paper and contains 30 percent postconsumer recycled content.

Contents

Series Introduction by Harold Bloom: Themes and Metaphors

1. Topos and Trope

What we now call a theme or topic or subject initially was named a *topos*, ancient Greek for "place." Literary *topoi* are commonplaces, but also arguments or assertions. A topos can be regarded as literal when opposed to a trope or turning which is figurative and which can be a metaphor or some related departure from the literal: ironies, synecdoches (part for whole), metonymies (representations by contiguity) or hyperboles (overstatements). Themes and metaphors engender one another in all significant literary compositions.

As a theoretician of the relation between the matter and the rhetoric of high literature, I tend to define metaphor as a figure of desire rather than a figure of knowledge. We welcome literary metaphor because it enables fictions to persuade us of beautiful untrue things, as Oscar Wilde phrased it. Literary *topoi* can be regarded as places where we store information, in order to amplify the themes that interest us.

This series of volumes, *Bloom's Literary Themes*, offers students and general readers helpful essays on such perpetually crucial topics as the Hero's Journey, the Labyrinth, the Sublime, Death and Dying, the Taboo, the Trickster and many more. These subjects are chosen for their prevalence yet also for their centrality. They express the whole concern of human existence now in the twenty-first century of the Common Era. Some of the topics would have seemed odd at another time, another land: the American Dream, Enslavement and Emancipation, Civil Disobedience.

I suspect though that our current preoccupations would have existed always and everywhere, under other names. Tropes change across the centuries: the irony of one age is rarely the irony of another. But the themes of great literature, though immensely varied, undergo transmemberment and show up barely disguised in different contexts. The power of imaginative literature relies upon three constants: aesthetic splendor, cognitive power, wisdom. These are not bound by societal constraints or resentments, and ultimately are universals, and so not culture-bound. Shakespeare, except for the world's scriptures, is the one universal author, whether he is read and played in Bulgaria or Indonesia or wherever. His supremacy at creating human beings breaks through even the barrier of language and puts everyone on his stage. This means that the matter of his work has migrated everywhere, reinforcing the common places we all inhabit in his themes.

2. CONTEST AS BOTH THEME AND TROPE

Great writing or the Sublime rarely emanates directly from themes since all authors are mediated by forerunners and by contemporary rivals. Nietzsche enhanced our awareness of the agonistic foundations of ancient Greek literature and culture, from Hesiod's contest with Homer on to the Hellenistic critic Longinus in his treatise *On the Sublime*. Even Shakespeare had to begin by overcoming Christopher Marlowe, only a few months his senior. William Faulkner stemmed from the Polish-English novelist Joseph Conrad and our best living author of prose fiction, Philip Roth, is inconceivable without his descent from the major Jewish literary phenomenon of the twentieth century, Franz Kafka of Prague, who wrote the most lucid German since Goethe.

The contest with past achievement is the hidden theme of all major canonical literature in Western tradition. Literary influence is both an overwhelming metaphor for literature itself, and a common topic for all criticism, whether or not the critic knows her immersion in the incessant flood.

Every theme in this series touches upon a contest with anteriority, whether with the presence of death, the hero's quest, the overcoming of taboos, or all of the other concerns, volume by volume. From Monteverdi through Bach to Stravinsky, or from the Italian Renaissance through the agon of Matisse and Picasso, the history of all the arts demonstrates the same patterns as literature's thematic struggle with itself. Our country's great original art, jazz, is illuminated by what the great creators called "cutting contests," from Louis

Armstrong and Duke Ellington on to the emergence of Charlie Parker's Bop or revisionist jazz.

A literary theme, however authentic, would come to nothing without rhetorical eloquence or mastery of metaphor. But to experience the study of the common places of invention is an apt training in the apprehension of aesthetic value in poetry and in prose.

Into the Living Labyrinth:
Reflections and Aphorisms

If there is a temple at the visionary center, then the circumference may well be a labyrinth. Canonical literature has William Shakespeare as its center, while at its circumference his works form a golden labyrinth, to adapt a phrase from one of my mentors, George Wilson Knight.

I first learned from Wilson Knight that Shakespeare pragmatically had erased the distinction between sacred and secular imaginative literature. Not an Old Historicist any more than I am a New one, Knight never recognized at time-bound Shakespeare, and that seems to me the beginning of critical wisdom in regard to the creator of Falstaff and Hamlet, Iago and Cleopatra, Macbeth and Prospero.

But why a labyrinth, however aureate and vital the Shakespearean cosmos turns out to be? The image of the labyrinth is far more prevalent in Ovid, Virgil, Dante, Chaucer, Spenser, Milton, Blake, Coleridge, Shelley, Dickens than it is in Shakespeare. Modern literature gives us labyrinth-haunted genius in Yeats, Joyce, Kafka, Calvino, among others, in overt manifestations. And yet the image of *A Midsummer Night's Dream* may be the ultimate literary labyrinth, as G. G. Chesterson argued.

Homer in the *Iliad* (Book 18, lines 590-592) gives a famous image of the battle-shield of Achilles, which pictures the labyrinthine dance-floor that the artificer Daedalus constructed for the Cretan princes, Ariadne. Virgil, Homer's greatest disciple, is obsessed with labyrinths in the *Aeneid*, particularly in Books 5 and 6. His hero, Aeneas, fuses Daedalus the labyrinth designer and Theseus, who with Ariadne's aid destroyed the Minotaur, for whom Daedalus had built the major Cretan labyrinth as prison-refuge. Penelope Doob deftly enlarges this fusion with the giant figure of Hercules, whose labors foreshadow those of the heroic founder of Rome.

It may indeed be, as Doob shrewdly implies, that all truly literary text is labyrinthine, interwoven, interlaced. The *Aeneid* can be termed the most literary of all texts, always anxiously over-aware of Homer's influence upon it. Dr. Samuel Johnson, the inaugural anxiety-of-influence critic, made merry with Virgil's bondage to Homer, in an essay on the imitators of Edmund Spenser. All literary influence is labyrinthine; belated authors wander the maze as if an exit could be found, until the strong among them realize that the windings of the labyrinth all are internal.

Does any other image so fuse (or at least connect) high literature and life as does the labyrinth? The ancient identity of rhetoric, psychology, and cosmology is preserved in the figuration of imaginative literature *as* a breathing, moving labyrinth. Rhetorically the maze of influencings *substitutes* an ever-earliness for belatedness. Psychologically the meandering windings are the defenses by which we—any among us—survive. Cosmologically our labyrinth is the second nature we share as readers of the strong writers.

The Olympian gods in Homer are marked by their beauty, vitality, and lucidity. So are Hamlet and the other grand Shakespearean protagonists, but all three qualities are edged by mortality. Gods do not walk labyrinths or perform labyrinthine dances: Hamlet and his peers do little else.

No critic, however generously motivated, can help a deep reader to escape from the labyrinth of influence. I have learned my function is to help you get lost.

Literary thinking is akin to walking a labyrinth. Shakespeare necessarily is the paradigm of literary thinking. In his twenty or so years of composition he relied upon a cognitive power largely beyond our apprehension, and became the clearest instance we have of the mind's influence upon itself. His defense against the labyrinthine windings of his mind's force was to become more and more cognitively and rhetorically *elliptical*. Shakespearean *praxis* at its most mature is *the art of leaving things out*.

Labyrinths are emblems of ellipsis. Exits/entrances are left out. But this has (or can have) a benign aspect in reading. The highest imaginative literature bids you to become utterly lost in it, with no

Ariadne's thread to get you out. What this labyrinth persuades you to do is just to keep reading, and not at all how to live or why.

Vico says we only know what we ourselves have made. If you inhabit a labyrinth, then you created it.

All of us have the experience of admiring a structure when outside it but then becoming unhappy within it.

Penelope Doob remarks that Dante's *Commedia* is a labyrinth. So, I would contend, is every sublime work on a cosmological scale.

Boccaccio said that every woman was a maze. Ben Jonson called love the "subtlest" (most intricate) maze of all.

The labyrinthine became an image for the confusions of a lost life, yet that negates the image's wealth. All labyrinths are illusory, in that they can be mastered, sometimes by cunning, other times by chance. Themselves metaphors, labyrinths substitute for accurate directions, but what is can accurate direction within a literary work? All directions ultimately are at home in the capable reader: she herself is the compass of that sea.

Borges asserts you can lose only what you never possessed, yet that we become aware of others only by their disappearance. Those are labyrinthine observations, and I think they are mistaken. He had dwelled too long in his mother's cynosure.

Literary influence and literature are what Shakespeare called "the selfsame."

Solitude is one labyrinth, literature another. You cannot be a guide to a labyrinth, but to be sagacious as to literary influence is possible.

Reading itself may be a labyrinth but not to read deeply and widely is to be entrapped in the invincible labyrinth of ignorance and absence.

THE AENEID
(VIRGIL)

"Virgil's *Aeneid*,"
by Penelope Reed Doob,
in *The Idea of the Labyrinth: From Classical Antiquity through the Middle Ages* (1990)

INTRODUCTION

In this chapter from her book-length exploration of the labyrinth in classical and medieval culture, Penelope Reed Doob argues that "the labyrinth constitutes a major if sometimes covert thread in the elaborate *textus* of the *Aeneid*, providing structural pattern and leitmotif." Tracing Aeneas's labyrinthine journey to found Rome, taking care to note recurrences of the labyrinth image and references to the mythology surrounding its creation, Doob concludes that the text contains a "network of allusions that gradually shape a vision of Aeneas's life as a laborious errand through a series of mazes.

Hic labor ille domus et inextricabilis error.
Here is the toil of that house, and the inextricable wandering.

Virgil, Aeneid 6.27

Doob, Penelope Reed. "Virgil's *Aeneid*." *The Idea of the Labyrinth: From Classical Antiquity through the Middle Ages*. Ithaca, N.Y.: Cornell UP, 1990. 227–53.

The *Aeneid*, one of the most influential works of Western literature, is the earliest major example of truly labyrinthine literature: It includes explicit images of the maze and references to its myth, employs a labyrinthine narrative structure, and embodies themes associated with the idea of the labyrinth (as defined in previous chapters).[1] Although the importance of the labyrinth in Books 5 and 6 has not gone unnoticed,[2] the full extent and significance of labyrinthine imagery and ideas in the *Aeneid* have not yet been explored. I hope to show that the idea of the labyrinth constitutes a major if sometimes covert thread in the elaborate *textus* of the *Aeneid*, providing structural pattern and thematic leitmotif. Three works of complex visual art are described in minute detail in the poem: the doors of the Temple of Juno in Carthage depicting the Trojans' *labores* (1.460), the Cumaean gates with their Daedalian memorial of the Cretan myth, and the shield of Aeneas, proclaiming the future of Rome. The centerpiece of this triptych, the first thing Aeneas sees when he lands in his country of destiny, depicts the history of the labyrinth; this fact surely hints at broad potential significance for the image and its myth within the poem.[3] As we shall see, the labyrinths of Books 5 and 6, discussed in Chapter 1, are only part of a network of allusions that gradually shape a vision of Aeneas's life as a laborious errand through a series of mazes.[4] First I trace the idea of the labyrinth in the poem; then I explore its significance for the work as a whole.

The *labor* and *error* associated with mazes are repeatedly emphasized in the *Aeneid*. The poem dwells on *labores* of various sorts: works of suffering, achievement, and art. The psychological and physical *labores* of Aeneas, his companions, and his descendants are necessary to build Rome, whose characteristic art will be government (6.851–854), bringing order to chaos. Through his labors, Aeneas becomes a second, more complex, version of Theseus, the maze-tamer king who knows how to handle *errores*, and of Daedalus, inventor, artist, exile, and shaper of chaos. Aeneas's labors also render him kin to Hercules, whose labors are celebrated in Arcadia, whose slaying of the giant Cacus foreshadows Aeneas's destruction of Turnus, and whose successful descent into Hades preceded that of Aeneas (6.392).[5]

If labyrinthine *labor* ("hic labor ille domus"—6.27) pervades the *Aeneid* thematically and verbally, so does its labyrinthine twin, *error*, whether as circuitous wandering or as mental misjudgment. For example, Book 3 is a narrative labyrinth describing Aeneas's *errores* (1.755) throughout the Mediterranean, wanderings whose goal is a stable *domus* and whose geographical pattern imitates the meanderings of the maze. After much tracing and retracing of steps in Troy, Aeneas sails first to Aeneadae and then to Delos, originally an *errans* isle that was eventually fixed in place only to instigate other errors by its ambiguous oracles to wanderers (3.76, 96–101); the labyrinth's characteristic shape-shifting from chaos to order and from stability to instability, a recurrent motif in the poem, is thus reflected in the portrayal of Apollo's birthplace just as the labyrinth itself will figure on his temple at Cumae. At Crete, ancient home of mazes and Trojans alike, the voyagers vainly wish to retrace their steps to Delos (3.143) and find the end of their labors (3.145). Despite divine and human guidance, they wander through blind waves (3.200, 204) to the Strophades, where the Harpies give directions but predict obstacles. At Buthrotum, Helenus prophesies a circuitous course (3.376) on pathless tracks (3.383) before Aeneas may find rest after labor (3.393) in Italy, so near in space yet so distant in time. Instead of taking the nearest path, Helenus advises, Aeneas must go the longest way round (3.412–413, 430), until finally the Sibyl shows the path and tells what *labor* to flee and what to follow (3.459–460).[6] Although the proper route is clearly defined, the Trojans take the shortest path despite Helenus's warning (3–507); soon they are lost, *ignari viae* (3.569)— the human condition in this poem's universe—and must retrace their steps (3.686–691), arriving at an illusory end of wandering labors in Drepanum (3.714). After further *errores* (1.32), they wander off course, driven to Carthage by Juno's storm. Throughout their erratic voyage the Trojans confront typically labyrinthine dangers: circuitous paths that near a goal only to turn away or reveal the goal as false; enforced delay and hesitation among uncertain choices; unreliable guides in the form of ambiguous visions and prophecies or uncertain helmsmen plagued by darkness; perils represented or announced by monsters as double in form as the Minotaur—the Trojan Horse, wooden animal concealing men; Polydorus, whose vegetable form has human blood; the bird-maiden Harpies; the dog-maiden Scylla. By such methods the text covertly establishes the image of the labyrinth: *labor* through blind *error*,[7] a seemingly endless search for a clear path to the perpetually deferred goal of *requies* after *labor*, a preordained *domes.* If *labor* is the content of Aeneas's mission, *errores* define its form: the two concepts are as intimately connected in the poem as in a maze. Success, therefore, demands both the persistent patience of the passive unicursal maze-walker and the active intelligence that can choose the right path in a multicursal maze.[8]

While the *errores* of Book 3 suggest the subjective experience of tracing a labyrinthine path, analogues to the labyrinth as an object and to the *monstrum biformis* within figure at the start of Book 2. In the proximate causes of Troy's downfall, the Trojan Horse and the serpents that kill Laocoon and his sons,[9] we may detect a constellation of words and ideas traditionally linked with the labyrinth. Like the Cretan labyrinth defined by Virgil himself in Books 5 and 6 (see Chapter 1), the horse is a monumental work of art linked with trickery (*dolus*: 2.15, 44—cf. 5.590, 6.29) and built by guileful Greeks (Calchas and Epeos vs. Daedalus). Both creations are intricately woven (*textum*: 2.16, 185—cf. 5.589, 593) and contain *error* (2.48, 6.27). Like the Cretan maze, the horse is dark and cavernous (*caecus*: 2:19, 5.89, 6.30; *caverna*, 2.19, 53—implicit in Books 5 and 6). Labyrinth and horse alike contain both danger and crafty Greeks: the Minotaur and the Athenians Daedalus and Theseus in the labyrinth, Ulysses and his companions in the horse. Each involves a hybrid *monstrum biformis*: the Minotaur is a fierce bull-man, the horse a wooden animal containing armed men. Both are prisons, the labyrinth intentionally and the horse temporarily (2.257–259), but both become extricable through treachery: Ariadne's and Sinon's (he too is a Greek master of artful deceit—2.195). Each structure was built to deceive and then to kill, and each bewilders its beholders (2.39, 5.589) before destroying them.[10] Confusion before a labyrinthine dilemma, and the question of how best to tackle that situation, will be a recurrent motif in the *Aeneid*, and its history starts here, as Aeneas begins his narration.

Confronted by the baffling and deceptive work of labyrinthine art, the Trojans hesitate, filled with doubt (2.39). In contrast, the hasty Laocoon charges forward, denounces the horse as a weapon, a hiding place for Greeks, or some other trick (*error*), and hurls his spear at its curved side. He sees the significance of the dangerous horse almost as clearly as Daedalus understood the maze, and his intended solution to the mystery is nothing if not direct. But while Laocoon's mind penetrates the horse, his spear does not: straightforward approaches and brute force may kill minotaurs, but they don't work with mazes. Had Theseus plunged into the labyrinth unprepared, death would have been certain, and almost throughout the poem, whenever Aeneas tries a direct route, he is forced into circuity. Laocoon's instincts are right: if Troy is to survive, the horse must be destroyed. But just as the Greeks have deceptively constructed their labyrinthine horse, so fate and the gods have shaped a labyrinthine trap for the Trojans; in the cosmic scheme of things, Troy must fall or Rome cannot be founded. Caught in the larger labyrinth crafted by the gods (a subject to which we will return), Laocoon cannot succeed.

The immediate instrument of Laocoon's downfall, and indirectly of Troy's—the twin serpents—also has something in common with mazes. With their vast coils (2.204), their sinuosity (2.208), their entanglements (2.215), their reduplicated windings (2.218), their knots (2.220), the snakes are as circuitous as the maze and, while not individually *biformis*, taken together they are as double as the Minotaur itself. When these monstrous beasts glide in from Tenedos, Laocoon is in the midst of sacrificing a bull, and the imperfect tense of the verb *mactabat* (2.202) is significant: while Laocoon has an accurate interpretation of the horse, his attempt to destroy it is futile, imperfect, incomplete, and similarly he can slay neither the bull nor the quasi-minotaurs within the horse. Instead, he himself is like a wounded bull half-sacrificed (2.223–224) as he falls victim to the mazy snakes.[11] Oddly enough, it is fitting that in his death throes Laocoon resembles the Minotaur as well as the bull he was trying to sacrifice: Laocoon must die if Troy is to be penetrated by the clever Greeks and Rome established. In this poem, Laocoon is unintentionally on the wrong side; trying to play Theseus's role and save his people, from the only perspective that finally counts he is the bull-man who must die.

Thus the narrative of Aeneas's *errores* requested by Dido (1.755–756) begins with two disguised manifestations of the labyrinth, though we may well see them as such only in retrospect: the deadly horse as a static parallel to the deceitful house of Daedalus and the serpents as a kinetic mirror of its fatal, convoluted duality, with Laocoon the tragic bridge between them. The crafty product and circling process normally united in the maze are initially broken into constituent parts,[12] but they come together when the terrible windings of the serpents open the horse's path to Troy.

Troy itself traditionally has labyrinthine associations: it gave its name to medieval and perhaps to ancient mazes and was, like some mazes, virtually impenetrable.[13] Ironically, the labyrinthine city is penetrated by labyrinthine trickery, and Aeneas, habitual treader of mazes, is driven from the labyrinth of Troy into labyrinthine *errores* thanks to the sinister manifestations of the maze in horse and serpents. Here we see that it is not only men who create labyrinths, but also nature and the gods: the human craft of the horse is supplemented by the terrible, divinely ordained serpents. The association of labyrinths with warfare, to be developed in the Trojan Ride and the battles in Italy, begins here, and perhaps too the idea that passion creates mazes, if there is a veiled parallel between the artfully built wooden cow (in which Pasiphae satisfied her lust and begot the monster that occasioned the maze) and the maze-like, minotaurish Trojan Horse, terrible consequence of the forbidden love of another *magna regina*, Helen, and Paris.

After Troy's walls are breached, Aeneas undergoes *labor, error*, and other labyrinthine experiences in the mazy city. He ignores Hector's injunction to wander over the seas—to seek foreign *errores*, as it were—and instead rushes about the city in blind fury, searching a path to the center (2.359–360) and undertaking untold *labores* (2.362). There is a covert allusion to the Cretan myth, and perhaps an implication that the tragic cycle of the labyrinth myth is destined for repetition, when Aeneas kills the Greek Androgeos, namesake of Minos's son, whose death caused the Athenian tribute to the Minotaur.[14] As Aeneas follows the path of Fortune rather than common sense (2.387–388), his *error* (2.412) in donning Greek arms leads to the death of many Trojans. He penetrates the labyrinthine house of Priam with its secret doors and fifty chambers, and his mother, Venus, promises an end to his *labores*, granting him a momentary privileged view above the labyrinth of Troy by revealing the gods themselves in combat. Leading his family to safety, he and his comrades seek one goal by many paths (2.716) as in a multicursal labyrinth; they almost achieve it (2.730–731), but Anchises alarms Aeneas, who runs confusedly through unknown byways (2.736), losing Creusa but reaching safety—escaping the maze of Troy, as it were. Immediately he retraces his steps into chaos (2.750–754) until Creusa's ghost sends him forth to Hesperia and a royal wife. Thus Aeneas's path within

and sets up the expectation that he
e maze after another, just as he has
ı. Significantly, he wanders *despite*
or and Venus and, once, *because* of
e dangerous but ultimately profit-
oks 3 (the journey to Crete), 5 (the
rney through Hades).

se adopting a perspective from
em a profound sense of human
a more detached overview, see
e *Aeneid* as in a labyrinth, both
ılly valid, and one might argue
e the odds are so long, fleeting
incide) are all the more laud-
...ʋıve chaos and order, destiny and
...ıor and triumph—all held in balance, all perspective-
dependent. In the *Aeneid*, that is simply how the universe is built.

Book I begins with Virgil's singing of Aeneas's quests for a stable
city and ends with another song by the Carthaginian Iopas: "hic canit
errantem lunam solisque labores" (1.742). "He tells of the wandering
moon and the sun's labors": the creation of man and beast, rain and
fire, the guiding *Triones*, haste and delay. Iopas's song, carefully
balancing one item against another, is a tightly structured *labor*, a
work of art like Virgil's, though in miniature. Iopas condenses and
crystallizes the labyrinthine meanings and cycles of the *Aeneid*: in
the beginning were *error* and *labor*, the moon and the sun, the twins
Diana and Apollo, who guard the double Cumaean doors. In the
beginning was the cosmic labyrinth. And the results? Man and beast,
the elements of the Minotaur. Rain and fire, life-giving and life-
destroying, elements of Aeneas's sea journeys and Dido's passion and
the Italian wars, elements coming together in the repeated image of
the storm. The "gemini Triones," the constellation of the plough-
oxen or the greater and lesser bears:[16] these celestial guides are also
beasts, one destructive, the other plodding but productive, the pairing
suggesting the minotaur that is man with his double nature. Speed
and delay, straightforward passage vs. the circuitousness of the labyrinth. In the world of the poem as in Iopas's song, all these dualities

are necessary and inescapable; together they define the cosmic labyrinth within which human history, before and after death, must also
be a story of journeys through the maze. As for the art that gives us a
privileged view of the labyrinth, we are left with an analogous vision:
Daedalus crafting a well-structured but unfinished sculpture that is
only partially studied by Aeneas in an elaborately constructed but
unfinished, or at least unpolished, poem.[17]

NOTES

1. In this [article] I [follow] the LCL Latin text of the *Aeneid*,
   trans. Fairclough, but translations are my own unless otherwise
   noted.
2. See Robert W. Cruttwell, *Virgil's Mind at Work: An Analysis
   of the Symbolism of the Aeneid* (1947; rpt. New York: Cooper
   Square Publishers, 1969), chap. 7, for a fairly comprehensive
   but bizarre examination of labyrinths in the poem; Mario di
   Cesare, *The Altar and the City: A Reading of Virgil's Aeneid* (New
   York: Columbia University Press, 1974), pp. 83–84 and chap.
   4; William Fitzgerald, "Aeneas, Daedalus, and the Labyrinth,"
   Arethusa, 17 (1984), 51–65 (the best study to appear to date);
   W.F. Jackson Knight, "Vergil and the Maze," *CR*, 43 (1929),
   212–213, and, following Cruttwell's work, *Roman Vergil*
   (London: Faber & Faber, 1944), pp. 167–169, and *Vergil: Epic
   and Anthropology* (London: Allen & Unwin, 1967), chaps. 8–9;
   Michael C. Putnam, *The Poetry of the Aeneid* (1965; rpt. Ithaca:
   Cornell University Press, 1989), pp. 85–88; and Clark, *Catabasis*,
   chap. 6.

   Focusing more narrowly on Daedalus and the Cumaean
   gates in Book 6: William S. Anderson, *The Art of the Aeneid*
   (Englewood Cliffs, N.J.: Prentice-Hall, 1969), pp. 55–62; A.J.
   Boyle, "The Meaning of the *Aeneid*: A Critical Inquiry, Part II:
   Homo Immemor: Book VI and Its Thematic Ramifications,"
   Ramus, 1 (1972), 113–151, esp. 113–119; Page duBois, *History,
   Rhetorical Description, and the Epic* (Cambridge: D.S. Brewer-
   Biblo, 1982), pp. 35–41; D.E. Eichholz, "Symbol and Contrast
   in the *Aeneid*," *Greece and Rome*, ser. 2, 15 (1968), 105–112;
   P.J. Enk, "De labyrinthii imagine in foribus templi cumani

insculpta," *Mnemosyne*, ser. 4, 2 (1958), 322–330; Cynthia King, "*Dolor* in the *Aeneid*: Unspeakable and Unshowable," *Classical Outlook*, 56 (1979), 106; Margaret de G. Verrall, "Two Instances of Symbolism in the Sixth *Aeneid*," *CR*, 24 (1910), 43–46; Brooks Otis, *Virgil: A Study in Civilized Poetry* (Oxford: Clarendon Press, 1964), pp. 284–285; Viktor Poschl, *The Art of Vergil*, trans. Gerda Seligson (Ann Arbor: University of Michigan Press, 1962), pp. 149–150; Eduard Norden, *P. Vergilius Maro Aeneis Buch VI* (Stuttgart: B.G. Teubner, 1957), pp. 121–130; Harry C. Rutledge, "Vergil's Daedalus," *CJ*, 62 (1967), 309–311, and "The Opening of *Aeneid* 6," *CJ*, 67 (1972), 110–115; John W. Zarker, "Aeneas and Theseus in *Aeneid* 6," *CJ*, 62 (1966), 220–226.

And, discounting the importance of the labyrinth even in Book 6: Robert A. Brooks, "*Discolor Aura*: Reflections on the Golden Bough," *AJP*, 74 (1953), 260–280, repr. in Steele Commager, *Virgil: A Collection of Critical Essays* (Englewood Cliffs, N.J.: Prentice-Hall, 1966), pp. 143–163.

3. See duBois, who argues that the *ekphraseis* in the *Aeneid* "define massive, significant thresholds that instruct those who pass through them" (p. 29) and represent Aeneas's past, present, and future, which Aeneas understands less and less fully.

4. In what follows, I generally ignore Homeric parallels, cross-relations with other classical literature (including Catullus 64), and the Augustan context. I assume that Virgil knew the traditions preserved for us by Pliny, Plutarch, and others, even though that assumption cannot be verified (but see Enk on Varro and Pliny). I read from a medievalist's perspective [. . . yet] I do not read as a medieval commentator would have done: I have looked at a broad range of published and manuscript commentaries and marginalia, from Servius through the fifteenth century, and have found little to support my interpretation.

However, the vastly popular *Histoire ancienne jusqu'à César* (early thirteenth century) makes the Daedalian sculptures the focus of its précis of Book 6, and at least three manuscripts of this work select the labyrinth (twice accompanied by the Minotaur) as one of only two or three illustrations of the

whole history of Aeneas: for Paris BN fr. 20125, see plate 19,
Appendix, MS. 6, and Monfrin, "Les *translations* vernaculaires
de Virgile au Moyen Age," pp. 189–249; for Paris BN fr. 9682
and Dijon Bibl. Municipale 562, see Buchthal, *Miniature
Painting in the Latin Kingdom of Jerusalem*, pp. 68–87 and
Catalogue (also my plate 18). Surprisingly, Jeanne Courcelle
omits these illuminations in her discussion of *Histoire ancienne*
manuscripts: Pierre Courcelle, *Lecteurs paäens et lecteurs chrétiens
de l'Énéide*, vol. 1: *Les Témoignages littéraires*, and vol. 2, by
P. Courcelle and Jeanne Courcelle: *Les Manuscrits illustrés de
l'Énéide du Xe au XVe siècle* (Paris: Institut de France, 1984).
For readers of the *Histoire ancienne*, then, text and sometimes
illuminations would point to the importance of the labyrinth in
the *Aeneid*. [Other] medieval readers also noticed and creatively
imitated the centrality of the labyrinth.

    For a far-ranging discussion of medieval Virgil
commentaries, see Christopher Baswell, "'Figures of Olde
Werk.'"

5. On Hercules, see Anderson, pp. 70–72; Camps, chap. 8; Otis,
   pp. 334–336: Putnam, p. 134; Kenneth Quinn, *Virgil's Aeneid: A
   Critical Description* (Ann Arbor: University of Michigan Press,
   1968), p. 123; and Di Cesare, p. 146. Pseudo-Bernard Silvester
   cites Hercules as an exemplar of the virtuous descent to Hades:
   J&J, p. 32, and S&M, p. 32.

6. The idea of fleeing vs. following, related to the continuous to-
   ing and fro-ing within a maze as well as to the idea of choosing
   the right path, is picked up at the end of Anchises' commission
   to Aeneas in 6.892.

7. The *errores* are both mental and physical: neither Aeneas's
   nor Anchises' judgment is always sound, as Anchises himself
   acknowledges (3.181). Indeed, Aeneas's *labores* and *errores*
   generally involve at least a temptation to mental error.

8. The theme of labyrinthine wanderings is subtly heralded upon
   Aeneas's arrival in Libya, when he speaks in the words of a
   maze-walker: he asks that Venus lighten his labor and tell him
   where he is, for he has wandered in ignorance (1.330–333).
   She responds by leading him into a metaphorical labyrinth
   of love by describing the *ambages* (1.342) of Dido's life;

the *ambages* of the Dido episode will delay Aeneas's own progress. Dido's history also suggests the labyrinth: it involves complexity (*ambages*), blind impiety, the concealing and then unweaving (*retexit*) of the blind crime of her house (*caecum domes scelus*). The collocation of blindness, crime, a house, and weaving connotes a labyrinth. Dido goes on to found her city through deception involving a bull; this *magna regina* has something in common with the abandoned Pasiphae and Ariadne abandoned.

9. On the imagery and significance of horse and serpents, see Bernard M.W. Knox, "The Serpent and the Flame: The Imagery of the Second Book of the *Aeneid*," *AJP*, 71 (1950), 379–400, repr. in Commager, *Virgil*, pp. 124–142; Boyle, "The Meaning of the *Aeneid*: A Critical Inquiry. Part I: Empire and the Individual: An Examination of the *Aeneid's* Major Theme," *Ramus*, 1 (1972), 63–90, here, 81–85, and part II, 136ff. (on serpents and the golden bough); Otis, *Virgil*, pp. 242–250; and Putnam, *Poetry of the Aeneid*, chap. 1, which also compares Aeneas's wanderings in Troy with his journey through the underworld and Nisus's and Euryalus's quest through the "malignant maze of the obscure wood" (p. 57)—a comparison he does not explore further.

10. Like the labyrinth (cf. 6.29), the horse is ambiguous, eliciting competing interpretations among the Trojans. Moreover, the description of the wooden horse may hold an aural echo of labyrinthine *ambages*. Frederick Ahl argues that to read classical writers as they read each other, we must be alert to puns and "included" words—collocations of letters in one or more adjacent words that spell out, or sound very much like, other words—see *Metaformations: Soundplay and Wordplay in Ovid and Other Classical Poets* (Ithaca: Cornell University Press, 1985). If Ahl is right, one might hear hints of "ambagibus" in *compagibus* (2.51).

11. My association of the Trojan Horse and the serpents with the labyrinth myth is obliquely supported in Dante's *Inferno* 12, where the Minotaur, conceived in a "false cow" (12.13), plunges back and forth in a simile generally assumed to be derived from *Aeneid* 2.223–224 (*Inferno* 12.22–24). Apparently, the combined

ideas of the wooden cow and the Minotaur brought Laocoon's death to Dante's (subconscious?) mind.

For the Sophoclean tradition that Laocoon deserved to die for impiety, see Joseph Gibaldi and Richard A. LaFleur, "Vanni Fucci and Laocoon: Servius as Possible Intermediary between Vergil and Dante," *Traditio*, 32 (1976), 386–397.

12. The structure of the first episode in Book 2—Trojan Horse, Laocoon, the treacherous Sinon, Laocoon's death, the Trojan Horse—constitutes a concentric panel, one common method of achieving what I would call a labyrinthine poetic structure. See Di Cesare, *Altar and City*, p. 40.

13. Cf. the Tragliatella wine-pitcher, chap. 1 above and plate 2, and the names for turf-mazes in chap. 5.

14. Also noted by Boyle, "The Meaning of the *Aeneid*: II," 116.

15. Thus I would finally disagree with Boyle, who values Turnus more highly than Aeneas simply because Aeneas aims higher and fails to reach that goal; even at his worst, I would argue, Aeneas is more admirable even though imperfect. Putnam, too, is disappointed in Aeneas: *Poetry of the Aeneid*, chap. 4, esp. pp. 192–193. See also Douglas J. Stewart, "Aeneas the Politician," *Antioch Review*, 32, 4 (1973) repr. in Bloom, *Modern Critical Views: Virgil*, pp. 103–118.

Taking more moderate positions on Aeneas's failure are Brooks, Clausen, Johnson (who gives perhaps the most sensitive refutation of Boyle's and Putnam's positions, pp. 114–134), Parry, Hunt, Quinn (esp. chap. 1), and George E. Dimock, Jr., "The Mistake of Aeneas," *Yale Review*, 64 (1975), 334–356. For generally positive views of Aeneas's achievement, see Otis, esp. pp. 313–382; Rutledge, "Opening of *Aeneid* 6" and "Vergil's Daedalus"; and Anderson, *Art of the Aeneid*. For an overview of the debate, as well as a discussion of inconsistencies in the poem, see Quinn, "Did Virgil Fail?" pp. 73–83.

16. Often called the Septemtriones rather than the two triones. Presumably the use of one form would evoke the other, and although Virgil stresses duality in Iopas's song, seven is an important number for the labyrinth, as the common Cretan design had seven circuits. In this context, the seven circles of Aeneas's and Turnus's shields, already noted, connote the

labyrinth. Similarly, that Aeneas is inconsistently described as having wandered for seven years both on his arrival in Carthage (1.755) and almost a year later in Sicily (5.626) suggests an intentional association of Aeneas's wanderings with the labyrinth. The sevenfold serpent winding around the altar in Sicily might anticipate the labyrinthine Trojan Ride. One might also see a succession of seven cities leading from Troy to Rome: Aeneadae, Pergamum in Crete, Buthrotum, Carthage, Acesta, Alba Longa, and finally Rome.

17. See Quinn, "Did Virgil Fail?"; that the *Aeneid* remained unfinished at Virgil's death was well known to later ages thanks to Donatus's *Life*.

THE FAERIE QUEENE
(EDMUND SPENSER)

"The Prophetic Moment,"
by Angus Fletcher, in *The Prophetic Moment:*
An Essay on Spenser (1971)

INTRODUCTION

In "The Prophetic Moment," Angus Fletcher focuses on what he calls the "two cardinal images for [Edmund Spenser's] prophetic structure: the temple and labyrinth." Accordingly, Fletcher says the temple and labyrinth are "poetic universals," which are "sufficiently large and powerful images to organize an immense variety of secondary imagery, leading thereby to an equally varied narrative." Calling the labyrinth "the image of terror and panic," Fletcher explains how the labyrinth in *The Faerie Queen* forms a kind of continuum between "Terror" and "Delight," two poles that describe the epic itself and the experience of reading Spencer's great poem, which Fletcher sees as the work of a prophet.

As the author of a romantic epic in which, as Richard Hurd claimed in the *Letters on Chivalry and Romance*, a complex design orders an

---

Fletcher, Angus. "The Prophetic Moment." *The Prophetic Moment: An Essay on Spenser.* Chicago: University of Chicago Press, 1971. 11–56.

even more complex action,[1] Spenser depends heavily on two cardinal images for his prophetic structure: the temple and the labyrinth. These two archetypes organize the overall shaping of *The Faerie Queene*, and while other archetypal images play a part throughout the poem, the temple and the labyrinth, as "poetic universals," are sufficiently large and powerful images to organize an immense variety of secondary imagery, leading thereby to an equally varied narrative.

Temples and labyrinths have a singular advantage to the poet, in that they both imply special layout and a typical activity within that layout. Furthermore, while both images suggest man-made structures—men have built temples and labyrinths—they each have a set of natural equivalents. Temples may rise out of the earth in the form of sacred groves, while labyrinths may grow up as a tangle of vegetation. The cardinal dichotomy of the two archetypes will permit the typical Renaissance interplay of art and nature. For both images the idea of design is crucial, and their stress on pattern as such gives Spenser's intricate poem a certain stability.

Yet design itself may play an ambiguous role when the two great images are set in counterpoint against each other, because whereas the image of a temple is strictly formalized, to frame the highest degree of order, the idea of a labyrinth leads in the opposite direction. The labyrinth allows a place, and would appear to create a structure, for the notable indeterminacy of the textural surface of *The Faerie Queene*. Labyrinthine imageries and actions yield "the appearance, so necessary to the poem's quality, of path-less wandering," which, as Lewis continued, "is largely a work of deliberate and successful illusion."[2]

The image of the temple is probably the dominant recurring archetype in *The Faerie Queene*. Major visions in each of the six books are presented as temples: the House of Holiness, the Castle of Alma, the Garden of Adonis, the Temple of Venus, the Temple of Isis, the sacred round-dance on the top of Mount Acidale. Even the Mutabilitie Cantos display this "symbolism of the center," as the trial convenes at the pastoral *templum* of Diana, Arlo Hill. In many respects the chief allegorical problems of each book can most easily be unwrapped if the reader attends closely to the iconography of such temples, and for that reason Lewis referred to them as "allegorical cores," while Frye calls them "houses of recognition."[3]

Together the temple and the labyrinth encompass the archetypal universe of *The Faerie Queene* and in that sense their meaning is more than allegorical. It is a narrative reality within the epic. Heroes come to temples, which they may enter and leave, and they pass through a labyrinthine faerieland. This archetypal scene of heroic action is not Spenser's own invention, though he develops it with great ingenuity. As Frye argued in the *Anatomy of Criticism*, apocalyptic and demonic imagery polarize the structures of a truly vast number of literary works.[4] On the other hand, for English poetry *The Faerie Queene* occupies a special place, since it is the "wel-head" of English romantic vision. Since it is romance, and not pure myth, it modulates the images of shrine and maze, to fit the scheme of romantic *entrelacement* and its chivalric manner.

In essence the temple is the image of gratified desire, the labyrinth the image of terror and panic. While in its originating form myth is "undisplaced," here the images of temple and labyrinth may be rendered in a more "realistic" or romantic guise, so that, for example, the purity of the temple is represented as the chivalric equivalent, a noble and chaste prowess. Spenser "romanticizes" the apocalyptic temple. Similarly he romanticizes the demonic labyrinth, which he does not hesitate to represent in undisplaced myth, as a twining monster or shape-shifting demon, but which he more often displaces into more romantic forms which better suit the romantic level of his mythography.

The archetypal and the displaced treatment of the temple and the labyrinth lead to a rich tapestry. Critics have done much to illuminate the interaction of the two archetypes, but in the following account I shall try chiefly to bring out the fact that when the dichotomy is narrowed, or forced into visionary union, prophecy results. This vatic nexus will be seen to imply a mode of visionary history, which keeps *The Faerie Queene* close to reality even when it seems to be reaching out to a distant world of spirit.

[. . .]

THE LABYRINTH

The opposite of the ideal templar form is the "perplexed circle" which a metaphysical poet, Henry King, described in his poem "The Labyrinth."[5]

> Life is a crooked Labyrinth, and wee
> Are dayly lost in that Obliquity.
> 'Tis a perplexed Circle, in whose round
> Nothing but Sorrowes and new Sins abound.

Christian dogma blamed this bewilderment on a blindness beginning with the Fall. Thus Ralegh's *History of the World* speaks of men who, having "fallen away from undoubted truth, do then after wander for evermore in vices unknown."[6] Orthodoxy held that Christ alone could save men from this "home-bred tyranny."

> Thou canst reverse this Labyrinth of Sinne
> My wild Affects and Actions wander in.

Beginning his epic with a Christian version of the classical *in medias res*, Spenser makes a labyrinth crucial to the first episode of *The Faerie Queene*. Redcrosse, the Lady Una, and the Dwarf are caught by a "hideous storme of raine," a tempest, as Spenser twice calls it.

> Enforst to seeke some covert nigh at hand,
>   A shadie grove not far away they spide,
>   That promist ayde the tempest to withstand:
>   Whose loftie trees yclad with sommers pride,
>   Did spred so broad, that heavens light did hide,
>   Not perceable with power of any starre:
>   And all within were pathes and alleies wide,
>   With footing worne, and leading inward farre:
> Faire harbour that them seemes; so in they entred arre.
>
> And forth they passe, with pleasure forward led,
>   Joying to heare the birdes sweete harmony,
>   Which therein shrouded from the tempest dred,
>   Seemd in their song to scorne the cruell sky. (I, i, 7 and 8)

There follows the famous Ovidian catalogue of trees, each given its proper use and therefore brought into line with a human culture. The catalogue is an epitome of order and syntax, and Spenser projects its systematic character by a strict procession of anaphoras and exemplary appositives. If we were not alerted to the overtones of "loftie" and "sommers pride," the rich leafage darkening the light of heaven, we might notice nothing untoward until the last line of the catalogue: "the maple seldom inward sound." Otherwise this would appear a fine plantation. If the forest misleads, it does so in spite of something the travelers can praise, that is, in spite of its mere *nature*. Spenser, however, is playing on the old proverb about not being able to see the forest for the trees. His exceedingly strict stanzaic game disguises the spiritual danger inherent in the darkness of the forest, the *selva oscura*. Instead the stanza becomes an agency in the deception, providing a fine instance, I would think, of the "rhetorical" function of verbal formulas, which Paul Alpers has recently stressed in *The Poetry of "The Faerie Queene."* The deception is gradual.

> Led with delight, they thus beguile the way,
> Untill the blustring storme is overblowne;
> When weening to returne, whence they did stray,
> They cannot finde that path, which first was showne,
> But wander to and fro in wayes unknowne,
> Furthest from end then, when they neerest weene,
> That makes them doubt, their wits be not their owne:
> So many pathes, so many turnings seene,
> That which of them to take, in diverse doubt they been.
>
> At last resolving forward still to fare,
> Till that some end they finde or in or out,
> That path they take, that beaten seemd most bare,
> And like to lead the labyrinth about;
> Which when by tract they hunted had throughout,
> At length it brought them to a hollow cave,
> Amid the thickest woods. (I, i, 10 and 11)

Una, the embodiment of Truth, at once recognizes the labyrinth for what it is: "This is the wandring wood, this *Errours* den, / A monster vile, whom God and man does hate." The turbulence of the "hideous storme of raine" persists in the description of the monster Errour. Like the tempest that wrapped itself around the travelers, the dragon would surround them in natural or unnatural fury.[7] Spenser gains something at once by making his first antagonist a dragon whose "huge long taile" is a grotesque incarnation of the twists and turns of the maze: "God helpe the man so wrapt in *Errours* endlesse traine." Errour can so tie herself in knots that she creates her own "desert darknesse."

The encounter with the dragon links the ideas of error and wandering, suddenly fixing the malevolent aspect of the maze. This forest is ominous, threatening, and should produce a wise, dwarfish panic. Seen in this light the labyrinth is a purely demonic image, the natural cause of terror. So strong is the aftertaste of this terror that the reader may at once forget how pleasantly the forest had beguiled the unwary travelers. This is our first introduction to an ambivalence that colors almost every episode in the poem. As to the baffling form of the maze there can be no doubt, once one is "in" it. Though all avenues are promising, none ever gets anywhere. While some winding passages enter upon others, those others turn into dead ends, or twist back to return the seeker to his starting point. In the garden of forking paths an opening is often the barrier to an openness.

The artist of the maze may, reversing the idea of a temple, grow high and formal walls of hedge, or he may baffle the quester by thickening and complicating a natural outgrowth of trees, plants, rocks or streams. Spenser is aware of both the artificial and the natural maze, both of which are models in *The Faerie Queene* for a rich iconography of motion. The sinuous lines of the maze can be reduced to a mythic essence, with such characters as Pyrochles or Cymochles, whose names and behavior imply the motion of waves and furious, redundant turbulence. (This Milton later chose as a metonymy for both Eve and Satan.) More largely, when the maze provides a perverse map, the hero finds himself following the antitype of the direct and narrow "way" of salvation. In the phrase of Spenser's early *Tears of the Muses*, the blinded hero deserves Urania's complaint, since he has gone astray: "Then wandreth he in error and in doubt." Even Truth itself, as Una, is forced to wander.

> Now when broad day the world discovered has,
> Up *Una* rose, up rose the Lyon eke,
> And on their former journey forward pas,
> In waves unknowne, her wandring knight to seeke,

With paines farre passing that long wandring *Greeke*,
That for his love refused deitie:
Such were the labours of this Lady meeke,
Still seeking him, that from her still did flie,
Then furthest from her hope, when most she weened nie.
(I, iii, 21)

The allusion to Odysseus sets two kinds of wandering against each other, the erroneous wandering of Redcrosse against the "true" wandering of Una, who is patterned partly on the hero who refused immortal life with Calypso ("the hider"). The *Odyssey*, with its inset tales of utopian vision, joins the idea of wandering with the idea of a finally targeted quest, the return home. Thus wandering may satisfy a benign form of nostalgia.

More usually Spenser associates the state of wandering with the idea of blank extension—words that typically accompany wandering are "wide," "deep," "long," and "endless." Wandering may also be "vain." To wander is to live in a state of continuous becoming (if such a paradox can be imagined), so that Spenser keeps errantry and error in process, by preferring the present participle, "wandering," to other grammatical forms.[8] Like Hobbinol in the June Eclogue, the hero, suffers from a "wandring mynde," and he must govern his "wandering eyes." The strange and the monstrous, like blindness and vanity, are further associations of the image of errantry, and it is not long before the reader forges a yet larger associative link with this wandering motif: resemblances met in this meandering life often strike the hero as uncanny, *unheimlich*.

By dramatizing the "image of lost direction," as Frye has named this archetypal cluster, Spenser is following long centuries of tradi-tional iconography. Besides the dense forest, where the labyrinth is all tangle, mythology can pursue this sinister logic to its conclusion, where it discovers the image Eliot used for his microcosmic epic of the modern world, the wasteland. If the labyrinth is the archetypal order of things outside the temple, if it is the basic image of profane space, then its form is to be defined not so much as a material setting (trees, rocks, streams, etc.) as a general condition of unmapped disorder. The poet born into a Christian world will often suggest that outside the temple lies the desert, the place of inevitable wandering. Without a guide, like a Guyon without his Palmer, man appears destined to wander forever. In the desert he may die horribly, alone, or he may fade away in gradual exhaustion. The wasteland is an unmarked wilderness. The Children of Israel would surely have been lost but that "the Lord went before them by day in a pillar of a cloud, to lead them the way; and by night in a pillar of fire, to give them light; to go by day and night." Without such signs a man deserted cannot choose but lose his way, and wandering becomes his destiny.

Common to these images of the deserted profane space, with their burning sands and feeble, inadequate shade "under the red rock," is a cosmic emptiness, a terror that man and god have withdrawn from the evil represented by the unbounded horizon. When the sea is depicted as an element of chaos, it too shares in this iconography of cosmic desertion, for then sailors wander over its "pathless wastes." In a somewhat comic vein Spenser suggests this sea-born confusion in his myth of Phaedria, who pilots her "wandring ship" over the Idle Lake until she reaches the floating island. How much more fearful is the waste sea that imprisons Florimell, or the mythologized Irish Sea crossed by the shepherd in *Colin Clouts Come Home Again.*

> And is the sea (quoth *Coridon*) so fearfull?
> Fearful much more (quoth he) than hart can fear:
> Thousand wyld beasts with deep mouthes gaping direfull
> Therin stil wait poore passangers to teare.
> Who life doth loath, and longs death to behold,
> Before he die, alreadie dead with feare,
> And yet would live with heart halfe stonie cold,
> Let him to sea, and he shall see it there.
> And yet as ghastly dreadfull, as it seemes,
> Bold men presuming life for gaine to sell,
> Dare tempt that gulf, and in those wandring stremes
> Seek waies unknowne, waies leading down to hell. (200–211)

If the terror of infinite space may be realized on land and sea during the Renaissance, an even wider sense of the vastness of outer space grows apace, and poets may now envision the receding horizon through the yet larger forms of space travel, as in *Paradise Lost.*

During the Renaissance material horizons were rapidly expanding, notably those of the tiny island power into a world explorer and world trader. In *The Merchant of Venice* the profane world is mapped by an inversion of the stillness of a perfect Belmont—the wandering of lost merchant ships.[9]

The Spenserian meditation might be expected to come down heavily on a pessimistic note, but it does not. The poet opposes his own demonic imagery. Because the labyrinth comes to be his dominant image for the profane space lying outside the temple, the labyrinth becomes the largest image for faerieland as a whole. Logically then, if we except the final apocalypse of the New Jerusalem, the heavenly City, the sacred temple space will always be found *inside* the labyrinth. The human temple assumes the existence of the labyrinth, where it finds itself. The labyrinth specifies the large and open extensions of faerieland, the temple its perfect enclosures. As in a Western, without the desert there can be no stockade, no Fort Bravo, not even a Dodge City.

In principle, therefore, the profane world is simply the world outside, or before, the temple; it is *pro-fanum*. It thus has a neutral aspect, into which we must briefly inquire. On this level the profane world appears to be the arena of business, of mundane commerce, of the Rialto, the marketplace, the undistinguished, ordinary, everyday scene of man's mortal life. News here means largely the ups and downs of gain and loss. Such was the "profit and loss" of Eliot's drowned Phoenician sailor, and such "the motive of action" in *East Coker*. On the whole, on this level, life simply goes on, with the individual and the species seeking its own survival, if not its fortune.

The truth is complicated here, as with other archetypal clusters. What emerges from *The Faerie Queene*, as from *The Wasteland* and the *Four Quartets*, is a labyrinth imagery which is only apparently dualistic. As a picturesque beauty may be intricate so may the beauty of this poetic maze called faerieland. Edward Dowden wrote that "*The Faerie Queene*, if nothing else, is at least a labyrinth of beauty, a forest of old romance in which it is possible to lose oneself more irrecoverably amid the tangled luxury of loveliness than elsewhere in English poetry."[10] Loveliness is not the whole story, but the tangle and luxury are truly Spenserian, and their form is mazelike. They are basic Spenserian facts chiefly because the labyrinth itself permits an ambivalence. The

temple may perhaps be unreservedly benign and desirable. The labyrinth is, by contrast, suspended between contraries.

The labyrinth is not a polarity, but a continuum joining two poles.
It might be constructed according to the formula: Terror—neutrality
(indifference?)—Delight. The terrifying is readily understandable as
one pole. The delightful is less easy to account for. But even here the
poet is traditional. Military defenses had been early transformed into
the fanciful form of magical protections thrown up around a sacred
spot.[11] Hostile beings and influences cannot penetrate the web of
mazed spells cast by the medicine man. Such visionary defenses are
understandable enough, since the defenders of a real city surrounded
by an intricate outwork, would know its turns and twists intimately,
while the attackers would not. Eliade has observed that frequently
the labyrinth protected the temple by providing a trial of initiatory
access to the sacred world within. Perhaps on this analogy it could be
argued that the "delightful land of faerie" is a maze surrounding the
series of temples which comprise the heart of each successive book,
and that in this sense faerieland "protects" each temple. The labyrinth implies a rite of passage. "The labyrinth, like any other trial of
initiation, is a difficult trial in which not all are fitted to triumph. In
a sense, the trials of Theseus in the labyrinth of Crete were of equal
significance with the expedition to get the golden apples from the
garden of Hesperides, or to get the golden fleece of Colchis. Each of
these trials is basically a victorious entry into a place hard of access,
and well defended, where there is to be found a more or less obvious
symbol of power, sacredness and immortality."[12] This perspective on
the continuum gives faerieland a double value which Spenser's readers
have often observed, that while its lack of structure is threatening
to the hero, he still persists in his quest, as if delighted by his good
fortune in being awarded the heroic trial. Though each quest moves
ambiguously "forward" in the manner of Redcrosse and Una ("at last
resolving forward still to fare"), each quest also assumes the goal of a
homecoming. Not surprisingly we find that the most Spenserian of
the Metaphysicals, Andrew Marvell, is fascinated by the idea of the
protective labyrinth. This image governs the form of "The Garden"
and makes it a lyric temple never fully detached from the profane
world, where men, amazed, wander about, seeking fame and fortune.

The truly green nature that surrounds one in England lends substance to this mythography.

In a revealing passage of his autobiography C.S. Lewis caught this natural perspective on the problem of the protective labyrinth. He was talking about youthful walks in Surrey, which he contrasted with walks in Ireland, his homeland. "What delighted me in Surrey was its intricacy. My Irish walks commanded large horizons and the general lie of land and sea could be taken in at a glance; I will try to speak of them later. But in Surrey the contours were so tortuous, the little valleys so narrow, there was so much timber, so many villages concealed in woods or hollows, so many field paths, sunk lanes, dingles, copses, such an unpredictable variety of cottage, farmhouse, villa, and country seat, that the whole thing could never be clearly in my mind, and to walk in it daily gave me the same sort of pleasure that there is in the labyrinthine complexity of Malory or *The Faerie Queene*."[13] Physical perambulation here provides a model for reading Spenser.

Such walking tours of *The Faerie Queene* will generate a growing atmosphere of centeredness, as each picture of the picturesque scene is framed in the mind's eye, becoming a momentary symbol of the center. At such times the essential emptiness of Faerieland fills with structured shapes, and the reader will feel the presence of the temple as the tempering harmony of order in disorder. [. . .]

NOTES

1. "It is an unity of *design*, and not of action. This Gothic method of design in poetry may be, in some sort, illustrated by what is called the Gothic method of design in gardening"—a view which bears directly on the present concern with the maze. Hurd's criticism perhaps inaugurates the line of thought which culminates in Tuve and Alpers, the former with her theory of Spenserian *entrelacement* (*Allegorical Imagery* [Princeton, 1966], 359–70), the latter with his method of "reading" *FQ*, by stressing its "rhetorical" and formulaic character. Further, it may be useful to notice that critics like Tuve and Alpers are particularly expert in the exegesis of the Spenserian labyrinth, and in this respect their work contrasts with those who are biased toward

a "templar" exegesis, for example Frye, Fowler, or even perhaps
Nelson. The reader will find selections from a wide range of
critics, including those mentioned above, in Paul Alpers, ed.,
Edmund Spenser: A Critical Anthology (Penguin ed., 1969).

2. C.S. Lewis, *English Literature in the Sixteenth Century* (Oxford,
1954), 381.

3. Lewis's habitual epithet, "allegorical core," is from medieval
exegesis. Frye suggests that recognition scenes in this vein
are the culmination, as with Shakespearian romance, of an
educational art in which "providential resolution" is a kind of
knowing, recognizing. See "The Structure of Imagery in *The
Faerie Queene*," in *Fables of Identity* (New York, 1963), 77 and
109. In the same context Berger would speak of an Orphic myth
of reflection, which he has analyzed in depth as the idea of a
"retrospect." Memory plays a key role, therefore, in the critiques
of Lewis, Frye, and Berger.

4. Frye sets forth the polarity of temple and its opposite, the
demonic labyrinth, with their analogical parallels in romantic,
realistic and ironic literature, in his "Theory of Archetypal
Imagery," in *Anatomy of Criticism* (Princeton, 1957), 141–58.

5. *The Poems of Henry King*, ed. Margaret Crum (Oxford, 1965),
173.

6. Sir Walter Ralegh, *The History of the World*, chap. VI, sec. iii
(1621 ed.), quoted from Witherspoon and Warnke, *Seventeenth-
Century Prose and Poetry*, 26.

7. The tempest is emblematically associated with Fortuna, as
chance events are the maze-happenings. Donne plays with this
idea in "The Storm" and "The Calm." As demonic parody of
the temple, the tempest (Spenser's "hideous storme") creates its
opposite, the calm of the shrine. *The Tempest* thus shows, in the
Boatswain's phrase, how men "assist the storm." The entrance
of Master and Boatswain in act V, i, 216 ff. prepares us for
Alonzo's final admission:

> This is as strange a maze as e'er men trod,
> And there is in this business more than nature
> Was ever conduct of. Some oracle
> Must rectify our knowledge.

8. In "Milton's Participial Style," *PMLA* 83, no. 5 (1968): 1386–99, Seymour Chatman shows that older poets, among them Marlowe, Shakespeare, and Spenser, preferred the present participle to the past, while Milton's marked preference for the past participle creates effects of finality, absolute loss, etc., in *Paradise Lost*. The general principle of participial usage applies to Spenser: ". . . participles are derived from underlying complete sentences, including the subjects, even when subject-deletion has taken place; and . . . more than any other parts of speech, the participles are characteristically subject to ambiguity of interpretation" (1386–87). Thus Josephine Miles, in *Eras and Modes in English Poetry* (Berkeley, 1964), 15: "But Biblical richness and the Platonic tradition early offered to such poets as Spenser and Sylvester, and then Milton, the idea of a poetic language as free as possible from clausal complication, as resilient as possible in richly descriptive participial suspension." Not all of Miss Miles's "signs of such a mode" are to be found in Spenser, but the participial is very much there. On sentence structure in Spenser, see Paul Alpers, *The Poetry of The Faerie Queene* (Princeton, 1969), 74–94. Alpers does not stress the controlling function of the present participle; in general he agrees with Empson that Spenser engages in deliberate syntactic mystification. H.W. Sugden, *The Grammar of Spenser's Faerie Queene* (1936; repr. New York, 1966), 141, cites "With pleasaunce of the breathing fields yfed" (I, iv, 38.2) as "a striking example of the license which Spenser allowed himself in the construction." The freedom resides in one central term of chivalry, the infinitive and participial errantry of the knight.

9. See D.W. Waters, *The Art of Navigation in England in Elizabethan and Early Stuart Times* (New Haven, 1958); E.G.R. Taylor, *Tudor Geography 1485–1583* (London, 1930); G.B. Parks, *Richard Hakluyt and the English Voyages* (New York, 1930), especially chap. 15, "The English Epic"; and R.V. Tooley, *Maps and Map-Makers* (1949; repr. New York, 1962), chap. 7, "English Map-makers; English Marine Atlases." Tooley reproduces various maps of the Elizabethan era, including the map of Dorset in Christopher Saxton's *Atlas*, 1579, (plate 38) and one plate from Robert Adams, *Expeditiones Hispanorum in*

Angliam vera descripto (1590) (plate 39), showing the Spanish and English fleets ranged opposite each other during the Armada engagement. The Spanish fleet (Spenser's Soldan, V, viii) here appears in a crescent formation.

10. "Spencer, the Poet and the Teacher," from Paul Alpers, ed., *Edmund Spenser*, 164–65.

11. I am paraphrasing W.F. Jackson Knight, *Vergil: Epic and Anthropology*, ed. J.D. Christie (London, 1967), 202. The protective labyrinth is familiar to Elizabethans through the story of the Fair Rosamond, as retold in Daniel's *Complaint of Rosamond* and Drayton's *Heroical Epistle* of Rosamond to King Henry. The original notes to the latter include the statement that "some have held it to have beene an Allegorie of Mans Life: true it is, that the Comparison will hold; for what liker to a Labyrinth, then the Maze of Life? But it is affirmed by Antiquitie, that there was indeed such a Building; though *Dedalus* being a name applied to the Workmans excellencie, make it suspected: for *Dedalus* is nothing else but, Ingenious, or Artificiall. Hereupon it is used among the ancient Poets, for anything curiously wrought." Michael Drayton, *Works*, ed. J.W. Hebel (Oxford, 1961), 2:138–39. Cf. Jonson's masque, *Pleasure Reconciled to Virtue*.

12. Mircea Eliade, *Patterns in Comparative Religion* (Cleveland and New York, 1963), 381.

13. *Surprised by Joy: The Shape of My Early Life* (1955; repr. London, 1969), 118–19.

"The Garden of Forking Paths" (Jorge Luis Borges)

"Borges and the Legacy of 'The Garden of Forking Paths,'"
by Jeffrey Gray,
Seton Hall University

Toward the end of his life, the Argentine writer Jorge Luis Borges (1899–1986) complained that he was fatigued with the discourse of labyrinths and mirrors he had set in motion and said that he hoped others would now relieve him of it. But the abundance of labyrinths in Borges's work—whether as titles, images, or figures—make inevitable his association with them and with the philosophical paradoxes and mysteries they generate. Labyrinths run through the poetry, from as early as 1940 in the poem "The Cyclical Night" ("La noche cíclica"), to "The Labyrinth" ("El Laberinto") and "Labyrinth" ("Laberinto") in 1967. In the prose, they figure more prominently, from the title of Borges's most widely known anthology in English, *Labyrinths* (1962), to stories such as "Ibn-Hakam Al-Bokhari, Murdered in His Labyrinth" and the story that it contains, "The Two Kings and the Two Labyrinths." Finally, labyrinths appear implicitly in works where they form a subset of a larger trope, that of recurrence, recursiveness, or doubling-back, as in the many works—such as "The Circular Ruins"—that include circular movements. Tlön, in "Tlön, Uqbar, Orbis Tertius," for example, is "a labyrinth devised by men, a labyrinth destined to be deciphered by men" (*CF* 81), unlike nature, which is undecipherable. Carlos Navarro observes that Borges's labyrinths frequently exist through the metaphors of "houses, cities, deserts, mirrors, photographs, and, of course, books and libraries" (403).

Borges's most famous labyrinthine story is "The Garden of Forking Paths," which first appeared in his collection of that title in 1941. (It was later added to another small book, *Artifices*, to form the volume *Ficciones* in 1944.) The book was much celebrated by Borges's own literary circle but was unfortunately panned by Argentine critics, who called it, among other things, "an exotic and decadent work," too indebted to "certain deviant tendencies of contemporary English literature" (Williamson 260), and instead gave that year's awards to books with safer, more familiar Argentine topics: gauchos, caudillos, and tales of the pampas. Borges would have to wait another twenty years for the fame (dating most conspicuously from 1961, the year he and Samuel Beckett were jointly awarded the International Formentor Prize) that would eclipse not only those now-forgotten gaucho stories but also the works and reputations of all Latin American writers before him.

The plot of "The Garden of Forking Paths" is easily summarized: Dr. Yu Tsun, a Chinese spy for the Germans during World War I, discovers that his presence in England has been detected by the authorities. Before he is apprehended, he must convey to his Berlin headquarters the location of a British artillery installation in the city of Albert so that it may be destroyed. He ultimately communicates this information by murdering a man named Stephen Albert, whose name he finds in the telephone directory. When his Berlin chief reads of Yu Tsun's arrest for the murder of Albert, he infers the location of the military site, which he then orders to be bombed. In an uncanny and perhaps unbelievable coincidence, Stephen Albert, before he is murdered, reveals himself to be a Sinologist who has devoted his life to the study of Yu Tsun's great-grandfather Ts'ui Pên, a man who renounced the world to write a novel and "to construct a labyrinth in which all men would lose their way. . . . His novel made no sense and no one ever found the labyrinth" (*CF* 122). Albert is the only one who has divined the truth: that the labyrinth and Ts'ui Pên's book, titled *The Garden of Forking Paths*, are one and the same. Ts'ui Pên did not believe in linear time but rather in time as infinitely bifurcating, "a growing, dizzying web of divergent, convergent, and parallel times.

That fabric of times . . . contains *all* possibilities" (127). His book's structure (or apparent lack of it) reflects this concept. Albert thus regards *The Garden* as a work not of madness but of genius, and his life's work has been to rehabilitate Ts'ui Pên's (and therefore Yu Tsun's family's) reputation. But Yu Tsun, seeing his persecutors' approach through the window, knows he must act. With "endless contrition, and . . . weariness" (128), he shoots Albert in the back, thus transmitting the logistic information—which he knows the next day's newspapers will carry—to the Germans. Tsun is immediately arrested and condemned to death. The story we have read has been his deposition from a prison cell.

The idea of branching plots central to "The Garden of Forking Paths" had been entertained by Borges previously in "A Survey of the Works of Herbert Quain," which examines the writings of an obscure and unsuccessful Irish writer (invented by Borges), who, Edwin Williamson suggests, Borges may have intended to stand for himself. Among Quain's works is a detective novel titled *The God of the Labyrinth*, which far from providing the satisfying arc of a detective story with its mystery, tension, and resolution, offers, as Ts'ui Pên's *The Garden* does, alternative possibilities that more or less negate the solution that the detective has found. Quain is also supposed to have written a novel called *April March*, in which he presents time as an infinitely branching labyrinth. Indeed, all four of Quain's wholly nonexistent literary works are self-undermining. Borges playfully claims to have derived his own story "The Circular Ruins" from the third Quain story, titled "The Rose of Yesterday." In "The Garden of Forking Paths," Borges seems to have joined the self-aborting detective plot of Quain's *The God and the Labyrinth* with the time labyrinth of *April March* (Williamson 259).

"The Garden of Forking Paths," while sharing traits of genre detective fiction—intrigue, duplicity, persecution, high tension, and murder—also involves more deeply philosophical questions, particularly the idea of the endless proliferation of text, which one sees also in stories such as "The Library of Babylon," "Funes the Memorious," "The Babylonian Lottery," and "Of Rigor in Science," stories in which everything is part of a constructed system, with nothing remaining *outside*. This idea of the constructedness of "reality" is arguably Borges's most significant legacy. It is, at any rate, what identified him as a "postmodern" at a time when that term was being applied mostly to prose fictions and what marked him as a chief influence of North American writers such as John Barth and Robert Coover when the postmodern novel in English began to emerge in the 1960s. It is also what makes Borges seem so much part of the furniture of popular postmodern works at the end of the twentieth and the beginning of the twenty-first century, his influence arguably pervading best-selling fantasies such as *The Da Vinci Code*, as well as such films as *The Matrix*, *The Truman Show*, and the films made from the stories of Philip K. Dick (*Minority Report, Blade Runner, Total Recall*, and *Through a Scanner, Darkly* among others), in all of which reality turns out to be a material construction, a text, whether implanted, developed by androids, or, virus-like, proliferating of its own accord.

This sense of a world embedded in textuality is also what places Borges firmly amid the landscape of late twentieth-century literary theory, most obviously the labyrinthine ideas of such postmodern thinkers as Jacques Derrida, Roland Barthes, and, perhaps especially, Jean Baudrillard. Such ideas are exemplified by the cartographers in Borges's brief "Of Rigor in Science." There, the cartographers, in the interest of accurate representation, end up making a map as large as the world itself and ultimately indistinguishable from it. Similarly, the philosophers of "Tlön, Uqbar, Orbis Tertius" imagine a world so complete and detailed that it eventually encroaches on the one the narrator reports as real. In the infinite and eternal "Library of Babel," the narrator spends his life (somewhat as Borges himself spent his life) in a library whose bookshelves hold *all* possible combinations of words, letters, and ideas: "the detailed history of the future, the autobiographies of the archangels, thousands and thousands of false catalogs, the proof of the falsity of those false catalogs, a proof of the falsity of the *true* catalog," and so on, without end (*CF* 115). In all these fictions, Borges explores the possibilities of the idea that our representations (maps, books, words, or signs) are indistinguishable from, and indeed ultimately supplant, what they are supposed to represent.

These characteristics, moreover, identify Borges as the chief precursor of the South American and Mexican "Boom" novelists of the 1960s—though Borges never wrote a novel—such as Gabriel García Márquez; Alejo Carpentier; Mario Vargas Llosa; Carlos Fuentes; the fellow Argentine Julio Cortázar, whose *Hopscotch* shares much of the labyrinthine quality of Borges's stories; and the later Isabel Allende. In a review written in 1926 of "Tales of Turkestan," Borges admires the way in which "the marvelous and the everyday are entwined" in those stories, with no distinction between fantasy and reality. "There are angels as there are trees: they are just another element in the reality of the world" (Williamson 176). Thus, decades before the movement emerged, Borges had already identified the principle, though he never used the term, of "magic realism."

Borges's scholarly style was elaborate—it was, as Andre Maurois noted, that of Poe, Baudelaire, and Mallarmé—and Borges loved English novels in which the story derives from a found, if fictitious, text: letters discovered in an attic, a log aboard ship, or a secret diary. The first paragraph of "The Garden of Forking Paths" provides a ready illustration, quoting as it does an obscure note in a history of the Great War. Thus, the more theoretical term "textuality" can also more commonly mean, where Borges the librarian is concerned, "bookish"—in the sense of his fascination with libraries, ancient volumes, spurious and conflicting editions, and "delinquent reprints, prophets, heresiarchs, and other interminable labyrinths," ("Tlön, Uqbar, Urbis Tertius" 68). But this is, at the same time, the sense in which Borges is contemporary: He did not believe in originality; for him, all texts, including invented ones, were found texts, and all texts were mutually derivative. He remarks, for example, on Henley's translation of Beckford's *Vathek*, 1943, "The original is unfaithful to the translation." Moreover, why write a book, he thought, when one can write a short fiction *about* that book? "The composition of vast books is a laborious and impoverishing extravagance. . . . A better course of procedure is to pretend that these books already exist, and then to offer a résumé, a commentary. . . . I have preferred to write notes upon imaginary books" (10 November 1941, www.themodern-world.com/borges).

Finally, in addition to Borges's legacy to postmodern fiction and film, to literary theory, and to the renaissance of Latin American fiction, his stories anticipate the Internet. This is a remark often applied to postmodern intertextual writers, but it is more than usually applicable to Borges. If the Internet is a vast, shallow sea, it is certainly also a garden of forking paths. "Surfing" is a form of oblivion, in which one moves from one site to another, making choices at each fork, until one's original impetus is lost, if one had any to begin with. Borges's work in general and "The Garden" in particular have long been recognized by Internet theorists to be print precursors of hypertext. One may find a hypertext version of the story at http://www.geocities.com/papanagnou/commentary1.htm, where numerous related Web sites are listed. Could any other story be more appropriately hypertexted? Multiple words fork off onto multiple paths that go on forever. Other sites and lists devoted to Borges include www.themodernword.com/borges, www.onelist.com/subscribe.cgi/JLB, www.egroups.com/group/Spiral-Bound, and clubs.yahoo.com/clubs/thesouth. The best is reputed to be http://www.hum.au.dk/Institut/rom/borges/ in Denmark.

The legacy I have outlined, infiltrating so many aspects of contemporary thinking, seems to identify Borges as an avant-garde, ultramodern (or postmodern) figure, if not in fact the avatar of a global paradigm shift. The labyrinth itself has been interpreted to indicate Borges's rejection of teleology in fiction. But several ironies arise as a result of seeing Borges in this way, even leaving aside the author's drift in later life toward a more and more conservative politics, a position that earned him considerable disfavor with his fellow writers and very likely prevented his being awarded the Nobel Prize. One of these ironies is that Borges, far from repudiating teleology, had been—prior to his writing "The Garden of Forking Paths"—frustrated by his inability to write a straightforward plot. He looked to the conventional detective story as a model, believing that the realist (not to mention the modernist) novel had lost the classical narrative order that crime fiction retained. In this sense, it is paradoxical that Borges once referred to "the labyrinths of the detective genre" (qtd. in Williamson 258), because, as he remarked in a lecture, we live in a chaotic age and therefore find relief in the "classical virtues" of the detective story, which "cannot be understood without a beginning, a middle and an end" (qtd. in Williamson 258). The even greater irony is that, in a story about a revolutionary labyrinthine literary structure, Borges should have created his first completely plot-driven story, one whose theme rejects linear, unified plot but whose form fully exemplifies it. "I had Chesterton behind me," Borges explained (*Conversations* 511).

Thus, as Borges scholars have trained their critical attention on elements such as the fictiveness of reality, they have tended to ignore

Borges's realist aspects. After all, as noted above, there is only *one* plot in "The Garden of Forking Paths." Robert L. Chibka remarks that Albert's concept of Ts'ui Pên's work is that it will be passed on through generations, each individual adding chapters and correcting the work of his predecessors, but there is nothing labyrinthine about such a concept (Chibka 117). It is true that one character proposes a theory of multiple plots, but that theory "while perhaps problematizing the story we read, does not govern it" (Chibka 116). In other words, Borges's "The Garden of Forking Paths" bears no resemblance to Ts'ui Pên's novel *The Garden of Forking Paths*. Moreover, while Albert may claim that the characters of Ts'ui's novel choose all imaginable alternatives and that therefore "in the work of Ts'ui Pên, all possible outcomes occur" (206), that is an impossibility. The alternatives Albert cites are all, Chibka notes,

> perfectly conventional, drawn from a stagnant pool of plot components collected from epic, tragic, and detective traditions. They embrace armies marching into battle and murderers knocking at doors, but no broken shoelaces or mediocre stir-fries, no ingrown hairs or wrong numbers.... (116).

To try to account for all possible outcomes would be never to leave the starting block, just as the idiot-savant Ireneo Funes in "Funes the Memorious," in his effort to avoid categories and generalities by naming not only every individual stone, leaf, and animal on the planet but also every moment of their existence, would not have been able to get past the first day in the life of a dog: Infinite possibilities *at any moment* require infinite time, i.e., eternity. In terms of a labyrinthine plot, the first set of forkings would induce paralysis: There would always be one more; it is not even necessary to speak of the forkings of every one of those forks.

In achieving what he had longed for, a story with a plot, Borges had to tell *one* narrative. That story's convergence—in one physical place and historical moment—of individuals, crimes, thoughts, and events performs the opposite of forking. Moreover, Chibka observes, even if time *did* resemble a labyrinth of infinite branches, anyone situated on any given branch at any given point will not perceive a labyrinth; his or her story is one story. Perhaps "The Garden of

Forking Paths" teaches us this refutation of its title thesis, since, after all, the story's protagonist and narrator *kills* the only living proponent of Ts'ui Pên's theory. In the end, Borges, fascinated by labyrinthine ideas of time, language, and the mind, comes down rather firmly on the idea of a world in which one must live one life in chronological time. Perhaps this is what he means when, at the end of his "A New Refutation of Time," Borges writes, "The world, unfortunately, is real; I, unfortunately, am Borges" (*Other Inquisitions* 187).

WORKS CITED

Borges, Jorge Luis, et. al. *Borges en Japón, Japón en Borges*. Buenos Aires: Eudeba, 1988.

———. *Collected Fictions*. Trans. Andrew Hurley. New York: Penguin, 1998.

———. *Ficciones*. Ed. Anthony Kerrigan. New York: Grove, 1962.

———. *Labyrinths: Selected Stories and Other Writings*. Ed. Donald A. Yates and James E. Irby. New York: New Directions, 1964.

———. "Los Laberintos policiales y Chesterton." *Sur* 10 (July 1935): 92–94.

———. *Other Inquisitions 1937–1952*. Trans. Ruth L.C. Simms. New York: Simon and Schuster, 1968.

———. *Selected Poems, 1923-1967*. Ed. Norman Thomas di Giovanni. New York: Delacorte 1972.

Chibka, Robert L. "The Library of Forking Paths." *Representations* 56 (Fall 1996): 106–122.

Navarro, Carlos. "The Endlessness in Borges' Fiction." *Modern Fiction Studies* 19 (1973): 395–406.

Williamson, Edwin. *Borges: A Life*. New York: Viking, 2004.

THE GENERAL IN HIS LABYRINTH
(GABRIEL GARCÍA MÁRQUEZ)

"Of Utopias, Labyrinths and Unfulfilled Dreams in *The General in His Labyrinth*," by Maria Odette Canivell, *James Madison University*

"El adolescente, vacilante entre la infancia y la juventud queda suspenso un instante ante la infinita riqueza del mundo. El adolescente se asombra de ser. Y al pasmo sucede la reflexión: inclinado sobre el río de su conciencia se pregunta si ese rostro que aflora lentamente del fondo, deformado por el agua, es suyo. . . . A los pueblos en trance de crecimiento les ocurre algo parecido. Su ser se manifiesta como interrogación ¿qué somos y cómo realizaremos eso que somos?"

"The adolescent, however, vacillates between infancy and youth, halting for a moment before the infinite richness of the world. He is astonished at the fact of his being, and his astonishment leads to reflection: as he leans over the river of his consciousness, he asks himself if the face that appears there, disfigured by the water, is his own. . . . Much the same thing happens to nations and people at certain critical moments in their development. They ask themselves: What are we, and how can we fulfill our obligations to ourselves as we are?"

—Octavio Paz, 9

At times, Latin American nations appear as if they still suffer from growing pains. Their liberation from the Spanish yoke was one of the bloodiest among independence wars. Although originally divided into what the imperial crown believed would be heterogeneous blocks, after independence the former Spanish viceroyalties splintered into different nations sharing a common past, a collective history, and a dream of unity. As the famed Mexican poet Octavio Paz intimates, adolescents grow up in the process of becoming conscious about themselves. Like their human counterparts, nations undergo a similar experience; in the process of emerging as a state, *nations* wonder who and what they are and how they can better serve their citizens.[1] Gabriel García Márquez's novel *The General in his Labyrinth* explores this rite of passage.

The novel operates in two planes. On the one hand it chronicles the actual geographical journey of the ailing *caudillo* (leader) Simón Bolívar from the city of Bogotá to San Pedro Alejandrino, a state in the outskirts of rural Santa Marta, Colombia; on the other it narrates the spiritual voyage of the dying head of state who realizes his hopes for national unity have been dashed by greed, political opportunism, and internal strife. In García Márquez's tale, Bolívar's death represents the death of the Pan-American utopia, embodied in the Bolivarian dream. Unlike the utopias of Europe, Latin America utopian thought has been characterized by its tight "relationship with the socio-political context and social praxis" (my translation, del Río, 5). Bolívar's vision of a united and perfect South American single state is a paradigm of the former. Utopias, however, perish in the very act of becoming alive as they represent "the concrete expression of a moment of possibility, which is however annihilated in the very process of being enunciated" (Bann 670).[2] Because of its very nature, then, the utopian dream of national unity Bolívar espoused ceases to exist once it becomes an actual project; thus in the journey from the mind of the caudillo to reality, his dream—and that of the Latin American nations—exhales its last breath.

The style of the narrative, a mixture of historical novel and fiction, is unremarkable in a geocultural area where historical novels abound; this is, however, the first venture of the Colombian Nobel laureate as historian and novelist. Writing history masked as fiction "has been a popular topic in Latin America as novelists share the notion that, through fiction, history becomes humanized" and, therefore, more accessible to everyday readers (Borland 439); nevertheless, the Colombian author confesses that he was not "troubled by the question of historical accuracy, since the last voyage along the Magdalene river is the least documented period in Bolivar's life" (*GL* 271). In spite of this avowed denial, the author spent two years studying his subject, reading biographies of the Venezuelan-born caudillo, indexing cards, researching historical accounts and linguistic turns of phrases, as well as plotting, with the help of friends, astrological charts to get a better feeling for Bolivar's mind-set. Perhaps due to the impression of historical accuracy, readers feel a sense of reality that is, at times, almost surreal. The phantoms gnawing Bolivar's once keen intellect traverse labyrinthine passages leading to madness. The doomed general, oblivious to the outside world, chastises himself for his failings even as he assures long-dead former soldiers their deaths were not in vain. Laced with regret, the text serves as an instrument of atonement, allowing Bolivar to re-examine his life and the political consequences of his actions until he finally is forced to conclude he has been lacking. The general's gravest trespass, García Márquez appears to suggest, is his failure to accomplish the Bolivarian dream that should have been left as a legacy to his people: the utopia of a united South America, from Panamá to Tierra del Fuego.

With a structure remarkably similar to Tolstoi's "The Death of Ivan Illych," García Márquez fictionalizes the last eight months of the life of the "Libertador," taking readers along a labyrinthine journey, detailing his last days in power and his death. Faithful to the biographical format of the leader's life, the narrative follows Bolivar who, mentally and physically ill, takes a boat trip through the Magdalena river (a metaphor for the Stygian crossing), departing from the capital of the would-be *grand Latin American empire* (the five republics of Venezuela, Ecuador, Bolivia, Perú, Colombia and part of Panamá) until he reaches the anodyne plantation where he will die. The trip is a nightmare; Bolivar faces the prospect of his own death, the scorn of his people, and the continuous reminders that the country is on the verge of civil war. Ghosts and citizens alike appear to contemplate the general with regret, silently accusing him for the political quagmire that his precipitous exit from Santa Fé de Bogotá caused. When he finally arrives in San Pedro, the gravely ill general has exhausted his will to live. As he lies in bed, riddled by pain and hardly conscious, he sighs: "It's the smell of San Mateo." It is only then that the caudillo realizes he will never set foot in the land of his birth, Venezuela, as he is destined to be buried away from home, an exile in his former empire. When the fragrant aroma of sugar, carried by the breeze, momentarily masks the stench of his rotting body, he whispers, "I've never felt so close to home." The dying man's heart contracts as he sees the "blue Sierra Nevada through the window . . . and his memory wandered to other rooms from so many other lives" (*GL* 254). Knowing he is so close to home and yet so far zaps his failing strength. On the verge of a coma, the Venezuelan caudillo utters one of the most enigmatic remarks on record: "Damn it," he sighed. "How will I ever get out of this labyrinth?" (*GL* 267).[3] García Márquez uses these famous last words in an attempt to reconstruct the Bolivarian labyrinthine mind, lost to us partly due to the caudillo's madness but also because of the paucity of historical evidence coupled with the many contradictory statements attributed to Bolivar. Attempting to fill in the blanks of the last days of the Libertador, the Colombian Nobel Prize-winner endeavors to recreate in the novel the "real nature of Bolivar's political thought amid his flagrant contradictions" (*GL* 272).

Bolivarian scholars and researchers alike have tried to piece together (with little success) the puzzle of these dying words. Was he bemoaning the fate of the empire, hopelessly lost with the disintegration of the central government in Santa Fé de Bogotá? Was he sorry about the execution of the popular *mestizo* general Piar, as well as regretting the deaths of his former friends and supporters, many of whom he betrayed? Is he contemplating eternal life? As more than two-thirds of his letters, personal mementos, and records of his military campaign were lost, Bolivar's thought comes to us incomplete—at best *reformulated*—most of the time. Historians, sociologists, politologists, in short, the entire range of social scientists, have co-opted the words of the Libertador for their own purposes.

García Márquez, however, steers clear of the political controversy. The narrative, although quite brutal at times, is sympathetic toward this visionary leader of the independence struggle, who polarizes now, as he did then, the affections of those who have studied his work. To some, the last great dictator, to others the savior of Latin America, Bolivar embodies the concept of the Latin American Utopia. As

Johnson claims, "from the beginning, then, dystopian subversions were always part and parcel of the onslaught of idealism and the attendant assault on paradise in the Americas" (686). Bolivar's dream of a united Latin America, that "great chimerical shoreless nation," is an impossible enterprise.[4] Using as mouthpiece the ill-fated South American leader, García Márquez bemoans: "For us America is *our own country*, and it's all the same, hopeless" (my emphasis, 165). Taking a cue from the intersection of life and death that labyrinths afford their sojourners, the narrative chronicles the trip down the river, a kind of infernal descent into hell, with the ailing general becoming progressively more and more paranoid, beset by nightmares, voices that speak to him about the sad fate of his crumbling empire, and physical symptoms (mimicking the illness of the empire) that include tears of pus and blood. In the text, we find the inevitable parallels between the death of the empire and the death of the leader who had a vision for *la Gran Colombia*: the utopia of the Latin American unity. The author goes back "to the beginnings of the Continent's history in order to expose the enactment, the imprinting of imperfect mourning in the cultural unconscious of Spanish America." Thus, "Spanish American history begins with the loss, the negation of Bolivar's dream of continental unity, and it is under this sign of that original absence that Spanish America's cultural existence has developed to the present day" (Alonso, 260).[5]

The narrative teases readers with peeks at the labyrinth of the general's mind, interjecting flashbacks of the rise and triumph of Bolivar and his accomplishments as a military and political leader. As if traversing the complex maze of Latin American politics, the flashbacks double upon themselves to reveal what may have happened to Bolivar's efforts to accomplish the united "Latin American nation." García Márquez uses as literary props the point of view of Bolivar's faithful followers, his servant, José Palacios; his lover, Manuelita Díaz; his soldiers; and even former mistresses who visit the ailing caudillo upon hearing about his forced exile. In that fashion, the reader is able to tag along through a confusing journey, plagued with interrupted passages leading to nowhere and jumps in time that conflate into a chronologically disjointed nightmare as revisited by the increasingly feeble mind of the general. Bolivar, who at one point shaves his head in a futile attempt to rid himself of all the ghosts inhabiting his brain, traverses this labyrinth of madness, the exit from which, paradoxically, results in death.

Perhaps for its assertion of the inevitable death of Pan-American unity, as well as its indictment of Bolivar, the novel was received with an equal mix of criticism and praise. García Márquez is a polemical author, both because of his political views and unquestioned support of Castro's antidemocratic policies (among others) and for the complexity and uneven quality of his literary work.[6]

Considering his familiarity with dictators and harsh judgment of tyranny (*The Autumn of the Patriarch, One Hundred Years of Solitude*), García Márquez is surprisingly lenient with Bolivar, who some scholars claim was a megalomaniac who destroyed the chances for Latin American unity by being invested as ruler against the wishes of his people. As Bushnell claims, "the final dictatorship of Simón Bolivar in Gran Colombia added little, if anything, to his glory, while embittering his days with personal disappointments and political frustration" (65). The convention of 1827—the historical event that García Márquez alludes to in the novel—served the purpose of healing "by means of constitutional reforms the strains which were already tearing the nation apart" (Bushnell, 66). The literary narrative, however, places Bolivar inside this maze of his own making. The failure of the convention to reunite the wills and hearts of Latin Americans is portrayed in the book as a conspiracy of the enemies of the Libertador, who could not agree to the project of a grand nation. As a result, the caudillo complains that "the only ideas that occur to Colombians is how to divide the nation" (*GL* 252). On this last statement alone, which the author attributes to Bolivar, it is possible to find an explication for the general's dying words. Bolivar can't find an exit from the political quagmire he has helped create *because it was he who sowed the seeds of failure.* When he disrupted the rule of law with the excuse of the imminent second invasion of Spain, he failed to keep agreement with the Colombian Constitution of 1821, thus giving his enemies an opening to start the campaign that would later culminate in his precipitous exit from power.

The fictionalized depiction of Bolivar is as complex and difficult to understand as his historical alter ego. In one of the well-documented incidents of the general's life, Bolivar refuses one million pesos—offered in gratitude by the Peruvian Congress—on the grounds that he does not deserve the reward, yet a short time later he volunteers to pay the state's debts out of his own pocket, claiming, "I despise debt more than I despise the Spanish" (*GL* 221). The Libertador contradicts himself constantly, renouncing the presidency of Colombia and then reclaiming power within a few days, until hardly anyone believes Bolivar will do as he promises. The general addresses the people of Colombia, offering to send troops to "defend the integrity of the nation." But when pressed for an answer to the question of whether he will accept the presidency of Colombia, he demurs, quashing the last hopes of those who saw him as the only viable alternative for the ailing nation.

In a sense, it is perfectly appropriate that García Márquez attempts this novel about utopia in 1989, when it would appear as if "at the end of the century there is not any more space for utopias" (del Río, 1). The Bolivarian utopia of unity cannot be called a failed project but rather an expression of the necessity for change in the Latin American reality. Like many Latin American authors, particularly on the left (Allende, Benedetti, Neruda), García Márquez *dreams* in the dreams of the Libertador, believing by necessity in a united Spanish-speaking America. Regrettably, utopias die in the process of becoming reality. Thus, like in the nightmare of Bolivar, the hope of a nation extending from Panama to the south dies even before the Venezuelan caudillo is buried.

Like his twenty-first-century dispirited co-nationals, Bolivar despairs about uniting this complex region joined by a colonial past, a shared language, and a common history. Sadly, the differences appear to be more than the shared traits. As Atwood claims, "had Bolivar not existed, Mr. García Márquez would have had to invent him." The general becomes a symbol of the desire of every Latin American to have strong, well-adjusted nations, leaving the eternal pangs of adolescence to enter well-adjusted adulthood. Latin American states, however, still suffer from growing pains. Like the former residents of *la Gran Colombia*, asking the caudillo for advice, many of us, tired of seeing how little improvement has been achieved for the majority of our citizens, feel compelled to repeat García Márquez's words: "We have independence, General, now tell us what to do with it" (*GL* 99). This, according to Bolivar himself, is the clue to all the contradictions present in Latin America.

NOTES

1. I use the word *nation* as a substitute for the Spanish *pueblo*, translated into the English version of Paz's quote as "nations and people." The meaning in the original quote is "people," but it also includes the connotations of nation and community.
2. Quoted in Reed, "From Utopian Hopes to Practical Politics: A National Revolution in a Rural Village." *Comparative Studies in Society and History* 37:4 (October 1995), pp. 670–691.
3. On Dec. 10, 1830, Bolivar dictates his last testament. When the physician insists that he confess and receive the sacrament, Bolivar says: "What does this mean? Can I be so ill that you talk to me of wills and confession? How will I ever get out of this labyrinth?" (Vinicio Romero Mártinez, brief chronology of Simon Bolivar; *The General in His Labyrinth*, appendix).
4. Quoted from *The Autumn of the Patriarch* (cited by Johnson, 696).
5. Although I would not go as far back as to claim that the novel initializes the beginning of history for Latin America, as the latter scholar claims, since that would imply that history before the Spanish empire came to America and during the *colonia* did not exist, I agree with Alonso that the intersection between the beginning of Latin America's independent history and Bolivar's death is central to the narrative.
6. Claiming that the Colombian author has spent 25 years trying and failing to live up to his own standards, Stavans concludes: "García Márquez's literary career is curiously disappointing" (58).

WORKS CITED

Alonso, Carlos J. "The Mourning After: García Márquez, Fuentes and the Meaning of Postmodernity in Spanish America." *Modern Language Notes.* 109:2, "Hispanic Issue." (March 1994): 252–267.

Atwood, Margaret. "A Slave to His Own Liberation." *New York Times Review.* 16 September 1990.

Bann, Stephen. *Utopias and the Millenium.* London: Reaktion Books, 1993.

Borland, Isabel Alvarez. "The Task of the Historian in el General en su Laberinto." *Hispania* 76:3 (September 1993): 439–445.

Bushnell, David. "The Last Dictatorship: Betrayal or Consummation." *Hispanic American Historical Review.* 63(1), 1983: 65–105.

Del Rio, Yohanka Leon. "Ensayo sobre la Utopia." Ponencia presentada al Diálogo Cubano Venezolano "Globalización e Interculturalidad: una mirada desde Latinoamérica." Escuela de Filosofía. Universidad del Zulia, Maracaibo, Venezuela, 28 al 31 de marzo de 2000 (www. icalquinta.cl/modules.php?name=Content&page=showpage&pid=180).

García Márquez, Gabriel. *The General and His Labyrinth.* New York: Knopf, 1990.

Johnson, Lemuel A. "The Inventions of Paradise: The Caribbean and the Utopian Bent." *Poetics Today.* 15:4 (Winter 1994).

Paz, Octavio. *El laberinto de la soledad.* México: Fondo de Cultura Económico, 1989.

———. *The Labyrinth of Solitude.* New York: Grove Press, 1961.

Posada-Carbo, Eduardo. "Fiction as History: The Bananeras and Gabriel García Márquez's *One Hundred Years of Solitude.*" *Journal of Latin American Studies* 30:2 (May 1998): 395–414.

Reed, Robert Roy. "From Utopian Hopes to Practical Politics: A National Revolution in a Rural Village." *Comparative Studies in Society and History.* 37:4 (October 1995), pp. 670–691.

Stavans, Ilan. "Gabo in Decline." *Transition* 62 (1993): 58–78.

GREAT EXPECTATIONS
(CHARLES DICKENS)

"The Poor Labyrinth: The Theme of Social Injustice in Dickens's *Great Expectations*," by John H. Hagan Jr. in *Nineteenth-Century Fiction* (1954)

INTRODUCTION

In his essay on social justice in *Great Expectations*, John H. Hagan Jr. details how Dickens's novel is a condensed guide to understanding the way nineteenth-century social classes operate and the way Pip is caught in a judicial system that perpetuates class prejudice, a kind of labyrinth created by Magwich. For Hagan, Pip is "not only a hapless young man duped by his poor illusions, but a late victim in a long chain of widespread social injustice." Similarly, Hagan finds Magwich a kind of victim of a "great social evil: the evil of poverty, and the evil of a corruptible judicial system." According to Hagan, Pip "becomes for both Magwitch and Miss Havisham a means by which, in their different ways, they can retaliate against the society that injured them." Thus Pip, "in becoming the focal point for Miss Havisham's and Magwich's retaliation—the one who is caught in the midst of the cross fire directed against

---

Hagan, John H. Jr. "The Poor Labyrinth: The Theme of Social Injustice in Dickens's *Great Expectations*." *Nineteenth-Century Fiction*, Vol. 9, No. 3. (December 1954), 169–178.

society by two of the parties it injured, who, in turn, display in
their desire for proprietorship some of the very tyranny and
selfishness against which they are rebelling—becomes society's scapegoat." As Hagan demonstrates, "Dickens opens a
great vista, a 'poor labyrinth,' through which we may see the
present as but the culmination of a long history of social evil."

On the surface *Great Expectations* is simply another very good example
of that perennial *genre*, the education novel. In particular, it is the
story of a restless young boy from the lower classes who comes into
possession of a fortune he has done nothing to earn, founds a host of
romantic aspirations upon it at the cost of becoming a snob, comes
to be disappointed both romantically and socially, and, finally, with
a more mature knowledge of himself and the world, works out his
regeneration. As such, the novel is what G.K. Chesterton once called
it, "an extra chapter to 'The Book of Snobs.'" But while admitting that
Pip is a fairly good specimen of a certain type of mentality so dear to
Dickens's satirical spirit, we cannot overlook the fact that Dickens
is using his character to reveal some still more complex truths about
society and its organization.

Though its shorter length and more compact organization have
prevented it from being classed with *Bleak House*, *Little Dorrit*, and
Our Mutual Friend, *Great Expectations* is really of a piece with that
great social "trilogy" of Dickens's later years. In the briefer novel
Dickens is attempting only a slightly less comprehensive anatomiza-
tion of social evil; thematically, the implications of Pip's story are
almost as large. Consider, for instance, how many different strata
of society are gotten into the comparatively small number of pages
that story takes up. In the first six chapters alone we meet members
of the criminal, the military, and the artisan classes, together with a
parish clerk and two well-to-do entrepreneurs. The principal difference between *Great Expectations* and the more massive panoramic
novels lies more in the artistic means employed than in the intellectual
content. In *Great Expectations* Dickens strips the larger novels to their
intellectual essentials. The point of one line of action in *Bleak House*,
we remember, was to show how Lady Dedlock had been victimized by

social injustice operating in the form of conventional morality and its hypocrisies. But into that novel Dickens also packed a great deal else; the Lady Dedlock action was but part of a gigantic network. In *Great Expectations* all such additional ramifications are discarded. Dickens concentrates with great intensity upon a single line of development, and, to our surprise, this line turns out to be remarkably similar in its theme to that of Lady Dedlock's story. For Pip's career shows not only a hapless young man duped by his poor illusions, but a late victim in a long chain of widespread social injustice.

The story's essential features make this fact plain. We learn in Chapter XLII that the prime mover, so to speak, of the entire course of events which the novel treats immediately or in retrospect is a man by the name of Compeyson, a cad who adopts the airs of a "gentleman." Significantly, he remains throughout the book shrouded in mist (literal and figurative), vague, remote, and terrifying, like some vast impersonal force. Through his actions two people once came to grief. First, after stripping her of a great deal of her fortune, he jilted the spoiled and naïve Miss Havisham, and thereby turned her wits against the whole male sex. Secondly, he further corrupted a man named Magwitch who had already been injured by poverty, and revealed to him how easily the law may be twisted into an instrument of class. The trial of Magwitch and Compeyson is so important a key to the novel's larger meanings that the former's description of it in the later pages of the book should be read in entirety. What the passage reveals is that impartiality in the courts is often a myth. Judges and jury alike may be swayed by class prejudice. The whole judicial system may tend to perpetuate class antagonism and hostility. In short, an important element at the root of Magwitch's career is great social evil: the evil of poverty, and the evil of a corruptible judicial system. Though not entirely so, Magwitch is certainly, in part, a victim. The conventional words Pip speaks over his corpse at the end—" 'O Lord, be merciful to him a sinner' "—remain merely conventional, for the man was more sinned against than sinning. From his very first appearance in the novel, when we see him shivering on the icy marshes, he is depicted with sympathy, and by the time we get to the end, he has risen to an almost heroic dignity.

The connection of all this with Pip is plain. The young boy becomes for both Magwitch and Miss Havisham a means by which, in

their different ways, they can retaliate against the society that injured
them. One of Miss Havisham's objects is, through Pip, to frustrate
her greedy relatives who, like Compeyson himself, are interested in
her for her money alone, and who, again like Compeyson, typify the
rapacious and predatory elements of society at large. Magwitch, on
the other hand, retaliates against society by striving to meet it on the
ground of its own special prejudices. Though deprived from childhood
of the opportunity to become a "gentleman" himself, he does not vow
destruction to the "gentleman" class. Having seen in Compeyson the
power of that class, the deference it receives from society, he fashions
a gentleman of his own to take his place in it. He is satisfied to live
vicariously through Pip, to show society that he can come up to its
standards, and, by raising his pawn into the inner circle, to prove that
it is no longer impregnable.

Thus Pip, in becoming the focal point for Miss Havisham's and
Magwitch's retaliation—the one who is caught in the midst of the cross
fire directed against society by two of the parties it injured, who, in
turn, display in their desire for proprietorship some of the very tyranny
and selfishness against which they are rebelling—becomes society's
scapegoat. It is he who must pay the price for original outrages against
justice, who must suffer for the wider injustices of the whole society
of which he is but a humble part. The result is that he too takes on
society's vices, its selfishness, ingratitude, extravagance, and pride. He,
too, becomes something of an impostor like Compeyson himself, and
thereby follows in the fatal footsteps of the very man who is indirectly
the cause of his future misery. Thus the worst qualities of society
seem inevitably to propagate themselves in a kind of vicious circle.
Paralleling the case of Pip is that of Estella. As Pip is the creation of
Magwitch, she is the creation of Miss Havisham. Her perversion has
started earlier; as the novel opens, it is Pip's turn next. He is to be the
latest heir of original injustice, the next to fall victim to the distor-
tions that have already been forced upon Magwitch, Miss Havisham,
and Estella. He is to be the latest product of Compeyson's evil as it
continues to infect life.

But injustice does not come to bear upon Pip through Magwitch
and Miss Havisham alone. There is injustice under the roof of his
own house. Throughout the first stage of Pip's career, Dickens presents dramatically in scene after scene the petty tyranny exercised

over the boy by his shrewish sister, Mrs. Gargery, and some of her friends, particularly Mr. Pumblechook, the blustering corn merchant, and Wopsle, the theatrically-minded parish clerk. It is the constant goading Pip receives from these people that makes him peculiarly susceptible to the lure of his "great expectations" with their promise of escape and freedom. But more important is the fact that it is Pumblechook and Mrs. Gargery who first put the treacherous idea into Pip's head that Miss Havisham is his secret patroness. One of the very reasons they insist upon his waiting on the old woman in the first place is their belief that she will liber-ally reward him, and thereafter they never let the idea out of the boy's mind. In short, Mrs. Gargery, Pumblechook, and Wopsle do as much as Magwitch and Miss Havisham to turn Pip into his erring ways. To be sure, the novel is not an essay in determinism. But despite the legitimacy of the reproaches of Pip's conscience, we cannot forget how early his impressionable mind was stamped with the images of greed and injustice—images that present a small-scale version of the greedy and unjust world of "respectability" as a whole. The tyranny exercised over Pip by his sister, Pumblechook, and their like is a type of the tyranny exercised by the conventionally "supe-rior" elements of society over the suffering and dispossessed. Theirs is a version in miniature of the society that tolerates the existence of the dunghills in which Magwitch and his kind are spawned, and then throws such men into chains when they violate the law. When Pumblechook boasts of himself as the instrument of Pip's wealth, he is truthful in a way he never suspects or would care to suspect. For the obsequious attitude toward money he exemplifies is, indirectly, at the root of Pip's new fortune. It was just such an attitude that resulted in the debasing of Magwitch below Compeyson at their trial, and thus resulted in the former's fatal determination to trans-form Pip into a "gentleman."

Injustice is thus at the heart of the matter—injustice working upon and through the elders of Pip and Estella, and continuing its reign in the children themselves. With these children, therefore, we have a theme analogous to one deeply pondered by another great Victorian novelist: the idea of "consequences" as developed by George Eliot. Both she and Dickens are moved by a terrifying vision of the wide extent to which pollution can penetrate the different, apparently separate and unrelated, members of society. Once an act of injustice has been committed, there is no predicting to what extent it will affect the lives of generations yet unborn and of people far removed in the social scale from the victims of the original oppression. Though on a smaller scale, Dickens succeeds no less in *Great Expectations* than in his larger panoramic novels in suggesting a comprehensive social situation. No less than in *Bleak House*, *Little Dorrit*, and *Our Mutual Friend*—and in *A Tale of Two Cities* as well—the different levels of society are brought together in a web of sin, injustice, crime, and destruction. The scheme bears an analogy to the hereditary diseases running throughout several generations in Zola's *Les Rougons-Macquarts* series. Dickens compresses his material more than Zola by starting *in medias res*, and showing Pip as the focal point for the past, present, and future at once. In him are concentrated the effects of previous injustice, and he holds in himself the injustice yet to come. The interest of the novel is never restricted merely to the present. Dickens opens a great vista, a "poor labyrinth," through which we may see the present as but the culmination of a long history of social evil. Society is never able to smother wholly the facts of its injustice. As Dickens shows in novel after novel, somehow these facts will come to light again: Bounderby's mother in *Hard Times* rises to reveal her son's hypocrisy to the crowd he has bullied for so many years; the facts of Mrs. Clennam's relationship to the Dorrit family, and of society's injury to Lady Dedlock, her lover, and her child, are all unearthed in the end. Immediate victims may be skillfully suppressed, as Magwitch, returning from exile, is finally caught and imprisoned again. But the baleful effects of social evil go on in a kind of incalculable chain reaction. It is the old theme of tragic drama read into the bleak world of Mid-Victorian England: the sins of the fathers will be visited upon the heads of their children; the curse on the house will have to be expiated by future generations of sufferers.

Thus it is fair to say that Pip's story is more than a study of personal development. In his lonely struggle to work out his salvation, he is atoning for the guilt of society at large. In learning to rise above selfishness, to attain to a selfless love for Magwitch, he brings to an end the chain of evil that was first forged by the selfish Compeyson. His regeneration has something of the same force as

Krook's "spontaneous combustion" in *Bleak House*, or the collapse of the Clennam mansion in *Little Dorrit*, or even the renunciation of his family heritage by Charles Darnay in *A Tale of Two Cities*. Just as Darnay must atone for the guilt of his family by renouncing his property, so Pip must atone for the evils of the society that has corrupted him by relinquishing his unearned wealth. And as Darnay marries the girl whose father was one of the victims of his family's oppression, so Pip desires to marry the girl whose father, Magwitch, is the victim of the very society whose values Pip himself has embraced.

In giving his theme imaginative embodiment Dickens used what are perhaps some of the most ingenious and successful devices of his entire career. With disarming suddenness, for example, *Great Expectations* opens with the presentation of a physical phenomenon almost as memorable as that of the fog in *Bleak House*: the marshes. More than a Gothic detail casually introduced to give the story an eerie beginning, the marshes reappear again and again, not only in the first six chapters, where indeed they figure most prominently, but throughout the book. They haunt the novel from start to finish, becoming finally one of its great informing symbols. The variety of ways in which Dickens manages unobtrusively to weave them, almost like a musical motif, into the texture of his tale is remarkable. At one time they may flicker briefly across the foreground of one of Pip's casual reveries; at another they may provide the material of a simile; or Pip may return to them in fact when he is summoned there late in the story by Orlick; or, again, he may see them from a distance when he is helping Magwitch make his getaway down the Thames. "It was like my own marsh country," Pip says of the landscape along the part of the river he and Magwitch traverse:

> ... some ballast-lighters, shaped like a child's first rude imitation of a boat, lay low in the mud; and a little squat shoal-lighthouse on open piles, stood crippled in the mud on stilts and crutches; and slimy stakes stuck out of the mud, and slimy stones stuck out of the mud, and red landmarks and tide-marks stuck out of the mud, and an old landing-stage and an old roofless building slipped into the mud, and all about us was stagnation and mud.

Mud is a peculiarly appropriate symbol for the class of society that Magwitch represents—the downtrodden and oppressed of life, all those victims of injustice whom society has tried to submerge. It is a natural image of the social dunghill in which violence and rebellion are fomented, the breeding place of death. Likewise, it is the condition of death itself upon which certain forms of life must feed. It is no accident on Dickens's part that when Pip and his companions stop at a public house on their journey down the river, they meet a "slimy and smeary" dock attendant whose clothes have all been taken from the bodies of drowned men. In fact, the motif of life thriving upon death is underlined more than once throughout the novel in a number of small but brilliant ways. On his first trip to Newgate, Pip meets a man wearing "mildewed clothes, which had evidently not belonged to him originally, and which, I took it into my head, he had bought cheap of the executioner." Trabb, the haberdasher and funeral director of Pip's village, is still another kind of scavenger. He, too, like the many undertakers in Dickens's other novels and Mrs. Gamp in *Martin Chuzzlewit*, profits hideously by the misfortunes of others. It is this condition that Dickens sums up most effectively in the repulsive image of mud.

But together with the marshes, he uses still another symbol to keep the idea of social injustice and its consequences before us. Chapter I opens with a description of the graveyard in which Pip's parents and several infant brothers are buried. Though less prominent as an image than the marshes, that of the grave presents much more explicitly the idea of the death-in-life state to which Magwitch and others in his predicament are condemned. We remember that it is from among the tombstones that Magwitch first leaps forth into the story; and when, at the end of the chapter, he is going away, Pip has been so impressed by his likeness to a risen corpse that he imagines the occupants of the graveyard reaching forth to reclaim him. This is not a merely facetious or lurid detail. The grave imagery suggests in a highly imaginative way the novel's basic situation. Magwitch, in relation to the "respectable" orders of society, is dead; immured in the Hulks or transported to the fringes of civilization, he is temporarily removed from active life. But when in the opening scene of the book he rises from behind the tombstone, he is figuratively coming back to life again, and we are witnessing the recurrence of an idea Dickens made a central motif of

A Tale of Two Cities, the idea of resurrection and revolution. When Magwitch looms up from the darkened stairwell of Pip's London lodging house at the end of the second stage of the boy's career, we are witnessing, as in the case of Dr. Manette's being "recalled to life" from the Bastille, an event of revolutionary implications. For what this means is that one whom society has tried to repress, to shut out of life, has refused to submit to the edict. He has come back to take his place once more in the affairs of men, and to influence them openly in a decisive way. The injuries society perpetrates on certain of its members will be thrust back upon it. Society, like an individual, cannot escape the consequences of its injustice; an evil or an injury once done continues to infect and poison life, to pollute the society responsible for it.

This is suggested by the very way in which the material of the novel is laid out. Within the first six chapters, Dickens regularly alternates outdoor and indoor scenes, each one of which is coincident with a chapter division. There is a steady movement back and forth between the shelter and warmth of the Gargery's house and the cold misery and danger of the marshes. Thus, while getting his plot under way, Dickens is at the same time vividly impressing upon us his fundamental idea of two worlds: the world of "respectability" and the world of ignominy; of oppressors and of oppressed; of the living and of the dead. In the first six chapters these worlds are separate; it is necessary to come in or to go out in order to get from either one to the other. But in his excursions from the house to the marshes and back again, Pip is already forging the link that is to bring them together at the end of the second stage of his adventures when Magwitch, refusing to be left out in the cold any longer, actually becomes an inhabitant of Pip's private rooms. The clearest hint of this coming revolution is given when the soldiers burst from the marshes into Joe's house, and disrupt the solemn Christmas dinner. The breaking in upon it of the forces of another world shows on what a sandy foundation the complacency of Pumblechook and his kind is based. Beneath the self-assured crust of society, the elements of discontent and rebellion are continually seething, continually threatening to erupt. Thus the alternation between worlds that gives the novel's first six chapters their order supplies the reader at once with the basic moral of the book as a whole: the victims of injustice cannot be shut out of life forever; sooner or later they will come into violent contact with their oppressors.

Moving from the early pages of the book to the larger pattern, we discover that alternation between two different locales is basic to the whole. Pip tries to make his home in London, but he is forced a number of times to return to the site of his former life, and each return brings him a new insight into the truth of his position, one progressively more severe than another. The alternation between London and the old village becomes for Dickens a means of suggesting what the alternation between outdoor and indoor scenes in the first six chapters suggested: pretend as one will, reality will eventually shatter the veil of self-deception. Like the individual who has come to sacrifice his integrity for society's false values only to find it impossible to deny indefinitely his origins and the reality upon which his condition rests, society cannot effectively stifle all the victims of its injustice and oppression. There will always be men like Jaggers—men to connect the dead with the living, to act as the link between the underground man and the rest of society. As a defender of criminals, Jaggers is the great flaw in society's repression of its victims; he is their hope of salvation and resurrection. Like Tulkinghorn, the attorney in *Bleak House*, he knows everybody's secrets; he is the man to whom the lines between the high and the low, the men of property and the dispossessed, are no barrier. A wise and disillusioned Olympian, Jaggers comments like a tragic chorus on the two great worlds that are the product and expression of social injustice, for the existence of which Pip and others must suffer the terrible consequences.

THE HISTORY OF TOM JONES, A FOUNDLING
(HENRY FIELDING)

" 'The winding labyrinths of nature':
The Labyrinth and Providential Order in
Tom Jones"
by Anthony W. Lee,
Kentucky Wesleyan College

In the cluster of stories surrounding the Greek myth of the labyrinth, King Minos of Crete charges the brilliant inventor Daedalus to construct an elaborate labyrinth to house the Minotaur, the half-human, half-bull monstrosity produced by the illicit union between Minos's queen, Pasiphaë, and a beautiful, snow-white bull given to Minos by Poseidon, god of the sea. The Athenian hero Theseus, with the assistance of Minos's daughter, Ariadne, destroys this creature in its lair. Later, Daedalus constructs wings for himself and his son, Icarus, to escape from Minos's enforced captivity at Crete, an event resulting in the unfortunate death of Icarus when he flies too near the sun:

> Grown wild, and wanton, more embolden'd flies
> Far from his guide, and soars among the skies,
> The soft'ning wax, that felt a nearer sun,
> Dissolv'd apace, and soon began to run (Ovid 250).

As a classically trained scholar who made frequent references to Greek and Roman authors in his writing, Henry Fielding would

have been well aware of the labyrinth myth. In the midst of his
1749 masterpiece, *Tom Jones*—a novel that literary scholar Leopold
Damrosch has characterized as "the greatest single literary work of the
eighteenth century" (221)—Fielding pauses to say:

> First, Genius; thou gift of Heaven; without whose Aid in vain
> we struggle against the Stream of Nature. Thou, who dost
> sow the generous Seeds which Art nourishes, and brings to
> Perfection. Do thou kindly take me by the Hand, and lead
> me through all the Mazes, the winding Labyrinths of Nature.
> Initiate me into all those Mysteries which profane Eyes never
> beheld. Teach me, which to thee is no difficult Task, to know
> Mankind better than they know themselves. Remove that Mist
> which dims the Intellects of Mortals, and causes them to adore
> Men for their Art, or to detest them for their Cunning, in
> deceiving others, when they are, in Reality, the Objects only of
> Ridicule, for deceiving themselves. Strip off the thin Disguise
> of Wisdom from Self-Conceit, of Plenty from Avarice, and
> of Glory from Ambition. Come, thou that hast inspired
> thy *Aristophanes*, thy *Lucian*, thy *Cervantes*, thy *Rabelais*, thy
> *Molière*, thy *Shakespear*, thy *Swift*, thy *Marivaux*, fill my Pages
> with Humour; 'till Mankind learn the Good-Nature to laugh
> only at the Follies of others, and the Humility to grieve at their
> own (Fielding 443-44).

This is an extraordinarily rich passage, one that can serve as a "key" to
unlock many critically important elements of *Tom Jones* and to ultimately understand the book's labyrinthine qualities.

Falling at the center of the prefatory chapter to book thirteen, this
passage is written in the voice of Fielding's governing narrative persona.
Formally, it is a parodic epic invocation, a textual maneuver reminding
the reader of the epic tradition underpinning *Tom Jones* and especially
recalling the Miltonic invocations in books one, three, and seven of
Paradise Lost. Structurally, this chapter occupies a crucial position. It
introduces the final six books of the novel, which themselves form
a unit containing the climax of the entire narrative. Furthermore, it
marks an important liminal point: the transition between the rural
setting of the previous twelve books and the bustling London world

Tom will enter in the following chapter. Congruent with this pivotal structural position, a number of important thematic points inform the passage, points that are briefly enumerated here but will be more fully developed later in this essay. One point is Fielding's plea for a guide, or "Genius," to help track the labyrinth. Like Milton in *Paradise Lost*, who issues similar pleas, Fielding's request is granted and hence he in turn becomes the Genuis who guides the reader through the labyrinth of *Tom Jones*—something that ultimately intimates the notion of Fielding as a Daedalus figure. The phrase "the winding Labyrinths of Nature" contains a double significance. On one hand it can refer to the narrative structure and complexity of the book itself. On the other it can refer to the goal of wisdom and moral improvement that this structure seeks to divulge, the labyrinthine "Mysteries" associated with knowing "Mankind better than they know themselves." Finally, the list of satirical works and authors the narrator invokes at the end of the passage hints at the subterranean intertextual complexity of Fielding's narrative.

A major implication of Fielding's adaptation of the labyrinth narrative paradigm lies in his authorial assumption of the role of Daedalus. Daedalus, of course, created the Cretan labyrinth, and Fielding, as author, analogically occupies the role of Daedalus as the constructor of his fictional edifice, *Tom Jones*. Fielding self-consciously embraced this inventive role in the manifesto of his "modern" fiction found in his earlier novel, *Joseph Andrews*:

> Now a comic Romance is a comic Epic-Poem in Prose; differing from Comedy, as the serious epic from Tragedy; its Action being more extended and comprehensive; containing a much larger Circle of Incidents, and Introducing a greater Variety of Characters (Fielding, x).

Fielding also echoes this observation in *Tom Jones* when he refers to this novel as "prosaic-comi-epic Writing" (137). The attentive reader will not miss the veiled allusion to the properties of the labyrinth in the formal shape suggested by the "larger Circle of Incidents" and the involved intricacy of "greater Variety of Characters." Furthermore, the passage betrays Fielding's adoption of the Daedalus role, with its emphasis upon newness, upon difference from earlier generic models of literature. While he holds allegiance to the Augustan neoclassicist program, Fielding is also aware that he is fabricating something quite new, the *novel*, with all the connotations of novelty that the word invites.

In *Tom Jones,* Fielding's embrace of innovation and novelty particularly emerges in the self-consciously ostentatious narrative voice he assumes. Each of the eighteen books is headed by an introductory chapter, in which Fielding foregrounds his authorial presence and narrative manipulation. He encourages, teases, cajoles, lectures, scolds, and seduces his reader in a protean variety of guises, such that his authorial persona itself becomes a major character in the novel. In this respect he occupies multiple roles that are analogous to different characters in the Greek myth. In the following comment, Fielding's narrative "character" embraces the role of the authoritarian dictator Minos: "For as I am, in reality, the Founder of a new Province of Writing, so I am at liberty to make what Laws I please therein. And these Laws, my Readers, whom I consider as my Subjects, are bound to believe and obey. . . ." (Fielding 53). But he is also an Ariadne, in that his numerous dispensations of advice, hints, and clues prepare the reader not only to enter the labyrinth but also to emerge from it victoriously. Fielding's thread, however, becomes more subtle as the narrative progresses. As he tells us in book 11, chapter 9: ". . . for thou art highly mistaken if thou dost imagine that we intended, when we began this great Work, to leave thy Sagacity nothing to do; or that, without sometimes exercising this Talent, thou wilt be able to travel through our Pages with any Pleasure or Profit to thyself" (397). While Fielding's narrative voice ultimately emerges as the "Genius" who leads the reader "through all the Mazes, the winding Labyrinths of Nature," it also is a genius that teaches and guides the reader. Thus *Tom Jones* is as much about the reader's education as that of its titular character, Tom: It constitutes a synthetic combination of a heuristic manual of ethics and an epistemological treatise. Like Alexander Pope's *Essay on Man* and John Locke's *Essay Concerning Human Understanding, Tom Jones* is concerned with the foundations and limits of human knowing. Fielding, however, approaches such inquiries from a pragmatic and immediately experiential frame of view rather than an austerely philosophical one.

First-time readers of *Tom Jones* may be permitted the impression that they have stumbled into not a labyrinth but a maze. Recent commentators have made a careful distinction between the two (Artress 50-51; MacQueen 13-20). Labyrinths are archetypal structures dating back at least 3,500 years and evident in numerous global cultures. Mazes are of more recent vintage, first appearing some 600 years ago in the landscape hedges of the European aristocracy. Labyrinths are unicursal; that is, they have one well-defined path. Mazes are multicursal, with many entrances and exits. Mazes are intentionally confusing, possessing numerous blind spots, dead ends, and cul-de-sacs, whereas labyrinths have a clearly defined beginning, middle, and end. Mazes are puzzles, challenging the individual's ingenuity, while labyrinths offer a secure, assured outcome, given that one stays on the proper path. If the maze emblemizes the messy, complicated secular world of individualism and competition, the labyrinth patterns a universe warmly suffused with a harmony, order, and certainty conferred by a benevolent, providential divinity.

Tom Jones possesses elements of both the maze and the labyrinth, as Fielding's remark suggests: "Do thou kindly take me by the Hand, and lead me through all the Mazes, the winding Labyrinths of Nature." The voluminous length of Fielding's great novel, the explosive congestion of its numerous characters, events, and places, and its leisurely suspension of its ultimate resolution, may contribute to the reader's disorientation. However, this perception is misleading. Like the great labyrinth at the Chartres Cathedral, *Tom Jones*, despite its deceptive local deployments of smoke and mirrors, follows with deliberate and precise resolution a single, true line tracing the movement from darkness to illumination, from confusing "Mysteries" toward intellectual and spiritual clarity. It intentionally disorients its reader, only to loosen him or her from the distractions of everyday life, thereby identifying and recommending a higher apprehension of wisdom. The narrative epicenter of Fielding's book, the center of the labyrinth, leads the careful reader into not only a glorious narrative climax but also initiates him or her into a fresh way of looking at human existence.

Many have written on the narrative structure of *Tom Jones* and its labyrinthine dimensions, where "the greatest Events are produced by a nice ["accurate in judgment to minute exactness" (Johnson)]

"Train of little Circumstances" (Fielding 597). Most famous of these is Samuel Taylor Coleridge, who observed a few weeks before his death, "What a master of composition Fielding was! Upon my word, I think the *Oedipus Tyrannus*, *The Alchemist*, and *Tom Jones*, the three most perfect plots ever planned" (Coleridge 672). More recently, critics have endeavored to elucidate this perfection. R.S. Crane has written an influential essay applying Aristotelian principles derived from the *Poetics* to the novel, finding within its plot a "total system of actions, moving by probable or necessary connections from beginning, through middle, to end" (Crane 689). Another important essay, Frederick Hilles's "Art and Artifice in *Tom Jones*," finds an emblematic pattern shaped like "a Palladian mansion" reflecting a "mathematical exactitude" (Hilles 786). Hilles identifies an intricately precise machinery dividing the novel into three major sections (books 1-6, 7-12, and 13-18), each of which is dominated by a single setting (Somerset, the open road, and London, respectively) and a major female character (Molly, Mrs. Waters, and Lady Bellaston, respectively). Inside of these three units are various structural subdivisions that contribute to the rich architectonic integrity of the book. Hilles's analysis convincingly demonstrates that, by virtue of its structural clarity and cohesiveness, *Tom Jones*, far from being a maze, is a deliberately constructed labyrinth. But the most fruitful way to analyze and understand the labyrinthine lucidity of *Tom Jones* emerges from the application of the heroic-quest model influentially articulated by Joseph Campbell.

In his classic study *The Hero with a Thousand Faces*, Campbell analyzes the Cretan labyrinth story, deriving from it, as well as numerous other literary and mythological sources, a basic ur-narrative of the heroic quest, which consists of three stages: departure, fulfillment, and return (Campbell 36). In the first stage, the hero departs from his or her everyday, familiar existence. For Tom, this occurs within the first section of Hilles's tripartite pattern, when he is expelled from the Edenic Paradise Hall and is violently separated from his beloved, Sophia. The second phase, a journey or quest in search of fulfillment, is located in the second part of Hilles's pattern, when Tom is on the road, in books 7-12. This part of the sequence is marked by encounters designed to instruct the hero: a series of trials, tribulations, losses, gains, and temptations that simultaneously impede and enrich the hero's experience. The final phase, the culmination of the journey in a personally transformative experience, is the fulfillment—be it moral, spiritual, or pragmatic—followed by the return of the hero to his or her point of origination, in order to bestow the "boon," the lesson learned from the quest, to the rest of the community.

Tom's departure and quest clearly correspond to Campbell's paradigm. After his involuntary expulsion, Tom must overcome obstacles of poverty, the elements, menacing blocking agents, temptations (especially those of the feminine sort), and so forth. The most intriguing aspect of the application of Campbell's scheme to *Tom Jones*, however, involves Tom's moment of fulfillment. An understanding of this pivotal moment will go a long way toward providing ultimate interpretation of the novel.

This fulfillment occurs in the prison scene (book 18, chapter 2), which is both the narrative and thematic climax of the novel. Here Tom's quest reaches an apparent dead-end, as his life reaches an absolute nadir. He is in prison for stabbing a man with a sword in a dispute over a woman. His beloved Sophia has rejected him after learning of his affair with a lady of fashion. His dubious behavior has alienated him from most of his family and friends. On top of all this comes even more devastating news:

> "I hope, sir," said *Partridge*, "you will not be angry with me. Indeed I did not listen, but I was obliged to stay in the outward Room. I am sure I wish I had been a hundred Miles off, rather than have heard what I have heard." "Why, what is the Matter?" said *Jones*. "The Matter, Sir? O good Heaven!" answered *Partridge*, "was that Woman who is just gone out the Woman who was with you at *Upton*?" "She was, *Partridge*," cried *Jones*. "And did you really, Sir, go to Bed with that Woman?" said he, trembling.—"I am afraid what past between us is no Secret," said *Jones*.—"Nay, but pray, sir, for Heaven's sake, sir, answer me," cries *Partridge*. "You know I did," cries Jones.—"Why then, the Lord have Mercy upon your Soul, and forgive you," cries *Partridge*; "but as sure as I stand here alive, you have been a Bed with your own Mother."
>
> Upon these Words *Jones* became in a Moment a greater Picture of Horror than *Partridge* himself. He was, indeed, for

some Time struck dumb with Amazement, and both stood
staring wildly at each other (Fielding 596).

Physically enclosed by the stone walls of the prison, Tom has entered
what Campbell calls the belly of the whale, based upon the biblical
story of Jonah. Additionally, Tom has arrived at the center of the
labyrinth. But here the Minotaur is not an externally menacing
monster; rather Tom is forced to face his own misdeeds, his own
character failings. In Fielding's retelling of the myth, the Minotaur
is Tom's shadow self, a coalescent formation of the hidden, darker
recesses of his psyche that he has hitherto refused to acknowledge.
It is only when he can confront his repressed self that he can truly
begin to grow into the complete, organically whole identity that it
is his quest to reveal and become. Campbell notes that this culmi-
nating moment "is a form of self-annihilation. . . . But here, instead
of passing outward, beyond the confines of the visible world, the
hero goes inward, to be born again" (Campbell 91). The appalling
prospect of having committed maternal incest (which we later learn
is untrue) jolts Tom out of moral complacency and self-delusion.
In Aristotelian terms, this is the moment of "anagnorisis," or self-
discovery. Tom, finally seeing himself as he truly is, is given the
opportunity to abandon his old ways and re-emerge into a new,
more evolved self. This moment of self-discovery and rebirth corresponds at the plot level to the "peripeteia," or sudden reversal of
fortune.

From this point on, things begin to dramatically improve for
Tom. He quickly reconciles with the center of moral gravitas in the
novel, Squire Allworthy, is soon reinstalled in Paradise Hall (this time
as master, rather than an adopted underling), and is happily married
to Sophia—whose allegorical name etymologically derives from the
Greek σοφια, through the Latin *sophia*, meaning "wisdom." Jones
has acquired the wisdom that constitutes the goal of his quest. He has
successfully threaded the labyrinth and gained his boon:

> Whatever in the Nature of *Jones* had a Tendency to Vice, has
> been corrected by continual Conversation with this good Man
> [Squire Allworthy], and by his Union with the lovely and
> virtuous *Sophia*. He hath also, by Reflexion on his past Follies,

acquired a Discretion and Prudence very uncommon in one of his lively Parts (Fielding 641).

The monosyllabic simplicity of Tom Jones's name suggests that he, too, is an allegorical character, an everyman figure that Fielding intends the reader to identify with. Tom's heroic quest, his threading of the labyrinth, thus offers a paradigmatic map urging the reader to explore similar possibilities in his or her own life—to acquire what Martin Battestin has identified as the central thematic message of *Tom Jones*, "prudence": "the supreme virtue of the Christian humanist tradition, entailing knowledge and discipline of the self and the awareness that our lives, ultimately, are shaped not by circumstances, but by reason and the will" ("Fielding's Definition of Wisdom" 738). In addition to this ethical dimension, the pristine clarity and symmetry of the plot suggest Fielding's use of the labyrinth to unfold a providential view of reality, a metaphysical world order where good is ultimately rewarded, evil found out and punished, and where, despite the appearance of untidy variegation, certainty and harmony prevail. To borrow from the language of Fielding's contemporary acquaintance, Alexander Pope, *Tom Jones* is "A mighty maze! But not without a plan" (Pope, 11).

In the early 1960s, a survey of American undergraduate college students identified *Tom Jones* as the most overrated classic in the Western canon. In 1990, the editors of the canon-defending *Great Books of the Western World* dropped *Tom Jones* from its ranks, 42 years after its initial inclusion. And recently *Tom Jones* was purged from the Literature Humanities reading list at Columbia University—the list that, dating back to the 1920s, formed the original catalyst of the Great Books program. On the face of it, these events might portend the dwindling of *Tom Jones*'s critical reputation. Nevertheless, the novel continues to attract many advocates. Kingsley Amis, most famous for his novel *Lucky Jim*—a book possessing wickedly mischievous satire worthy of Fielding's art—offers in a later novel this observation, pronounced in the voice of a character standing before Fielding's Lisbon grave:

> Perhaps it was worth dying in your forties if two hundred years later you were the only non-contemporary novelist who could

be read with unaffected interest, the only one who never had to be apologised for or excused on the grounds of changing taste (Amis 185).

Despite any ostensible drop in contemporary prestige, *Tom Jones* itself remains its finest recommendation. If, in an age when the mass media has shortened the attention span of many, the spacious capacity of *Tom Jones*—a tome requiring weeks of careful, sustained perusal—appears forbidding, few labyrinthine novels will better repay the reader's attention. *Tom Jones* is a great novel because of the pungent earthiness of its humor, because of its unflinching embrace of the realities of human experience, both light and dark, because of its satirical penetration into social corruption, and because of its enduring grasp of the deep essentials of human psychology. These qualities make *Tom Jones* an inexhaustible text; its concerns are our concerns, and we cannot help but be absorbed by Fielding's darkly bittersweet, but ultimately affirmative, observations upon our shared human condition.

WORKS CITED AND SUGGESTIONS FOR FURTHER READING

Amis, Kingsley. *I Like It Here.* New York: Harcourt Brace, 1958.

Artress, Lauren. *Walking a Sacred Path: Rediscovering the Labyrinth as a Spiritual Tool.* New York: Riverhead, 1995.

Baker, Ernest A. "*Tom Jones.*" *The History of the English Novel, Vol. 4.* New York: Barnes and Noble, 1936, 1968. 123–54.

Battestin, Martin C. *A Henry Fielding Companion.* Westport Conn.: Greenwood, 2000.

———. "Fielding's Definition of Wisdom: Some Functions of Ambiguity and Emblem in *Tom Jones.*" *English Literary History* 35 (1968): 188–217; reprinted in *Tom Jones*, ed. Sheridan Baker: 733–49.

———. *The Moral Basis of Fielding's Art: A Study of Joseph Andrews.* Middletown, Conn.: Wesleyan UP, 1959.

———. *The Providence of Wit.* Oxford: Clarendon P, 1974.

———. *Twentieth-Century Interpretations of Tom Jones.* Englewood Cliffs, N.J.: Prentice-Hall, 1968.

———— and Ruthe R. Battestin. *Henry Fielding: A Life*. London and New York: Routledge, 1989.

Bloom, Harold, ed. *Modern Critical Views: Henry Fielding*. New York, New Haven, and Philadelphia: Chelsea House, 1987.

Booth, Wayne C. "'Fielding' in *Tom Jones*." Originally published as Chapter 8 of *The Rhetoric of Fiction*. Chicago: Chicago UP, 1961. 94–96; reprinted in *Tom Jones*, ed. Sheridan Baker: 731–33.

Campbell, Jill. "Fielding and the Novel at Mid-Century." In *The Columbia History of the British Novel*. Ed. John Richetti. New York: Columbia UP, 1994: 102–26.

Campbell, Joseph. *The Hero with a Thousand Faces*. Princeton: Princeton UP, 1949, 1968.

Chalmers, Alexander. *The Works of the English Poets from Chaucer to Cowper*. 21 vols. London, 1810; reprinted, Hildesheim and New York: Georg Olms Verlag, 1971.

Coleridge, Samuel Taylor. "Notes on *Tom Jones*," *Tom Jones*. Ed. Sheridan Baker. 2nd ed. New York: Norton, 1995. 671–2.

Crane, R.S. "The Plot of *Tom Jones*." Originally published in *The Journal of General Education* 4 (1950): 112–30; reprinted in *Tom Jones*, ed. Sheridan Baker: 677–99.

Damrosch, Leopold, Jr. "*Tom Jones* and the Farewell to Providential Fiction." In *God's Plots and Man's Stories*. Chicago: Chicago UP, 1985; reprinted in Bloom: 221–48.

Empson, William. "*Tom Jones*." Originally published in *The Kenyon Review* 20 (1958): 217–49; reprinted in *Tom Jones*, ed. Sheridan Baker: 711–31.

Fielding, Henry. *Joseph Andrews*. Mineola, N.Y.: Dover, 2001.

————. *Tom Jones*. Ed. John Bender and Simon Stern. New York: Oxford UP, 1998.

————. *Tom Jones*. Ed. Thomas Keymer and Alice Wakely. New York: Penguin, 2005.

————. *Tom Jones*. Ed. Sheridan Baker. 2nd ed. New York: Norton, 1995.

————. *Tom Jones*. Ed. Martin C. Battestin and Fredson Bowers. 2 vols. *The Wesleyan Edition of the Works of Henry Fielding*. Middletown, Conn., and Oxford: Wesleyan UP and Oxford UP, 1975.

————. *Tom Jones*. Ed. Martin C. Battestin and Fredson Bowers. New York: Modern Library, 2002. Contains corrections to text of Battestin and Bowers, 1975.

Fussell, Paul. *The Rhetorical World of Augustan Humanism; Ethics and Imagery from Swift to Burke.* Oxford: Clarendon Press, 1965.

Goldsmith, Oliver. *Collected Works of Oliver Goldsmith.* Ed. Arthur Friedman. 5 vols. Oxford: Clarendon Press, 1966.

Hahn, H. George. "Main Lines of Criticism of Fielding's *Tom Jones,* 1900–1978." *The British Studies Monitor* 10 (1980): 8–35.

Hilles, Frederick W. "Art and Artifice in *Tom Jones.*" *Imagined "Worlds: Essays on Some English Novels and Novelists in Honour of John Butt.* Ed. Maynard Mack and Ian Gregor (London: Methuen, 1968). 91–110; reprinted in *Tom Jones,* ed. Sheridan Baker. 786–800.

Hunter, J. Paul. *Occasional Form: Henry Fielding and the Chain of Circumstances.* Baltimore and London: Johns Hopkins UP, 1975.

———. "*Tom Jones*: Rethinking Ideas of Form." Henry Fielding at 300: Tercentary Reflections Panel Session. American Society for Eighteenth-Century Studies. Sheraton Colony Square Hotel, Atlanta, Ga. 23 March 2007.

Iser, Wolfgang. "The Role of the Reader in Fielding's *Joseph Andrews* and *Tom Jones.*" *The Implied Reader: Patterns of Communication in Prose Fiction from Bunyan to Beckett.* Baltimore and London: Johns Hopkins UP, 1974. 29–56.

Johnson, Samuel. *A Dictionary of the English Language.* 1st ed. London, 1755; facsimile reprint, Burnt Mill, Harlow, Essex: Longman, 1990.

Karpuk, Susan Price. *Tom Jones: An Index.* New York: AMS, 2006.

Kermode, Frank. "Richardson and Fielding." *Essays on the Eighteenth-Century English Novel.* Ed. Robert D. Spector. Bloomington and London: Indiana UP, 1965. 64–77.

London, April. "Controlling the Text: Women in *Tom Jones.*" *Studies in the Novel* 19: 3 (Fall 1987): 323–33.

MacQueen, Gailand. *The Spirituality of Mazes and Labyrinths.* Friesens, Altona, Canada: Northstone, 2005.

Miller, J. Hillis. *Ariadne's Thread: Story Lines.* New Haven and London: Yale UP, 1992.

Ovid. "The Story of Daedalus and Icarus." *Metamorphoses.* Trans. Croxall. Hertfordshire: Wordsworth Editions, 1998. 249–52.

Pope, Alexander. *An Essay on Man: Epistle I. The Twickenham Edition of the Poems of Alexander Pope, Vol. 3.* ed. John Butt, et al. New Haven: Yale UP, 1939–69.

Rawson, Claude, ed. *Henry Fielding*. London: Routledge and Kegan Paul, and New York: Humanities P, 1968.

———. "Henry Fielding." In *The Eighteenth-Century Novel*. Ed. John Richetti. New York and Cambridge: Cambridge UP, 1996. 120–52.

Rizzo, Betty. "The Gendering of Divinity in *Tom Jones*." *Studies in Eighteenth-Century Culture*. 24 (1995): 259–77.

Ronald Paulson. *Fielding: A Collection of Critical Essays*. Englewood Cliffs, N.J.: Prentice-Hall, 1962.

Watt, Ian. "Fielding as Novelist: *Tom Jones*." *The Rise of the Novel*. Berkeley and Los Angeles: U of California P, 2001 (1st pub. London: Chatto and Windus, 1957): 239–89.

Weinbrot, Howard D. *Augustus Caesar in "Augustan" England: The Decline of a Classical Norm*. Princeton: Princeton UP, 1978.

THE HOUSE OF THE SPIRITS
(ISABEL ALLENDE)

"Of Labyrinths in Isabel Allende's
The House of the Spirits"
by Maria Odette Canivell,
James Madison University

The French novelist Alain Robbe-Grillet claims that as soon as "a modern architect is given a project, he draws a labyrinth" (in Stolzfus 292). Mankind appears to be fascinated by the image of labyrinths, these connecting networks of intricate winding passages where the exploration of life and death is made possible and the study of the human soul can take place. Artists, writers, and philosophers have used the image of the maze to symbolize man's struggle, the perpetual conflict between mind and soul, our fears and hopes, as well as the inexplicable paradox of mankind's fate. Labyrinths are a locus of spiritual growth, magical quests and representations of human struggle where past, present, and future conflate into a single unit, an archetype for the inner world. Confusing and disorienting, mazes represent "a symbol of human consciousness, a metaphor of the mind coping with experience" (Privateer 92), where complex systems of preordained rules allow safe passage to the center. A careful reading of Isabel Allende's *The House of the Spirits* will highlight her masterful use of the archetype to tell a story of family and country.

Allende's labyrinth is a site of hope. The Chilean author suggests that "creativity and innovation require a transgression of fixed boundaries" (Levine 34); therefore her mazes defy the stereotype of the labyrinth as a place of despair. Instead, in the many mentions of labyrinths from the pages of *The House of the Spirits*, a sense of peace prevails. Allende's warrens serve as shelter from the storm, as well as safe places for hiding the family's magical secrets. The writer's characters take refuge inside the hearts of these labyrinths, where their minds wander (and wonder) without being subjected to scorn and prejudice.

During the Middle Ages, mazes safeguarded the inhabitants of cities and burgs from the perils of the outside world. Chartres Cathedral houses one of the most famous labyrinths of early modern Europe. As its location might suggest, this labyrinth offered more than physical protection. After reaching the maze's center, pilgrims finally found spiritual enlightenment. In *The House of the Spirits*, Allende returns to this medieval Christian idea of the maze as a magical instrument of protection. The many labyrinths of the novel, both mental and physical, shield Alba, Clara, Nívea, and Blanca from evil.

Alba, the novel's main narrator, transports fugitives to friendly embassies in a car covered in brightly painted yellow flowers, which call to mind the rosette in the center of the Chartres labyrinth. In other places, the author casts the motif as a path to magical sanctuary away from the madness and cruelty of the exterior world. Alba exorcises her own demons by reliving the unfortunate events that led to her incarceration and subsequent rape at the hands of her grandfather's bastard. Like Theseus, who voluntarily travels the maze to destroy the Minotaur, Alba voluntary relives—and thus rewrites—the story of her loved ones so she, and other members of her family, can finally find peace.

In addition to serving as sanctuary for the novel's characters, the labyrinth also determines the novel's structure. The narrative follows a circular pattern beginning and ending with the same sentence: "Barrabás came to us by sea." The dog Barrabás presages the political violence that will accompany readers throughout the book. The accidental murder of Rosa at the hands of a political foe of her father will embitter the young Esteban Trueba, who will (many years later) turn to Rosa's sister, Clara, for solace. The internal politics of Chile, reflected in the incarceration of Alba after the bloody coup of September 11, 1976, will deliver the young girl to prison. As Ambrose Gordon suggests, the book is not a single, linear story about a family but rather several seemingly independent stories pieced together by the narrator, who gathers *memories* and *memoirs* as a way to reclaim the labyrinth's center (531). The political component of each individual narrative becomes more accentuated as the story progresses, until we see the last female protagonist, Alba, sent to prison on trumped-up political charges. As she languishes in her cell, beaten, physically violated, and starved, the prisoner tries to recapture the sense of freedom that labyrinths afford. Despite her horrible situation, Alba "made a superhuman effort to remember the pine forest and Miguel, but her ideas got tangled up and she no longer knew if she was dreaming or where this stench of sweat, excrement, blood and urine was coming from" (406). When the heroine is ready to give up, awaiting a death that will not come, her dead grandmother Clara pays her a visit. Dressed in all her finery, Clara proposes to her grandchild a way to reclaim the center of the labyrinth: Alba must write the story of her family. In doing so, not only will she find solace from the mental and physical pain she is subjected to, but she will provide fellow sufferers with the means to exorcise ghosts and thus "overcome (their) terrors" (1). In Spanish, the phrase "*curarse de espantos*" means to prevent evil thoughts, as well as the more literal meaning "to cure oneself from fear and terror." The English translation uses "overcome terrors." The word *espanto* has the double meaning of spirits and terror. It is not a coincidence that Allende uses this term, as it implies the reconciliation of Alba with all the spirits, good and bad. This testimony, Alba's grandmother suggests, will be a tribute to those who suffer the indignities of the Chilean dictatorship, those sharing "the terrible secret" of degradation in prisons and concentration camps, whose existence is concealed from the world by their jailers. It will also remind Alba and the other prisoners who languish in cells everywhere in the world that "the point is not to die, since death came anyway, but to survive, which would be a miracle" (414-15).

From the first pages of the novel, the author introduces the idea of literature as redemption. Alba saves herself by writing her family's story. Allende suggests, "writing is a matter of survival. If I don't write I forget, and if I forget it is as if I had not lived" (*Conversations* x); writing, the author claims, allows me to "prevent the erosion of time, so that memories will not be blown by the wind"

(*Conversations* x). Like her character Alba, the Chilean novelist acknowledges that literature is both a form of therapy and salvation, providing an escape from madness and physical deprivation. Taking her cue from Clara, who suggests to her granddaughter "the saving idea of writing in her mind, without paper or pencil, to keep her thoughts occupied and to escape from the doghouse and live," the narrator-protagonist of the book recovers her sanity (414).

Using the grandmother's forceful personality as an anchor, Alba finally finds the courage to fight for her life. Clara does not believe in self-pity. The ghost scolds Alba, who is feeling sorry for herself, telling her to stop thinking about the past. She advises Alba to drink some water, ignore the pain, and begin to write her memoirs. Clara's admonishment seems to be that keeping one's mind occupied is the best way to escape madness. Alba initially struggles with the chore, as "the doghouse (was) filled with all the characters . . . ," speaking out of turn and interrupting each other; in time, however, the voices converge into a chorus, allowing the captive to finally remember and rewrite her family's history:

> She took down their words at breakneck pace, despairing because while she was filling a page, the one before it was erased . . . but she invented a code for recalling things in order, and then she was able to bury herself so deeply in the story that she stopped eating, scratching herself, smelling herself, and complaining, and overcame all her varied agonies. (405)

Writing the story within her head allows the girl to find the inner strength she needs to survive. Aided by the tales of her ancestors and a fierce desire to trump the will of her jailers, she transcends the filth and degradation of the prison and finds peace within the center of the labyrinth.

Linda Levine argues that Allende's writing eludes genre classification, in part due to her way of "weaving life into fiction." Just like Alba collects memories and *memoirs* to tell the story of her family (and that of her land of birth, Chile), *The House of the Spirits* blends elements of the historical novel, testimonial literature, the *Bildungsroman* and the memoir. In Spanish, the word for story and history is the same; public and private *historias* are one and the same. Thus, the lives of the

Chilean people, horrified by the terrible events after the coup d'état, are tightly woven with episodes from the story of the Trueba family. Personifying its suffering in the tale of Alba, the family's collective historical memory is kept alive. The author acknowledges that the novel blends both fact and fiction:

> "A novel is made partly of truth and partly fantasy.... In *The House of the Spirits* the phantoms of the past are so intermeshed with the events that have left such a mark in my country that it is very difficult for me to separate reality from fiction" (Agosin 38).

Although Allende cleverly bypasses any allusion to the identity of the historical cast woven inside the novel, it is easy to identify key left-wing political actors who figured prominently in the modern history of Chile. Among these secondary characters, it is worthwhile to mention The Poet (the allusion to Pablo Neruda, who was also Allende's mentor, is unmistakable) and Pedro Tercero García (Victor Jara, the composer and singer). The historical allusions do not end with the inclusion of these central figures in the political history of the country, but rather, as Ramblado-Minero claims, the novel's first part, the family's story, is an allegory for the novel's second part. Thus, the last four chapters can be easily read as the history of Chile, while the first nine could be seen as the personal story of the family. Embracing the Pan-American ideal that Neruda espoused in his *Canto General,* Allende toys with this idea of fictionalized history being used as a catalyst for the suffering of all the people in Latin America. The author claims sisterhood with the rest of the countries of the continent, stating that: "my country is all of Latin America, (and) all of us who live in this continent are brothers and sisters" (Agosin 42). It is thus that Alba's memoir becomes, in Allende's words, the bond between countries and people who share a common, yet sometimes terribly painful, history.

Characters, like the readers of the novel, must travel through strange and at times surreal spaces, with boundaries that are not clear. Tránsito, Jaime, Nicolas, and Rosa are ethereal beings suspended between worlds. The first, as her Spanish name indicates

(the meaning is "way," "path," but also "transitory"), occupies a
liminal place within a structure of dominance and dependence
(Levine 26). The effeminate twins commune with spirits, refusing
to take their rightful place in "the man's world" their father envi-
sions for them. They roam the house's "labyrinth of icy corridors,"
acting more like ghosts than living souls (240). Jaime lives in "a
tunnel of books" that forms a perfect nest for spiders and mice, with
his bed, an army cot, placed at the center (221). Nicolás devotes
his energies to yoga, flamenco, and creating a spiritual center for
abused souls, while Jaime reads and silently pines for his brother's
girlfriend, Amanda. The girl, blind to his devotion, treats him and
his precious books "without the slightest sign of reverence," until
she finally takes leave of him with a kiss, "a single terrible kiss on
which he built a labyrinth of dreams where the two of them were
a prince and a princess hopelessly in love" (237-238). All of these
characters meander through labyrinths—some physical, others
psychological—searching for the center. Regrettably, the spirits
must wait until Alba weaves their history into a complete tapestry
to find the way back home.

Clara, hoping to find refuge from the madness of the outside
world, uses the motif of the maze to take flight from reality. Alba's
grandmother adds room after room to the manor "until the big house
on the corner soon came to resemble a labyrinth" (224). In the back
rooms, safe from the prying eyes of her husband, Mrs. Trueba and
her retinue establish "an invisible border [arising] between the parts
occupied by Esteban Trueba and those occupied by his wife" (224).
Férula fills the gaps of her sister-in-law's mind "with gossip about the
neighbors, domestic trivia, and made up anecdotes that Clara found
very lovely and forgot within five minutes" (98), allowing Férula to
tell her the same stories repeatedly, reinforcing the circular pattern of
the narrative. Living within such a disorienting physical structure, it
is not surprising that the actions and thoughts of the family also take
on labyrinthine qualities. Although initially the narrator, doubling as
one of the main characters, tells her family's story from the perspective of an outsider, we soon realize that she is the grandchild of Clara
and the one who has delicately assembled the pieces of the puzzle for
us. Clara, the narrator says, "was in the habit of writing down important matters, and afterwards, when she was mute, (she) also recorded

trivialities, never suspecting that fifty years later I would use her note-books to reclaim the past" (1).

Taking back from the dead, however, is seldom an easy task; thus, the tone of the novel set in the very first chapters presages what will happen to the rest of the family. The continuous travel between past and present strikes readers as confusing, almost labyrinthine. It is only when we learn the sad fate of the members of the family that the story/history begins to make sense. Allende's deceased female char-acters will return to the narrative as ghosts, destined to live forever repeating the same mistakes. All of the novel's females exhibit a "runaway imagination," which makes it very difficult for them to live within the reality principle (4). Alba, Blanca, Clara, and Nívea share the same psychological traits; paradoxically, their Spanish names are derivatives of "white," "clear" and "pure." The literary homonym, however, refers to the purity of the love they share with one another and the men in their lives.

In contrast to the women, the men of the Del Valle-Trueba family have been cursed with emotional barrenness by their female relatives ever since cousin Jerónimo, who was blind, died while climbing a tree in his backyard. The men's obsession with proving their manhood is to blame for Jerónimo's death; therefore, they must atone for the crime. As penance for their misdeeds, they are unable to emotionally connect to their female partners, who tirelessly nurture and love them in spite of this.

Both male and female characters share this pattern of repetition: the men using violence as a means to obtain what they want, and the women loving emotionally stunted males who seldom return the bounty of love they receive. Even the twins, the most feminine male characters in the narrative, cannot escape their destinies. Nicolás disappears in an industrialized city, making money as a spiritual guide. He ends up, however, alone. Jaime dies protecting the presi-dent, taking to his death the memory of the love of his childhood, Amanda. None of them, until Esteban Trueba dies, manage to retrieve the key that allows them to find the way to the center of this labyrinth of their own emotions, as only the women can find the thread leading them to a better world. It is only at the end of the novel that Alba finally understands "nothing that happens is fortuitous" (431). She sees that the tragic events in the life of her family were the only way to break the chain of violence and madness present in the Trueba clan. Trying to explain to her young grandchild why every member of the Trueba-del Valle family appears to be beset by some kind of lunacy, the stoic grandmother says that "the madness was divided up equally and there was nothing left over for us to have our own lunatic" (281). Thus, lunacy is a general family trait, inherited along with hair color (green for Alba and Clara), height, and weight.

In writing the family's history and thus "her-story," Alba, the last in this line of extraordinary women, breaks the walls of the labyrinth and exposes the center for all the men to find. It is only then, after recording the deeds of her family in the form of narrative, that she enables her grandfather to reclaim the dead spirit of his wife, who appears to him from then on looking as lovely and loving as when they first met. As the novel closes, Alba's grandfather dies in peace, calling out the name of his beloved: "Clara, clearest, clairvoyant." In this poignant last scene, the author plays with the Spanish derivative of the word *clara*, the feminine form of clear, transparent, understood. By using the term *clarísima*, Allende alludes to the epiphany visited upon Trueba, who finally manages to understand and accept the woman who was the love of his life. It is thus that he reaches the center of the labyrinth of his stunted emotional life, finding in the center, like his female kinfolk did, the peace he had always sought.

WORKS CITED

Agosin, Marjorie. "Pirate, Conjurer, Feminist." In *Conversations with Isabel Allende*. Ed. Rodden, John. Austin: U of Texas P, 1999.

Allende, Isabel. *The House of the Spirits*. New York: Dial Press Trade, 1986.

———. *La casa de los espíritus*. New York: Harper Collins, 2001.

———. "Foreword." Rodden, John. Ed. *Conversations with Isabel Allende*. Austin: U of Texas P, 1999.

Freud, Sigmund. "Creative Writers and Daydreaming." *Critical Theory Since Plato*. London: Harcourt Brace, 1992.

Gordon, Ambrose. "Isabel Allende on Love and Shadow." *Contemporary Literature*, 28:4 (Winter 1987): 530–542.

Hildburgh, W.L. "The Place of Confusion and Indeterminability in Mazes and Maze-dances." *Folklore* 56:1 (March 1995): 188–192.

Levine, Linda. *Isabel Allende*. New York: Twayne, 2002.

Neruda, Pablo. *Selected Poems*. Boston: Houghton Mifflin, 1990.

———. *Canto General*. Berkeley: University of California Press, 2000.

Privateer, Paul. "Contemporary Literary Theory: A Thread Through the Labyrinth." *Pacific Coast Philology* 18:1/2 (November 1983): 92–99.

Ramblado-Minero, María de la Cinta. *Isabel Allende's Writing of the Self: Trespassing the Boundaries of Fiction and Autobiography*. Lampeter, Wales: The Edward Mellen Press, 2003.

Stoltzfus, Ben. "Robbe-Grillet's Labyrinths: Structure and Meaning." *Contemporary Literature* 22:3 (Summer 1981): 292–307.

IF ON A WINTER'S NIGHT A TRAVELER (ITALO CALVINO)

"Italo Calvino's *If on a Winter's a Night a Traveler* and the Labyrinth"
by Aimable Twagilimana,
Buffalo State College, SUNY

Greek mythology has it that King Minos of Crete built an intricate structure, the labyrinth, which was designed by Daedalus to imprison the Minotaur. The structure was so complex that the designer himself got lost in it, and Theseus, the eventual Minotaur slayer, needed a clue from Ariadne to find his way to the exit. From this mythological imagination to the present, the labyrinth has been used as a metaphor to convey various ideas such as quest, pilgrimage, travel, turnings, shifts, mapmaking, games, contemplation, meditation, mutability, openness, multiplicity, complexity, encyclopedia, anthology, inter-disciplinarity, confusion, and even defeat. The literary incarnations of this maze of ideas has found echoes in the work of well-known writers such as Umberto Eco, Jorge Borges, and Italo Calvino.

For Calvino, the labyrinth was a metaphor for the complex realities of the 1960s characterized by the crisis of decolonization, globalization, and late capitalism and its new technologies. In his 1963 article "La sfida al labirinto" ("The Challenge to the Labyrinth"), he argued that, faced with these new realities, the modern man needed to rethink his identity, his originality, and his way of relating to the new world; he needed a new "formal-moral choice," that is, a new way of writing reflecting the labyrinthine nature of his time. Italo Calvino's use of the labyrinth, both as a human condition and a type of narrative, in his work in general and in *If on a Winter's Night a Traveler* in particular conveys his faith in the imaginative possibilities of literature, in its ability to challenge, not surrender to, the labyrinth and find the exit. This essay explores Calvino's labyrinth as a complex network of stories, genres, critical theories, and authors and readers and a tour de force revision of these categories, each captured as a complex, plural entity. He saw literature not only as storytelling but also as a reflection on the nature of storytelling, on the role of the author, the reader, and the text, as well as on the values it promotes. In his articulation of a new narrative, he adopted the postmodern aesthetic with its experimental techniques, its embrace of information technology and popular culture, its rejection of modernist elitism and essentialist ideologies, its questioning of authority and binary opposi-tions, its penchant for parody, and its acceptance of identity, truth, and understanding as constructs in continuing flux.

"No one says a novel has to be one thing," a character in post-modernist writer Ishmael Reed's *Yellow Back Radio Broke-Down* says, "[i]t can be anything it wants to be . . ."(36). Calvino's *If on a Winter's Night a Traveler* pushes this idea to the nth degree to test the limits of fiction only to suggest that no such limits exist, and the fictional space presents potentially infinite possibilities. As a result, "we encounter an extraordinary collection of literary forms and genres, including a love story, a mystery, a political satire, a mock literary biography and a parody of the campus novel. In addition, Calvino offers us a medi-tation on the current state of fiction and a wry commentary on the publishing trade" (Washington xi). Furthermore, the novel surveys literary and critical theories from Horace's "*dulce et utile*" to linguistic theory, postmodernism, feminism, and reader-response theory, with other theories in between. Both writing and reading become acts of communication, a new epistemology of the novel that tests, enriches, and transforms the genre, questioning the author's authority and enhancing the reader's interpretive possibilities. In this carnivalesque encounter of elements, someone randomly opening the book may read Calvino exalting the pleasure of reading; another may get pages that read more like literary, linguistic, or philosophical treatises; another may catch a story in progress to see it lead to empty pages or to similar pages repeated over; and so on and so forth. Through this experimental blend, Calvino seems to make a commentary comparable to Paul Ricoeur's contention that "literature is a vast laboratory in which we experiment with estimations, evaluations, and judgments of approval and condemnation through which narrativity serves as a propaedeutic to ethics" (Ricoeur 115) or even to Toni Morrison's suggestion in her 1993 Nobel lecture that narrative is not "mere entertainment" but also one of the ways "in which we absorb knowledge" (7). In *The Uses of Literature* and other essays, Calvino develops the same idea of fiction as a significant and relevant category, an epistemological system, or a way of knowing, different from but complementary to other systems of knowledge.

Questioning traditional genre boundaries, Calvino constantly juxtaposes the author, the text, and the reader and creates a space where the three are in constant communication, negotiating their roles, each readily invading the other's space—for example, a character wondering if his creator (the writer) is reading him correctly: ". . . whether the author interprets in this way the half sentence I am muttering" (21). The novel reproduces the author-text-reader triangle in other triangular relationships. Calvino does this, for example, through three love stories: the Reader's pursuit of the complete text, Ermes Marana's attempt to "regain" Ludmilla, and the Reader's own pursuit of Ludmilla. The Reader's quest for the text parallels his love affair with Ludmilla. Marana's manipulation of texts through his translation started as a way of gratifying Ludmilla's expectations about texts. Concerning the Reader and Ludmilla, their first love-making is also an act of reading: "Ludmilla, now you are being read. Your body is being subjected to a systemic reading, through channels of tactile information, visual, olfactory, and not without some intervention of the taste buds" (155). The Reader himself is being read: "The other Reader is now receiving your body as if skimming the index, and at some moments she consults it as if gripped by sudden and specific curiosities, then she lingers, questioning it and waiting till a silent answer reaches her" (155). The erotic pursuit mirrors the rubbing of the ten stories against each other. The unfinished stories form complex connections like those found in a real labyrinth: They allude, parody, and echo one another and other texts. They form a network of texts that enlace a network of texts that intersect. "What makes lovemaking and reading resemble each other most," Calvino tells us, is that within both of them times and spaces open, different from measurable time and space" (156). The opening is to the vast, immeasurable space beyond language and the infinite universe of texts. The symbolic rubbing of the author-text-reader, like lovemaking, is an erotic activity, one whose climax begins the promise of another reading, which requires a new beginning . . . endlessly.

Rather than telling one story, the novel offers ten fragments of stories, one branching on the next one in unexpected and sometimes bizarre turns, including pages that are inserted more than once, missing pages, or blank pages. Calvino's narrative is the story of what we do each time we embark on reading a novel: We may pause after the opening sentences, reread the same story, focus on the ending, and think about connections to other books we may have read in the past. Each fragment of the story is preceded by a chapter that reflects on the nature of reading; on theories of writing, language, and literature; on the quest for a missing, incomplete, or misplaced book; and on the network of readers who haunt the pages of the novel. All in all, a good portion of the book is about the author constantly interrupting our reading and reminding us that we are reading fragments of stories; it is a reflection on the book as a construct aware of its own artifact.

Most readers go to a book expecting a beginning, a middle, and an end, which gives a sense of closure, a conclusion, a resolution, or sets of answers to conflicts. Calvino makes it a point to remind readers of conventions and expectations only to challenge them, blatantly refusing to gratify them, or purposefully playing with them. At the end of the book, for example, after he has flouted all the traditional conventions, he playfully has one reader say: "'Do you believe that every story must have a beginning and an end? In ancient times a story could end only in two ways: having passed all the tests, the hero and the heroine married, or else they died. The ultimate meaning to which all stories refer has two faces: the continuity of life, the inevitability of death'" (259). Suddenly he playfully decides to marry the Reader and Ludmilla, reminding the reader of the centrality of delight (Horace's "dulce") in the act of reading, an idea he foregrounded at the outset by advising "the most comfortable position" to read (3) and that he dexterously explores throughout the text. Even though the author seems to have the upper hand in the end, he continuously gives something back to the reader: the playful teasing in the sense of "what if I changed or fulfilled your expectations, reader?" when the reader least expects it.

This delight permeates the novel and comes in different forms, including the way in which the readers are imagined. In spite of the unsettling turns and shifts in the novel, Calvino wants readers to have a pleasurable experience as he takes them through the labyrinth of interrupted stories, structural shifts, geographical mobility, ideological struggles, technological innovations, and even love imbroglios. The author and the reader share ownership of the story. In this sense, Calvino agrees with Roland Barthes's idea of the "death of the author." In "The Death of the Author," Barthes argues that "a text consists not of a line of words, releasing a single 'theological' meaning, but of a multidimensional space in which are contested several writings, none of which is original" (53). As such, a text "is a fabric of quotations resulting from a thousand sources of culture" (53). Having been intellectually informed by everything he or she read, watched, listened to, or experienced, the author's life becomes potential material for his or her yet-to-be-created text. The author thus becomes simply an assembler and distributor of previously told or written texts. "His sole power," Barthes argues, "is to mingle writings to counter some by others, so as never to rely on just one" (53).

Calvino's novel starts with a frame and then multiplies fragments of stories tenfold. These stories literally branch like the design of a labyrinth: A story line starts, to be later abandoned at a turn for the beginning of another story and so on and so forth. The reference to *Arabian Nights* in the novel is perhaps the clearest indication to the reader as to how to approach the text. In a fashion reminiscent of *If on a Winter's Night a Traveler*, *Arabian Nights* consists of a collection of stories from various Arab countries and periods. Collected and translated by different people, they tend to end at climactic moments, a choice that Shahrazad (Scheherazade) makes every night to keep the curiosity of the king alive, since her life depends on his willingness to let her live another day to finish an unfinished story. Unlike Shahrazad, in her life-and-death situation, Calvino does not finish his stories, but this intertextual linkage gives a strong indication to readers that they also have the responsibility to answer questions and finish the stories, if they so choose. It is Calvino's way of putting in practice what his friend Barthes suggested about a text as "a device to undo the reader's passivity and actively engage him in the creative process of literature by letting him discover solutions to the story" (Markey 117).

Calvino's readers zigzag through the world of *incipits*, each with parallels and connections to others, as the Reader searches for the complete story. This quest mirrors the world of texts, a world of plurality and intertextuality, the idea that texts refer to, retell, dialogue with, parody, question, interrogate, transform, and enrich other texts. As Barthes writes,

> a text is made of multiple writings, drawn from many cultures and entering into mutual relations of dialogue, parody, contestation, but there is one place where this multiplicity is focused, and that place is the reader, not, as was hitherto said, the author. The reader is the space on which all the quotations that make up a writing are inscribed without any of them being lost; a text's unity lies not in its origin but in its destination. Yet this destination cannot any longer be personal: the reader is without history, biography, psychology. (54)

The author is the scriptor, the creator of the text, "the writing hand that gives words to existences too busy existing" (Calvino 181), and the reader is the explicator, the creator of meaning: "I read, therefore *it* writes," Silas Flannery puts it in his diary, which reads like a narrative theory (176). Flannery's statement is a parody of René Descartes's "*cogito ergo sum*" (I think, therefore I am), an essentialist proposition that assumes the existence of reason as the condition of being in the Enlightenment philosophy. Flannery's (and Calvino's) revision of the Cartesian slogan points to the reader's active engagement of a story and its meaning. As Markey argues, "it is the reader himself who . . . actually generates the fiction, simply by rereading, grasping a thought and then forming his own impressions" (119).

Like Silas Flannery, the fictitious Irish author in Calvino's novel, Calvino's Reader is a Barthesian reader. We know nothing beyond his quest for the text. While we learn something of the female readers, Ludmilla and her sister Lotaria, we do not know much about the Reader. We understand for sure that he is the meeting point of all the fragmented stories. His quest for the complete text mirrors our own, and all the texts intersect with him, echoing the way each text we read intersects with every other text we have read before or we might read in the future.

The Reader is also a composite individual, or a community of readers if you will, as reflected in the convention of six readers in Chapter 11 who share their ways of reading, creating a session that resembles a meditation on the nature of reading or a meeting that recalls what Stanley Fish called "interpretive communities." Each of the seven readers, having been shaped by different subjective experiences, represents a different interpretive community. For the first reader, an incipit of a few pages is sufficient to create "whole universes" (254). The second reader needs the whole book, but he or she "read[s] and reread[s], each time seeking the confirmation of a new discovery among the folds of the sentences" (255). Like the second reader, the third reads entire books, but "at every rereading, I seem to be reading a new book, for the first time" (255), suggesting that each reading of the same book creates a different story altogether. For the fourth reader, all books constitute one book, as "every new book I read comes to be a part of that overall and unitary book that is the sum of my reading" (255). As for the fifth reader, all books originate from and echo one elusive book. The sixth reader only needs incipits, first sentences, or just "the promise of reading" (256). Finally, for the seventh reader, "it is the end that counts" (256). The Reader is a traditional reader, who requires a book with a beginning, a middle, and an end and who just came back from a fruitless quest for the complete text. This maze of ways of reading represents some of the cognitive processes involved in the complex activity of any reader's own creation and interpretation of the story.

The Reader is also the fraudulent reader cum translator Ermes Marana. Ermes is a homonym of Hermes, the Greek god who serves as a messenger from the Olympian gods to the humans. As such, he is a translator, but he is also known for manipulating his messages. In the Homeric hymns, he is referred to as a true dissembler, a master of irony (an *eiron*), a messenger with many shifts, a liar, and a thief. Likewise, hired to translate, Marana creates new stories, following his belief that "literature's worth lies in its power of mystification, in mystification it has its truth; therefore a fake, as the mystification of a mystification, is tantamount to a truth squared" (180). He is the founder of a secret society called the "Organization of Apocryphal Power" (OAP), which he uses to cause the confusion we observe in Calvino's novel. As translator, instead of conveying the meaning of the original text, he creates new ones and thus multiplies texts and meanings. Like the fifth reader in the previous paragraph, Marana claims, in one of his letters probably written by himself to con an editor but supposedly sent to him by Cerro Negro in South America, that there is a single source for all stories: "a local legend . . . an old Indian known as the Father of Stories, a man of immemorial age, blind and illiterate, who uninterruptedly tells stories that take place in countries and in times completely unknown to him. . . . The old Indian, according to some, is the universal source of narrative material, the primordial magma from which the individual manifestations of each writer develop; according to others, a seer . . ." (117); to others yet, the Father of Stories is the incarnation of great writers of the past such as Homer, Alexandre Dumas, and James Joyce (117).

Translation is another idea that complicates the narrative and helps to convey Calvino's writerly labyrinth. It is significant that, except for the frame story *If on a Winter's Night a Traveler*, the rest of the stories are translations from languages such as Polish, Cimmerian, Cimbrian, French, Japanese, Irish, Spanish, and Russian. If the reader is on a quest for the text, it must be the pure text, the pre-Babel text as it were, the elusive text that the Reader is looking for, which is analogous to the pre-Babel language that Walter Benjamin talks about in "The Task of the Translator." In this seminal essay, Benjamin argues that translating transforms, enriches, and enhances the target language as well as the language of the original text. Each translation contributes to the quest for the pure language. In his lies, Ermes Marana claims to have traced the text back to the Father of Stories, even though it could also be the Organization of Apocryphal Power or the Organization for the Electronic Production of Homogenized Literary Works (OEPHL). In reality, Ermes Marana, the cunning and eloquent trickster figure, is the source of all the confusion. Carter thinks that Marana may refer to "fraud," "riffraff," "garbage," "swamp," "frog," "the devious-devising mouthpiece of stories translated, stolen, or otherwise plagiarized, who somehow roams the world" (131) and who feeds the book market with all the ten fragments in Calvino's book.

The labyrinth in *If on a Winter's Night a Traveler* is also conveyed through the language and symbols of network used throughout the novel. The bookstore is one such symbol, particularly in its incarnation of intertextuality. The Reader navigates a labyrinth of a "thick barricade of Books," "Books You Haven't Read," "Books You Needn't Read," and "Books Read Even Before You Open Them Since They Belong to the Category of Books Read Before Being Written" (5). In this last case, as Barthes argues and as Calvino's Reader's labyrinthine search shows, any text yet to be written has already been written somewhere. The books mentioned in this section of the frame mirror the fragments encountered later on, for example, "Books You've Been Hunting For Years Without Success" (5) and "Books Read Long Ago Which It's Now Time to Reread" (6).

Professor Uzzi-Tuzii's library in Chapter Four continues the bookstore symbol. The location that the Reader and Ludmilla visit is situated in the basement of the university library. The two readers are looking for a text to complete *Outside the Town of Malbork* only to get the incipit of *Leaning from the Steep Slope*, a simultaneous translation from Cimmerian by Professor Uzzi-Tuzii. The three involved in this scene are buried underneath the library whose landscape usually has the shape of a labyrinth, a network of shelves. Shifts also occur here: a shift from story to story, a shift from language to language, and a shift from reading the written text to (simultaneous) oral transmission (as Professor Uzzi-Tuzii translates and orally transmits the story to the Reader and Ludmilla), and a shift in interpretive ideologies (from Uzzi-Tuzii to Galligani). The two professors' bickering keeps the story moving. As Barthes argues in "The Rustle of Language," the library represents language in motion, which rustles when it is working to perfection, but when the machine dies, it is distressing (76) because it recalls the Reader's demise, as he glimpses into silence and the void, if the possibilities of interpretation die. Flying, which is metonymic of reading, leads to that void: "you cross a gap in space, you vanish into the void" (210). For Ermes Marana also, "behind the written page is the void: the world exists only as artifice, pretense, misunderstanding, falsehood" (239). This fits Marana well as he believes that "'something must always remain that eludes us. . . . As long as I know there exists in the world someone who does tricks only for the love of the trick, as long as there is a woman who loves reading for reading's sake, I can convince myself that the world continues'" (240). "Beneath every word there is nothingness" (83), we read earlier in the novel, a reflection of what happens to the ten stories and that forces shifts in the Reader's quest for the text. As a result, beyond the confines of Calvino's novel, there is the possibility of the Reader's potentially endless quest for the text, a claim supported by Calvino's forced ending.

The void is potently conveyed in the second fragment (by Bazakbal): At one point, Bazakbal's book leads to blank pages, thus to a void or maybe to possible contemplation of what might have been there. The Reader experiences that void, the vertigo at the end of the ten fragments of stories in the novel, but this void is already experienced at the outset with the title. Titles are usually fragments (mostly noun phrases), but Calvino's title is a blatant fragment, the beginning of a sentence, a conditional, dependent clause that calls for completion. The "if" clause is a promise of completion that we hope to see in the novel, but this promise is betrayed at the end of the first chapter when the Reader realizes that the story suddenly stops on page 32. As playful as Calvino can be, however, he seems to offer a complete sentence toward the end of the novel, but it is only a concatenation of the titles of the unfinished stories (258). Calvino puts together titles of works that canceled each other out in the first place and produces the semblance of an acceptable sentence, but it is just the promise of another beginning, thus leading into the void again. Suddenly, Calvino throws in a *deus ex machina* to extricate the Reader from the quagmire he has created: He marries the Reader and Ludmilla. Do we want a conventional ending? Well, there we have it!

In *The Uses of Language*, Calvino refers to the "deep-rooted vocation in Italian literature, handed on from Dante to Galileo: the notion of the literary work as a map of the world and of the knowable, of writing driven on by a thirst for knowledge that may by turns be theological, speculative, magical, encyclopedic, or may be concerned with natural philosophy or with transfiguring visionary observation" (32). He offers that way of knowing in *If on a Winter's Night a Traveler* in the form of a labyrinth, a metaphor that conjures up a complex juxtaposition of stories, genres, critical perspectives, historical moments, geographical places, and a community of authors and readers, to name a few examples. To navigate this labyrinth, Calvino left us with five values in his last set of writings before he died: *Six Memos for the Next Millennium*; he died before he could define the sixth ("consistency"). These are "lightness" (possibility of intellectual elevation), "quickness" (literature's ability to move us to higher intellectual desires), "exactitude" (linguistic precision), "visibility" (literature's ability to make reality vivid to readers, notably through the use of images), and "multiplicity," which refers to "the contemporary novel as an encyclopedia, as a method of knowledge, and above all as a network of connections between the events, the people, and the things of the world" (105) and which best captures the labyrinth in *If on a Winter's Night a Traveler*.

Works Cited

Barthes, Roland. "The Death of the Author." In *The Rustle of Language*. Trans. Richard Howard. Berkeley: University of California Press, 1989. 49–55.

_____. "The Rustle of Language." In *The Rustle of Language*. Trans. Richard Howard. Berkeley: University of California Press, 1989. 76–79.

Benjamin, Walter. "The Task of the Translator." In *Selected Writings*. Volume 1. Cambridge, Mass.: Harvard University Press. 253–263.

Calvino, Italo. *If on a Winter's Night a Traveler*. Trans. William Weaver. San Diego: Harcourt Brace & Company, 1981.

_____. *The Uses of Literature*. Trans. Patrick Creagh. San Diego: Harcourt Brace & Company, 1986.

_____. *Six Memos for the New Millennium*. Cambridge, Mass.: Harvard University Press, 1988.

Carter, III, Albert Howard. *Italo Calvino: Metamorphoses of Fantasy*. Ann Arbor: UMI Research Press, 1987.

Fish, Stanley. *Is There a Text in This Class? The Authority of Interpretive Communities*. Cambridge, Mass.: Harvard University Press, 1980.

Markey, Constance. *Italo Calvino: A Journey Toward Postmodernism*. Gainesville, Fla.: University Press of Florida, 1999.

Morrison, Toni. *The Nobel Lecture in Literature, 1993*. New York: A. Knopf, 1994.

Reed, Ishmael. *Yellow Back Radio Broke-Down*. Normal, Ill.: Dalkey Archive Press, 2000. [1969].

Ricoeur, Paul. *Oneself as Another.* Trans. Kathleen Blamey. Chicago: University of Chicago Press, 1992.

Washington, Peter. "Introduction." In *If on a Winter's Night a Traveler.* Trans. William Weaver. San Diego: Harcourt Brace & Company, 1981. ix–xxiv.

"IN THIS STRANGE LABYRINTH HOW SHALL I TURN?" — #77 (LADY MARY WROTH)

"The Maze Within: Lady Mary Wroth's 'strang labournith' in *Pamphilia to Amphilanthus*" by Margaret M. Morlier, *Reinhardt College*

Exploring the twisting paths and labyrinthine turns of emotional experience, Lady Mary Wroth's *Pamphilia to Amphilanthus* (1621) established a place for the feminine voice in the love-sonnet tradition. Pamphilia, whose name means "all loving," expresses joy, grief, desire, and loss. Embedded in this collection of 103 sonnets and songs is a self-contained poetic crown of sonnets or *corona*, a sonnet sequence in which the last line of each poem becomes the first line of the next. Wroth's *corona*, poems 77 through 90 in the collection, begins and ends with the speaker, Pamphilia, asking the question, "In this strange labourinth how shall I turn?" Although Wroth drew the image of the labyrinth from classical literature, she reworked key elements of the stories. Traditionally the ancient maze is a place of entrapment. In Wroth's poetic *corona*, however, it becomes a site of personal discovery, an opportunity for growth, and an image for understanding the role of art in human experience.

By the time that Wroth composed her sonnets in the seventeenth century, the image of the labyrinth as a structure had accumulated several metaphorical meanings. In literature, the pattern of the maze, with its twisting paths, became a metaphor for psychological complexity. In religion, some medieval churches had mazes drawn on

the floors, and a penitent pilgrim would work his or her way through
the elaborate lines to find the right path to a specific ending place,
sometimes crawling on hands and knees to signify the difficult progress of the soul through earthly life. Puritan thinkers of the English
Renaissance reinterpreted the image. For Puritans, earthly experience
seemed to be a series of puzzles or mazes to be negotiated by an individual, who should be guided by the inner light of faith. Given all of
these metaphorical and spiritual meanings, the image can represent
both a process of confusion and a product of artistry, depending, as
Penelope Reed Doob has discerned, on perspective (1). From inside,
the way to proceed is confusing. From outside, the labyrinth might
appear as a highly structured design. Wroth's sonnets invoke both
of these perspectives to have the labyrinth represent the confusion
of emotional experience and the order that language can provide to
clarify this confusion.

Like a labyrinth, with its enclosures and restricted paths, the sonnet
form has its own formal restrictions, and *Pamphilia to Amphilanthus*,
with its 103 poems, is a tour de force of sonnet writing. The word
"sonnet" derives from *sonnetto* or "little song" in medieval Italian
literature. Although there was a minor tradition of heroic sonnets,
the dominant theme of Italian sonnets was love, most famously in
Petrarch's fourteenth-century collection *Il Canzoniere*. In English
literature, the sonnet has two main forms: Italian and English. The
Italian sonnet form has fourteen lines with a two-part structure,
an octave (eight lines with a rhyme scheme *abba abba*) and a sestet
(six lines with a varied rhyme scheme, often *cd cd cd* or *cde cde*); the
English sonnet form has three quatrains of alternating rhyme (*abab
cdcd efef*) and a closing couplet (*gg*). Either form requires compression in thought and feeling. Wroth demonstrated mastery of both
forms in her collection, with the further impressive achievement of an
embedded *corona* of fourteen English sonnets.

In her *corona*, Wroth drew on specific elements from the classical stories of Ariadne, which involve a labyrinth, a golden thread,
and a circular coronal, wreath, or crown. In *The Metamorphosis*, Ovid
presented the builder Daedalus as "an artist / Famous in building,
who could set in stone / Confusion and conflict, and deceive the eye
/ With devious aisles and passages" (Ovid 8. 159–62). The maze—a
place of "deceptive twistings" (Ovid 8.168) and "innumerable

windings" (Ovid 8.166)—holds the Minotaur, a monster that is half-bull and half-man. According to Ovid's narrative, King Minos feeds the beast "each nine years" with a "tribute claimed from Athens, / Blood of that city's youth" (8. 170–71). However, the bloody ritual ends when Theseus arrives from Athens to enter the maze and slay the beast (Ovid 8. 172).

Ariadne now enters the narrative. Because she falls in love with Theseus, she supplies him with a "thread / Of gold, to unwind the maze which no one ever / Had entered and left" (Ovid 8.173–75). Theseus escapes using this thread. Although he takes Ariadne with him, he soon abandons her. Significantly, however, as the story ends, Bacchus finds her, bringing her love and taking the circular "chaplet" that she wears to set it "spinning high, its jewels / Changing to gleaming fire, a coronal / Still visible, a heavenly constellation" (Ovid 8. 179–82). In some earlier versions of the story, Theseus has a wreath that he, in turn, gives to Ariadne to wear; this wreath becomes the constellation of the corona. In other earlier versions, Ariadne gives Theseus a wreath that serves to light the darkness of the labyrinth to help him escape. Wroth drew an important theme from these stories of Ariadne's abandonment: the value of constancy in love. Yet Wroth revised key motifs and symbols from the classical versions. Most importantly, her persona, Pamphilia, does not escape from the labyrinth but is able to grow psychologically and spiritually from engaging with difficult, even conflicting emotions, such as jealousy and joy.

With the linked poems of Wroth's *corona*, a path unfolds, taken one step, or one sonnet, at a time through precarious emotional terrain. Subtitled "A crowne of Sonetts dedicated to Love," the sequence begins with a question:

> In this strang labourinth how shall I turne?
> Wayes are on all sids while the way I miss:
> If to the right hand, ther, in love I burne;
> Lett mee goe forward, therin danger is;
> If to the left, suspition hinders bliss,
> Lett mee turne back, shame cries I ought returne
> Nor fainte though crosses with my fortunes kiss;
> Stand still is harder, allthough sure to mourne (1–8).

The "strang labourinth" (1) in the opening question might refer to "Love" in the subtitle. After the first line, the speaker sees each possible direction as a different emotional path. To the right, the speaker would "burne" (3) in passion. To the left is "suspition" that "hinders bliss" (5). Turning back, the speaker might encounter "shame" (6). As the second quatrain ends, the speaker complains that to stand still also makes her "sure to mourne" (8).

Then the language itself becomes a kind of labyrinth or puzzle for readers to explicate. The first three questions about right, forward, or left are direct, with parallel syntax that implies the logic of cause and effect (if . . . then). The fourth question introduces more contorted syntax. Pamphilia laments, "Lett mee turne back, shame cries I ought returne / Nor fainte though crosses with my fortunes kiss" (6–7). Here Wroth exploits the poetic line breaks to create ironic meanings in diction and syntax. Read by itself, the first line of Pamphilia's lament might mean that she should turn back ("Lett mee turne back") because "shame cries" that she "ought [to] returne [backward]." At the same time, the line might mean that if Pamphilia turns back, then shame will cry that she ought to return to the forward path. The enjambment with the next line creates a third possible meaning: "shame cries [that] I [ought neither] to returne [backward] / Nor [should I] fainte though crosses [or mistakes, obstacles] with my fortunes [are brushed] kiss" (Wroth 6–7). In these two lines, Pamphila considers her options. Does shame tell her go back? Will she confront shame if she goes back? Does shame tell her to go forward with courage? Mirroring Pamphilia's confusion, the poetic syntax creates confusion for the reader.

Mary B. Moore finds a similar parallel: "The phrase *this strang labourinth* [in the first line] may refer to the poem itself—the most immediate *this*—or the word *this* may refer to the poet, her life, her erotic experience, even to all of these" (Moore 143). The sonnet's poetic style, Moore continues, creates the effect of "contracted energy" and even "forced containment" like the labyrinth itself (143). In fact, in Moore's analysis, the ending of the second quatrain—"Stand still is harder, although sure to mourne" (8)—might suggest that "standstill itself mourns, apparently confusing the poetic subject and her feelings with the action of negotiating the labyrinth" so that the "fusion of place, action, and speaker . . .

represents the labyrinth as subjectivity" (143). Wroth's skillful use of poetic techniques like elided words, inverted word order, and poetic syntax provokes interpretive confusion so that the sonnet establishes in form as well as content the theme that experience can present perplexing choices.

Just as language can create and express confusion, it can also clarify experience. The word *labourinth*—and its pun on "labour"— can refer to the advantage of working with language. After the confusing syntax of the second quatrain, the language of the sonnet begins to become clearer. The third quatrain and final couplet have short, direct phrases: "Thus lett mee take the right, or left hand way; / Goe forward, or stand still, or back retire" (9–10). Pamphilia realizes that she "must thes doubts indure with out allay / Or help, butt traveile find" for her "best hire" (Wroth 11–12). The word *traveile* means "work," reinforcing the meaning of "labourinth" as labor. However, in the sixteenth and seventeenth centuries, *traveile* might also refer to a journey or a finished literary work (OED *sb*1, I 3 and II). On one level, then, Pamphilia seeks a path in the labyrinth; on another, as a persona for the poet, she seeks a literary vehicle for the "best hire" in understanding emotions. The opening sonnet of the *corona* introduces this theme about the interplay of experience and language. In the final couplet, Pamphilia concludes that there is no way to escape the engagement with emotions, so she chooses "to leave all" attempts at rationalization and "take the thread of love" through the maze (Wroth 14).

The thread image incorporates another key element from the classical stories. The rest of Wroth's *corona* follows a thread of Pamphilia's thoughts, each sonnet taking its direction from the closing words of the preceding sonnet. Set against the classical stories, Pamphilia is both Theseus, potentially lost in a deadly maze, and Ariadne, the feminine voice of love who provides the guiding thread to allow for escape. Nevertheless, unlike the males of classical tradition, Pamphilia does not escape or transcend the enclosure. Instead she seeks a steady path through it. In an analysis of Wroth's achievement for giving a feminine voice to the sonnet tradition, Naomi J. Miller observes that "Pamphilia's voice itself becomes her thread of love expressed," guiding her through the "fluctuating behavior" of the beloved as well as her own emerging subjectivity (43).

Thus, while Pamphilia reacts to the inconstancy of the beloved, the sonnets also explore her own fluctuating emotional states. Heather Dubrow has noted that the mention of "chaste thoughts" in the third sonnet of the *corona* "signals . . . the focus on the internal, on the mind of the lover" instead of the "relationship between lovers" (153). Wroth's sonnets infuse these emotional states with theological significance by modifying the associations of the labyrinth from medieval and Puritan theology. In the second sonnet of the crown, the "thread of love" (1) leads to "the soules content" (2). When "chaste thoughts" (5) guide the mind, then love can lead to "blessings" (9), "peace" (10), "right" (11), and "fayth" (12). Pamphilia declares that the "Light of true love, brings fruite which none repent" (7) and that love is the "fervent fire of zeale" (10), with diction alluding, as Moore reminds us, to Puritan inner light of faith (145). In the fourth and fifth sonnets of the *corona*, the thread of love can provide a kind of redemption, and the "fires of love" are apocalyptic:

> Never to slack till earth noe stars can see,
> Till Sunn, and Moone doe leave to us dark night,
> And secound Chaose once againe doe free
> Us, and the world from all devisions spite (5–8).

Given these spiritual implications, the "affections" should "Governe our harts" (Wroth, P 80.9 and 10). The paths of experience, although fraught with complex emotions, can bring enlightenment and personal growth. Love becomes a "profitt"—with a pun on profit and prophet (Roberts 130, n14)—and "Tuter" (Wroth, P 81.14). Yet as Dubrow indicates, Wroth's sonnets promote "spiritual love" and "heightened spiritual peace" without "turning away from human love in favor of the worship of God" as other sonnet sequences might (153).

In this sense, Wroth's sonnets record engagement with experience, primarily psychological experience. Moreover, putting experience into words can bring further surprising psychological and philosophical insights. Dubrow makes the point that the "repetitive enchaining" of a corona "incorporates some narrative qualities in what is predominately a lyric sequence" (141). In other words, the sequence presents a psychological narrative. The labyrinth, then, becomes an appropriate image of how language can bring personal revelations through the twists and turns of composition. In the sixth and seventh sonnets of the poetic crown, for example, love can "inrich the witts, and make you see / That in your self, which you knew nott before" (9–10). In the eighth sonnet, love influences perception: It draws on human goodness to make the devotee a "painter" who can "drawe your only deere / More lively, parfett, lasting, and more true / Then rarest woorkman" (9–12). Love of another person can lead to self-knowledge so that "Hee that shunns love doth love him self the less" (14). The tenth sonnet of the *corona* proposes a distinctive relationship between love and reason. In classical and Puritan philosophies, reason should rule emotions. Pamphilia, in contrast, asserts that "Reason adviser is, love ruler must / Bee of the state which crowne hee long hath worne" (5–6). After idealizing various parts of the experience of love, the poetic crown ends by acknowledging the reality of "Curst jealousie" (11) that cannot be idealized. Therefore, the words that began the *corona* also end it: "Soe though in Love I fervently doe burne, / In this strange labourinth how shall I turne?" (13–14). Although Pamphilia remains within the labyrinth of emotional experience, her journey through language has brought her insights along the way.

Several scholars have noted that the labyrinths in Wroth's poems build on medieval and Renaissance symbolism. Doob, for example, discusses the common medieval spelling of labyrinth as *laborintus*, which reinforces the concept of labor or work. She explicates several possible etymological implications of this spelling, but the significant one for the present analysis is "difficult process" (Doob 97). Doob also explains that the hero's usual escape from the labyrinth might occur literally with the golden thread or metaphorically though some kind of transcendence like a "privileged—*and an accurate*—overview of the world, whose random confusion is revealed as the perfect physical and moral order of a divine architect" (312–13). The only exception she finds before the seventeenth century is Chaucer's *House of Fame*, a work in which the labyrinth "becomes an emblem of the limitations of knowledge in this world, where all we can finally do is meditate on *labor intus*" (313). Chaucer's poetry, in fact, celebrates the labyrinthine "confusion and complexity" of life (Doob 338). Similarly, Wroth's feminine hero, Pamphilia, does not escape the maze but seems to engage her experience within it as a source of knowledge.

Other scholars propose that Wroth's use of the labyrinth looks forward to modern philosophies. Huston Diehl describes "an anxiety in the Protestant image of the maze that differentiates it from the medieval and the Counter-Reformation labyrinths and anticipates the post-modern maze" (Diehl 288). After analyzing visual and literary representations of the labyrinth, Diehl argues that the Protestant Reformation was a "transitional term" when the concept of life as a maze became internalized, preparing the way for modernist and postmodern doubt of the twentieth and early twenty-first centuries (289). The maze of Wroth's poetic crown is certainly more existential—a philosophy from the twentieth century—than Puritan. The Renaissance Puritan tended to see the labyrinth as "analogous to the serpent—evil, satanic—trapping man in the sinful world, the corrupt body, the narcissistic self" and to look for an escape from worldly confusion in divine providence (293). In contrast, the twentieth-century existential hero often looks for meaning through experience, working within a restricted set of earthly choices in a way that parallels Pamphilia's paths within the labyrinth of emotional states.

Still, even with the formal poetic crown, which ends by repeating its first line, Worth's speaker is not walking in endless circles. Miller has a similar view: "The question in the fourteenth line of the fourteenth sonnet echoes the question on the first line of the first sonnet, completing the circle only to continue it" (Miller 158). Indeed, the next poem in the collection of 103 poems shifts in tone to images of light, imploring "Sweet lett mee injoye thy sight / More cleere, more bright then morning sunn" (1–2). The speaker continues to develop dynamically in the following poems, as *Pamphilia to Amphilanthus* concludes. In the final poem of the collection, Pamphilia declares her silence but hopes to inspire "young beeginers" (10). In Moore's words, this ending seems to be one of "calm resignation, of achieved form, perhaps of achieved knowledge" (Moore 148). Even further, the collection ends by firmly acknowledging a place for the feminine voice in lyric poetry.

Wroth's *corona* looks forward to postmodern literature in two senses: as a feminist response and as a work that presents language as a source of meaning. Dubrow makes the point that in the tradition of Petrarchan love sonnets, the "woman is an object to be investigated," yet Wroth revises the tradition "to investigate her own emotions and thus wrest agency from objectification" (159). The *corona*, the third key element from the classical stories, symbolizes praiseworthy value or achievement. In response to the classical myth, in which Bacchus set the crown in the sky as a constellation to honor Ariadne, Wroth creates her own crown with the fourteen sonnets.

The "strang labourinth" of Wroth's sonnets becomes a site for a dynamic quest as well as a highly wrought poetic design. Like Dubrow and Moore, both Jeff Masten and Nona Fienburg argue that Wroth reveals a developing feminine subjectivity throughout *Pamphilia to Amphilanthus*. Indeed, the linking of sonnets in the crown mimics the linking of thoughts in associative meditation. Masten even proposes that the finesse of the *corona* seems to be a kind of performance, to "stage a movement which is relentlessly private, withdrawing into an interiorized space," so that the polished poems can only "gesture" toward subjectivity (69). By embedding this well-wrought design in a larger collection of poems, Wroth encourages readers to step back and see the *corona* as a self-enclosed whole. The labyrinth in this enclosure provided Wroth with a vehicle for representing and exploring an emotional journey. The journey might not be over at the conclusion of the *corona*, but the processes of art allow for surprising, valuable revelations along the way—in the twisting paths and sudden turns of language.

WORKS CITED

Diehl, Huston. "Into the Maze of Self: The Protestant Transformation of the Image of the Labyrinth." *Journal of Medieval and Renaissance Studies* 16 (1986): 281–301.

Doob, Penelope Reed. *The Idea of the Labyrinth from Classical Antiquity Through the Middle Ages*. Ithaca, N.Y.: Cornell UP, 1990.

Dubrow, Heather. *Echoes of Desire: English Petrarchism and its Counterdiscourses*. Ithaca, N.Y.: Cornell UP, 1995.

Fienberg, Nona. "Mary Wroth and the Invention of Female Poetic Subjectivity." *Reading Mary Wroth: Representing Alternatives in Early Modern England*. Ed. Naomi J. Miller and Gary Waller. Knoxville: U of Tennessee P, 1991. 175–90.

Masten, Jeff. "'Shall I turne blabb?': Circulation, Gender, and Subjectivity in Mary Wroth's Sonnets." *Reading Mary Wroth: Representing Alternatives in*

Early Modern England. Ed. Naomi J. Miller and Gary Waller. Knoxville:
U of Tennessee P, 1991. 67–87.

Miller, Naomi J. *Changing the Subject: Mary Wroth and Figurations of Gender in
Early Modern England*. Lexington, Ky.: UP of Kentucky, 1996.

Moore, Mary B. *Desiring Voices: Women Sonneteers and Petrarchism*. Carbondale,
Ill.: U of Southern Illinois P, 2000.

Ovid. *Metamorphosis*. Trans. Rolfe Humphries. Bloomington, Ind.: Indiana UP,
1958.

Roberts, Josephine A. Introduction and Notes. *The Poems of Lady Mary Wroth*.
Baton Rouge, La.: Louisiana State UP, 1983.

Wroth, Lady Mary. *The Poems of Lady Mary Wroth*. Ed. Josephine A. Roberts.
Baton Rouge, La.: Louisiana State UP, 1983.

INFERNO
(DANTE ALIGHIERI)

"The Poetry of the *Divine Comedy*,"
by Karl Vossler,
in *Medieval Culture: An Introduction to Dante and his Times* (1929)

INTRODUCTION

Navigating Dante's labyrinthine *Inferno*, with its many interpretive layers and its many circles, Karl Vossler provides a guide to Dante's great poem. As a journeyer through the horrors of hell, Dante, the author and pilgrim, is both artificer and maze walker, the one who must navigate the complex structure of the poem and the labyrinth of the self. As an important overview of Dante's work, Vossler's essay demonstrates the way the poem's intricate details are related and invites the reader to enter an interpretive labyrinth. Below are three sections from the essay.

Vossler, Karl. "The Poetry of the *Divine Comedy*." *Medieval Culture: An Introduction to Dante and his Times*, Vol. II. Trans. W.C. Lawton. New York: Harcourt Brace, 1929. 207–300.

THE STAGE SETTING OF HELL

If in Heaven pure and appropriate form has its abode, no completely lawless unfitness and lack of form rules in Hell; for Hell also is a divinely ordained world. But the aberrations from law and form do attain there their maximum.

The earthly sphere is the incomplete and concrete likeness of the heavenly sphere, a form filled out with matter in a fortuitous fashion, an irregular sphere whose outer surface is determined by Heaven, its content by the material.

Since Heaven is the realm of form, and Hell the realm of matter, Hell has its place in the interior of the earthly sphere, indeed in its inmost centre.

This centre, as the abode of the absolutely material, is just as extreme and abstract as spacelessness, regarded as the abode of absolute form.

The stage of the *Commedia* lies between the outmost limits of the divine and of the infernal world. The Inferno is the most dismembered, but still divinely ordered, landscape, inhabited by devils. This funnel, with its cliffs, abysses, shattered rocks, dilapidated bridges, streams, torrents, lakes, and morasses, with rain, snow, and hail, with firebrands and ice, with wildernesses and forests, in short with all the terrors of wild and hostile Nature, is one of the mightiest creations of poetic imagination.

In the midst of this disordered, unfettered, self-mutilating natural world, there stands a city, resembling human handiwork and enlightened effort. But this city of the Devil is no creation of civilized human hands, but a demoniac construction, a work and an instrument of inhumanity, no barrier nor bulwark against savage nature, but organized savagery itself; a deliberately and intentionally created inhumanity, which, because it is conscious and organized, is far more hellish than the hellish natural world.

The subterranean constructions: the gate of Hell, the city of Dis, graves, fountains, dams, etc., are not in contradiction with subterranean nature, but present themselves as exaggerations and supplements of it, so that there is nothing capricious or unpoetical about them. The order and intent which they reveal are just as devilish and inhuman as the apparent disorder and irrationality of Nature.

For, in the last analysis, even the natural phenomena of Hell have in them nothing accidental, but are essentially hostile to man, and torture is the purpose they attain; their cruelty is only less systematic than the hellish constructions. Therefore the poet has placed the infernal city, with its organization and administration, in the lower section of the Inferno, the purely natural transgressions in the upper portion.

Accordingly, the infernal scenery is the poetic expression of an ever-increasing enmity toward man. First we see Nature against man, then man against his neighbour and against himself; after that we behold Nature grown conscious, the city of Dis turned against man until finally, in deepest Hell Nature, man's neighbour, the city, and the ego itself unite in hostility to man so that the drama comes to a standstill.

The scenery is therefore essentially dramatic, is part of the action, and often becomes the action itself. We have in the *Inferno* a drama wherein not only the players but even the scenery actively participate.

Only in poor dramas does the scenery harden into mere useless decoration; in the Inferno, however, furious rain, howling wind, tongues of flame, biting cold, stench, light, gloaming, darkness, and even the motionless stones are things alive that give pain and are malicious. Out of all the shadows of the abysses horrors are grimacing, and behind every rock agony lurks. The earth, the walls of a room, the air, are all spiteful, uncanny, bewitched, enchanted, unaccountable.

To pass through a region so unfathomably strange and hostile would be a perilous venture, and material for a romantic poem. But Dante is no errant knight, and his *Inferno* is no romance. His intention is not to sing the horrors of Hell, but to comprehend them, to master them with reason.

The *terra infernalis* is to be explored and explained, not to be enjoyed and conquered, as an Alpine peak is by a tourist.

The scenery endowed with life, filled with malice, alive with rage and trickery, has its counterpart in human reason, and especially in Virgil. He, the wanderer's guide, reveals the malice, thwarts the magic, explains and puts to flight the terrors of the infernal world, preserves the order and law which this savagery obeys. His opposition brings Hell's game to a standstill.

Now since Virgil is himself a prisoner in Hell and can offer the How but not the final Why of the mystery, he can calm the action of Hell, indeed, but not destroy it, can show the scenery to be limited, finite, measurable, and purposeful, and strip it of its romantic charm, but must, nevertheless, leave it its actuality and its picturesque reality. He is himself only a part, an inhabitant, even though the wisest, of this kingdom.

Provided Virgil remains true to himself, he still cannot, with the most abstract didacticism and good sense, destroy the poetic life of Hell. He is subject to it.

His character, as we have analyzed it, signifies for the poem no dangerous negative, but one of its most fruitful, liveliest resources.

THE INFERNAL DRAMA

As the scenery of Hell takes part in the infernal drama, it is to be expected that the actors also, on their side, should become part of the scenery and decoration. In fact, a succession of monsters, devils, sinners, and beasts serve as players and supernumeraries at once; and most, if not all, are so merged in the drama that neither the mechanician nor the stage manager can dispense with them.

These minor figures—and all in Hell except Dante and Virgil are minor figures—are yet so fully taken up with their own affairs that the passage of the two wanderers must appear to them a strange, sometimes desirable, sometimes indifferent or unwished-for, interruption of their own toils. So, instead of being the echo, the chorus, or the decorative environment to the chief action, they carry on a variety of independent minor actions.

But in this very multiplicity and diversity of byplay lies a great danger to the unity of the poem. The chief action threatens to become empty and to sink to the level of a mere journey or wandering, the motive of which is but the crossing of the infernal realm, in accordance with a program. Curiosity and haste would then be the only spring of the main action; and in this express-train fashion of travelling, the inhabitants of the land, with all their own peculiar interests, must seem mere fleeting phantoms; somewhat in the manner that human beings, houses, cities, rivers, mountains and forests, signboards, and milestones go whirling by those who sit in a swiftly rushing railroad train.

The danger that the drama may degenerate into tourist sight-seeing exists throughout the entire *Commedia*. At the close of the poem the mind of the hasty reader retains no sense of development, but a maze of pictures. The majority of readers of Dante actually remember, not the course and progress of the poem in its entirety, but only certain brilliant episodes. In order to remember the passage, the connection, and the manner in which such meetings, such little dramas, are woven into the chief one, one needs a long and intimate acquaintance with the *Commedia*. It is customary to say that Dante's wealth of pictures and figures is too great for the memory to grasp them all easily. But wealth beyond our powers of enjoyment may become want. So it comes to pass that, at the present day, in most Italian cities where Dante is publicly read and expounded, the poem is cut to pieces, and only single cantos are treated, never the poem as a whole. Such dissection may be due to the scanty capacity of the readers, but to some extent it is a natural result of the construction of the poem.

Just as we plan a long journey, calendar and map in hand, so Dante arranged the successive stops of his pilgrimage through Hell and the hours of the day with such detail and exactness that the expounders find themselves compelled to prepare Dante charts and Dante clocks. To be sure, like all the maps and clocks in the world, they fit only approximately and in a general fashion.

For the comprehension of poetry, which by nature is incommensurable, these attempts at orientation can give no adequate aid. As we do not want to memorize but to understand the poem, we renounce artificial mnemonic aids.

This does not mean that Dante's arrangements and divisions are merely such aids and have a wholly inartistic and pedantic import, or fall outside the poetic action. Since the *Inferno* does describe a pilgrimage or journey, clocks and maps are an essential part of the illusion, and the efforts at orientation by the travellers are, just as much as their most exciting adventures or poetically enlivened action, aesthetically effective, justified, and correct. When Dante, in the eleventh canto of the *Inferno* and in the seventeenth of the *Purgatorio*, makes Virgil explain the moral order of these realms, and when Virgil, at almost every cornice of Hell or Purgatory, inquires for the shortest way, the situation cannot, to an intelligent critic, appear inartistic.

But when Alighieri makes the claim that his divisions and orien-
tations have been fully tested as to their mathematical accuracy and
validity, and when his expositors accept this assertion, all this has no
longer any relation to poetry and aesthetic criticism. We need not
concern ourselves, now that we have left the study of the sources
behind us, with the question of the scientific value that is to be
accorded to the chronology, astronomy, moral philosophy, and geography of the *Commedia*.

But we shall have to raise the question whether the chronology,
astronomy, moral philosophy, and geography within the poem itself,
within the limits of the poetic illusion, are consistent with each other;
or, in other words, whether this exactitude, after it has once entered
into the poetry and has become poetry, is also taken seriously and
maintained throughout.

For just by means of this exactitude the poet has overcome the
danger that the main and the subordinate actions may fall apart.
So it is not that the poet has turned mathematician: it is the mathematician that has become a poet. Chiefly because the divisions and
ordering of the journey are taken so seriously by the travellers, the
numerous impressions, the many little dramas, acquire their fixed and
fitting place, and ceasing to be mere episodes, which might at will be
rearranged or even omitted, are built up one upon another, so that
the earlier are presupposed and explained by the later. So it is the
memory not of the reader, but of the poet and traveller, that holds
together the chief and the minor actions. If the reader's memory is
unable to follow the poet's, so much the worse for him, so much the
better for Dante's glory. For recollection is, in its essence, intellectual
will and inward sympathy. Through such sympathy and receptivity on
the traveller's part all the scenery and minor action are absorbed into
the main theme, all externals become experience, are treasured up
and elaborated. The chief action is, accordingly, no hasty trip or mere
sightseeing journey, but an orderly, attentive, and profound process of
grasping and recasting all minor incidents and scenery.

To be sure, with a companion who forgets nothing, who has the
entire past before his eyes and with it the present in all its details,
whose spirit keeps pace with each new impression and, like a stream
fed by a hundred brooks, widens and grows until at last he becomes
superhuman—with such a comrade, travelling is uncomfortable. I

know of no other poem that makes larger demands on the reader. The whole *Commedia*, from beginning to end, fully understood and lived through, is an extraordinary task, which only extraordinary people accomplish. Yet even the poet himself as he step by step with scrupulous care, with the strictest inner connection, without digression, without anticipating what is to come, goes on from known to unknown, makes no unjustified demand on his companion.

The division of the infernal region and of the journey through it is therefore no abstract scheme, but a frame that sets off and unites the whole, arrays it and defines it, and permits all the episodes to appear both separately and collectively, a frame which is a part of the picture, because it was planned with it and is viewed with it. It is like the frame of masterly mediaeval altarpieces, whose extent and borders were planned by no ordinary artisan, but by the painter himself.

Scenery and plot, main and minor action, are held together by Dante's inmost sympathy and rapt attentiveness. Sometimes he forgets himself so completely in conversation with a sinner, or at the sight of a monster, that this sinner, that monster, becomes the centre of interest and the chief action; sometimes he is so keenly and clearly aware of his own position, so collects himself and becomes so thoroughly absorbed in himself, that the whole of Hell seems drawn and engulfed into this inward swirl. In Dante's *Inferno* there is no definite distinction between chief and subordinate action, chief and minor figures, scenery and drama: for the one passes unceasingly into the other, and this transition is poetic life.

THE GENERAL TONE OF THE "INFERNO"

Such an alternation of outwardness and inwardness, objectivity and subjectivity, self-forgetfulness and self-comprehension, renunciation and appropriation, of individualizing and abstracting, such an exchange between the Ego and the non-Ego, may be more or less violent and abrupt, or natural and regular. It makes a difference whether I am journeying across a plain, where land and people are alike to the point of monotony, or whether I am wandering through a precipitous mountain region where the landscape is varied and inhabitants of diverse race and temperament are thrown together. Both environments, however, the monotonous as well as the varied, offer

difficulties to the observer. The former may easily be found monotonous, the latter bewildering. In order that there may be between
Nature and its artist lover a rhythmic interchange, a give and take, an
easy flow of intercommunication, there is need of a tempered environment, of a region or landscape such as we call congenial.

To be sure, every people, every century, every individual, every
instant, finds a different side of the environment especially congenial,
and befitting its own nature.

What is the elemental tone and mood of the *Inferno?* And is it
possible that a spirit like that of Dante could feel at ease there?

That elemental tone has been recorded powerfully and clearly by
the poet himself, in the famous inscription over the Gate of Hell;

> "Through me the way is to the city dolent;
> Through me the way is to eternal dole;
> Through me the way among the people lost.
> Justice incited my sublime Creator;
> Created me divine Omnipotence,
> The highest Wisdom and the primal Love.
> Before me there were no created things,
> Only eterne, and I eternal last.
> All hope abandon, ye who enter in!"[1]

It is the mystery of eternal life, seen from its most agonizing
side. For no less eternal and fathomless than life is its most faithful
companion, pain. By the force of relentless justice it trickles forth out
of the noblest sources of life, out of strength, wisdom, and love.

This divine origin gives Hell its hopeless eternity and unconquer-
able power. He who thus harbours torture within himself despairs. But
he who has the power to draw it forth from his bosom and to gaze on
its interminable duration, such a man has conquered it: and nothing
of life's sorrow lingers still within him except the lofty consciousness
of dread eternity. An awesome shrinking from an eternity of pain is
the keynote of the *Inferno*.

That is why its scenery is conceived as hostile to life, cruel, diabol-
ical, and always on the offensive against mankind: an agony made
visible and ennobled by its eternal duration; a fixed threat against
the Ego. Therefore the main action of the *Inferno* is a stirring, an

appealing and attentive contemplation and inward experience of that scenery.

That Alighieri was never in his life better prepared and emotionally more adapted for such an undertaking and for the full comprehension of hatred, cruelty, and all the agonies of earth than in the days when he had himself undergone his bitterest griefs, the death of Beatrice and of Emperor Henry, and when he could not but doubt his own worth—all this we know full well. The conception of the *Inferno* fits into those years and moods of despair, and every canto bears traces of them.

Not merely external events, however, but his temperament also provided the fitting mood for the *Inferno*. The stuff of which he was made contained more gall than milk. If he did, nevertheless, struggle upward to the hopefulness of the *Purgatorio* and to the cheerfulness of the *Paradiso*, he drew the strength therefor out of the agonized depths of his nature.

In the *Purgatorio*, and especially in the *Paradiso*, the lyrical element as the expression of the poet's mood becomes more and more independent, rises here and there above the narration, action, and scenery, leaves the circumstantial and external, withdraws within itself, so that only the soul and light of those cantos breathes and lives, while the outer features grow pale and fade away.

But in the *Inferno*, the lyric is rarely distinguishable from the epic and the dramatic, and just because it is omnipresent, does not appear as lyrical. The *Inferno* with its tangible realism is like a monster whose soul has no definite organ, and in which not only the limbs but the hair and claws are endowed with life, coiling and writhing like snakes and scorpions.

NOTE

1. *Inferno*, III, 1–9.

"Kubla Kahn"
(Samuel Taylor Coleridge)

"Symbolic Labyrinths in Coleridge's 'Kubla Khan'"
by Robert C. Evans,
Auburn University at Montgomery

Samuel Taylor Coleridge's hypnotic poem "Kubla Khan" is set in an exotic locale, features an all-powerful architect, and describes one of the most magnificent building projects ever undertaken (at least in the human imagination). The entire poem, in fact, can be understood as itself a kind of labyrinth—one that is full of puzzling turns, unexpected twists, and literally mysterious passages. Symbolically, too, the poem itself fulfills many of the traditional and figurative functions often associated with labyrinths and mazes: It leads us both into and through a strange and confusing new place; it initiates us into a bewildering but also fascinating kind of experience; it is figuratively associated with paradise but also contains threatening or disturbing elements; and it is explicitly linked with the holy, the sacred, and the inscrutable (Cooper 92–93). Reading the poem, like passing into and out of a labyrinth, functions almost as a rite of initiation in which the reader, like any initiate, is transformed, so that by the end of the process he or she has achieved a new and deeper kind of knowledge, although it is knowledge that cannot be simply explained, logically expressed, or easily understood. Before considering the ways in which "Kubla Khan" can be read as a kind of symbolic labyrinth, however, it may be useful to survey quickly the traditions of labyrinthine imagery in the history of Western civilization.

I.

Over the centuries and in different cultures, labyrinths have been interpreted and understood in a wide variety of ways. Michael Ferber notes that the "original labyrinth of classical mythology was the vast maze under the palace of King Minos of Crete, inside which was the Minotaur, product of the monstrous lust of the queen for a bull. It was built by Daedalus and finally entered and exited (after he killed the monster) by Theseus, with the help of Ariadne and her ball of string" (102–03). As Ferber reports, this story was widely imitated in classical, medieval, and even later literature (103), but it seems to have had no visible impact on Coleridge's poem, which lacks (among other things) both a monster and a death-defying hero.

Indeed, one of the most striking aspects of Coleridge's palace and gardens is how relatively unpopulated they seem; Kubla Khan himself and the mysterious "damsel with a dulcimer" (l. 37) are the only two real (as opposed to figurative) humans mentioned as actually present (other than the speaker himself), and it is not even clear that the damsel is present at Xanadu per se. Moreover, for a place that is full of "wood[s] and dale[s]" and that features a river and sea, Kubla's magnificent grounds seem curiously lacking in wildlife. No birds, beasts, or fish appear, and even the palace or "pleasure-dome" itself (l. 2) is given short shrift. Coleridge's lyric, in other words, has little in common with the story of perhaps the most famous labyrinth in Western culture; even the quest motif that is so obviously a part of the myth of Daedalus's labyrinth is much more implicit and subtle in Coleridge's poem. In "Kubla Khan," it is the actual landscape—rather than any human or even mythical agent—that provides the main source of action and interest. The river plays a far more active role in the poem than does even Kubla himself. He is, in a sense, the poem's "unmoved mover"—the being who creates through his "decree" (l. 1) an alternate universe but who then sits back and merely (or mostly) watches it function.

By the time of the Christian Middle Ages, labyrinths had often come to represent (in the words of Wendy B. Faris) "the entangling layers of worldly sin surrounding man." According to this view, "God perceives order in the design and may endow man with the Ariadne's thread of grace he needs to reach the divine center of the pattern." Labyrinths during Christian periods thus often symbolize "man's wanderings and temptations" (Faris 692) as well as the complexities of human life, "with all its trials, tribulations and digressions"; thus, "for this reason, the middle [could] often symbolize the expectation of salvation in the form of Holy Jerusalem" (Becker 171). Christians also sometimes perceived labyrinths as emblems of "divine inscrutability," and the movement through such designs (especially when they were depicted, as they often were, on the floors of cathedrals) could be treated as a "symbolic substitute for a pilgrimage to the Holy Land" (Cirlot 174). Of these standard Christian associations, the latter two seem most relevant to Coleridge's lyric: Kubla's character and purposes are certainly inscrutable, and the mini-universe he creates is explicitly and repeatedly associated with such terms as *sacred* (ll. 3, 24, 26), *holy* (l. 14, 52), and *Paradise* (l. 54). Once again, however, the most intriguing aspect of "Kubla Khan," when it is studied in conjunction with the history of traditional labyrinths, is how much it differs from previous treatments of such symbolism. The poem offers little emphasis on either sin or salvation (at least as those terms are usually and conventionally conceived). No great moral threat is emphasized; no great ethical challenge is stressed; no great matters of right or wrong are either openly stated or clearly implied; and no profound spiritual danger or achievement is suggested. Coleridge does not create an obviously Christian (or even anti-Christian) atmosphere; issues of conventional religion, conventional morality, and conventional spirituality seem largely irrelevant to this poem.

Coleridge was writing, in fact, during a time when the imagery of labyrinths seems to have lost many of its standard classical and Christian overtones and when, indeed, "the popularity of the labyrinth as a symbolic title seems to decline" (Faris 694). This shift may have been due in part "perhaps . . . [to] a greater degree of realism" in the literature of this time, so that "labyrinthine structures appear [figuratively] as forests or cellars" in much writing of the 1700s and 1800s (Faris 694). During this period, literature featuring labyrinths (whether literal or symbolic) tends to emphasize "the dark, hidden aspects of the design, causing it to suggest not political or social life so

much as the hidden emotional, even unconscious life of individuals"
(Faris 694). Certainly these comments seem relevant to Coleridge's
text; the poem's relative neglect of social and political issues (except
in its vague and passing allusion to the possibility of "war" [l. 30])
has already been mentioned, while the whole final third of the piece
seems to emphasize the potentially profound inner transformation of
the speaker rather than any concern with society or politics as such.
Coleridge's focus seems to be much less on society than on the individual and much less on social morality than on the private imagination. Later, in the twentieth century, labyrinths would often come to
represent a sense of man's existential confinement or the absurdity
of human existence, but neither of these meanings seems especially
relevant to Coleridge's poem. Thus in its labyrinthine aspects, as in
so much else, the work seems for the most part *sui generis*, or quite
literally one of a kind.

II.

Having briefly surveyed the history of symbolic uses of labyrinths
in different periods of Western culture and suggested the ways in
which such uses compare and contrast with the labyrinthine aspects
of Coleridge's lyric, it now seems worthwhile to discuss the multiple
ways in which images of labyrinths and mazes have been more
generally interpreted by students of human psychology and myth.
J.C. Cooper, for instance, nicely summarizes many of these interpretations when he notes that labyrinths have often been associated
with such meanings as "the return to the Centre; Paradise regained;
attaining realization after ordeals, trials and testing; initiation; death
and rebirth and the rites of passage from the profane to the sacred;
the mysteries of life and death; the journey of life through the difficulties and illusions of the world to the centre as enlightenment or
heaven; a proving of the soul; the path of travel and escape to the next
world (this world being easy to enter, but once entered into difficult
to leave); a knot to be untied; danger; difficulty; [and] fate" (92–93).
"The labyrinth," Cooper notes, "is often presided over by a woman
and walked by a man," and it "is also said to symbolize the world;
totality; inscrutability; movement; [and] any complex problem,"
while "its continuous line is [often associated with] eternity, endless

duration, [and] immortality" (93). Cooper, summing up the work of many other scholars, reports that the "labyrinth, at one and the same time, permits and prohibits," functioning as a "symbol of both exclusion in making the way difficult and of retention in making the exit difficult; only those qualified and equipped with the necessary knowledge can find the centre, [while] those venturing without knowledge are lost" (93). He further notes that the labyrinth is frequently "related to the symbolism of the cave [and] with the idea of an underworld, mysterious journey, or the journey to the next world" (93). Many of these meanings seem pertinent to "Kubla Khan," particularly Cooper's emphases on the recovery of paradise, symbolic rebirth, and the presence of a mysterious woman, but even Cooper's splendidly detailed overview of labyrinth symbolism is hardly exhaustive. There are still other aspects of the potential meanings of labyrinthine imagery to mention.

Thus, Udo Becker notes that labyrinths "painted on Etruscan vases" have sometimes been "interpreted as representations of a womb" (170)—a meaning which would support the pervasive view that movement into and out of a labyrinth symbolizes a kind of rebirth. Beverly Moon suggests that the labyrinth often "signifies a movement from what is outside and visible to what is inside and invisible" (68), while Donald Gutierrez conveys a real sense of the potential complications of labyrinthine symbolism when he notes that a maze can involve such various connotations as "difficulty, fun, perplexity, anxiety, hope, despair, fear, horror, transcendent release or realization. Thus it is a complex state or condition that engenders hardship, persistence, frustration, imperilment, liberation, or death" (3). Finally, Jean Chevalier and Alain Gheerbrant (although under the heading of "Maze" rather than "Labyrinth") provide a comprehensive overview that resembles Cooper's in some ways but differs from his in others. Of particular interest is their comment that the existence of a maze, almost by definition, "proclaims the presence of something precious and holy," so that the

> centre protected by the maze is the preserve of the initiate, the person who has passed the tests of initiation (the windings of the maze) and has shown him- or herself worthy to be granted the revelation of the mystery. Once that person reaches the

centre, he or she is, as it were, made holy, entering the arcane and bound by the secret (643).

As will soon become apparent, these comments seem especially relevant to Coleridge's poem, particularly to its concluding passages.

III.

From its very opening line, Coleridge's lyric seems strange, exotic, and mysterious. Both the place ("Xanadu") and the person ("Kubla Khan") mentioned in that line sound foreign and unusual, yet the poet refuses to pause to explain anything about either; he merely takes their existence for granted, as if both Kubla and his homeland are well-known. Thus, just as Kubla Khan brings an entire alternate universe into existence by simple decree, so, in a sense, does Coleridge himself. We are never given a chance to question or ponder who, exactly, Kubla is or where, precisely, Xanadu may lie; no sooner is Kubla mentioned than his power and creativity are immediately implied: He orders the existence of a "stately pleasure-dome" (l. 2), and, in the combination of that adjective and that noun, Coleridge initiates a pattern of provocative ambiguity that will continue throughout the entire lyric. The word *stately* suggests something princely, noble, majestic, and imposingly dignified, while the term *pleasure dome* is intriguingly vague. What, exactly, *is* a "pleasure dome"? What kinds of pleasures are associated with it? Coleridge doesn't say, but the phrase *stately pleasure-dome* manages to combine hints of luxury and self-indulgence with an emphasis on grandeur and dignity, and in that respect the phrase is typical of the paradoxical qualities of the entire poem, which is full of sensual imagery but also manages to sound lofty and sublime. There is, from the very beginning of this lyric, an air of tantalizing inscrutability that makes reading the poem an experience similar to entering a labyrinth full of strange twists and unexpected turns.

No sooner is the "pleasure-dome" mentioned, however, than it is immediately forgotten; a different sort of poem might have spent a long stanza elaborating on the details of the building, but *this* poem immediately shifts to describing the natural landscape. Just as the existence of Xanadu and Kubla Khan were merely taken for granted, so is the existence of "Alph," which is described not simply as "a" venerated stream but as "*the* sacred river" (l. 3; italics added) as if Alph in particular, and such things in general, were simply matters of fact. Once again, then, Coleridge (like Kubla himself) creates by simple fiat—by mere decree—and it is with the introduction of the river that we have our first real hint of potentially labyrinthine imagery. The river runs through "caverns" (a term also traditionally associated with labyrinths), and these caverns are "measureless to man" (l. 4); that makes them, like labyrinths, seem mysterious, bewildering, and even a bit frightening. The opening lines thus balance a sense of Kubla's power with a sense of the limitations faced by most humans: Kubla can create by decree, but, to most ordinary humans, nature can seem "measureless" and thus somewhat intimidating. That the river moves through the caverns and then plunges down into a "sunless sea" not only reinforces the labyrinthine overtones of the opening lines but also suggests the immensity of the cave into which the waters flow: It is huge enough to prevent an entire "sea" from being touched by the rays of the sun (l. 5). The opening lines imply the power of Kubla (including his ability to impose his designs on nature), but those lines imply the even greater power of nature itself.

This delicate balance of the human and the natural continues in the ensuing lines, which describe how Kubla had "walls and towers" built to enclose an immense area full of "fertile ground"—an area containing not only "forests ancient as the hills" (phrasing that suggests nature in its unmanaged, untamed state) but also "gardens bright with sinuous rills" (ll. 5–10, phrasing that suggests nature that has been domesticated by human cultivation). Does the phrase *sinuous rills* refer to streams designed for irrigation, or were the streams present before Kubla imposed his design? Whatever the case, the word *rills* not only contributes to our sense of the fertility of the grounds and gardens and contrasts with the immensity of the "sunless sea," but it also adds to the impression of the labyrinthine complexity of Xanadu. What is most striking in this respect, however, is how little Coleridge says about the details of the walls, the towers, the gardens, the pleasure-dome, or any other aspects of the man-made designs that have been imposed upon the landscape. We are given no precise information about the appearance of any of these things, nor are we provided with any information about how they were constructed. No workers are mentioned, and no history of the process of enclosing such an immense tract of land is offered. No descriptions are given of the inhabitants of the place or of the people who maintain it; indeed, Kubla himself is mentioned merely in passing. No one—except (by implication) the poem's speaker and reader—ventures into this mysterious landscape or moves through it. In contrast to much literature associated with labyrinths, this poem describes no literal journey or quest, and yet despite the relative absence of references to either human or animal life, the poem seems powerfully dynamic and vital.

Most of the dynamism of "Kubla Khan" is associated not with questing persons or the movements of other creatures but with the landscape itself, especially the energetic flowing of the "sacred river." Thus, in a passage that has often been seen as depicting a kind of symbolic orgasm, the speaker describes how "A mighty fountain momently was forced" from out of ground that seems almost to be "breathing" in "fast thick pants" (ll. 17–19). Suddenly the poem is full of paradoxes, including an inanimate landscape that somehow seems almost alive but also the idea that this landscape is at once both "savage" and also "holy and enchanted"—the kind of place in which it might be easy to imagine a "woman wailing" for a literally paradoxical "demon-lover" (ll. 14; 16). Everything about this passage of the poem is mysterious and intriguing but also full of a kind of bizarre balance; thus the peacefulness stressed earlier is now balanced by an almost frightening sense of violence. The river that once plunged down into a sunless sea now forces itself up again into the light of day, and the earlier imagery of walls and towers (associated with creative construction) is now balanced by the idea of "Huge fragments" of rock being "vaulted" forth "like rebounding hail" (l. 21). When the river suddenly re-emerges from the darkness, the speaker describes it (in one of the most explicitly labyrinthine of all passages in this lyric) as "meandering with a mazy motion / Through wood and dale" until it once again reaches "the caverns measureless to man" and then sinks once more "in tumult to a lifeless ocean" (ll. 25–28). In some ways the poem here seems, like a labyrinth or a maze, to have circled back upon itself: Imagery mentioned earlier is now repeated (and thus inevitably takes on even greater symbolic significance). And, just as the earlier river imagery led to a passage of almost volcanic force, so the newest introduction of that imagery leads to a passage that implies the potential of true destructiveness: "And 'mid this tumult Kubla

heard from far / Ancestral voices prophesying war!" (ll. 31–32). Up
to this point, Kubla has seemed all-powerful, but now even he (or at
least his creation) seems potentially under threat. The natural tumult
just described seems, perhaps, merely a prelude to a violently destructive human tumult involving people who are, nevertheless, never
mentioned (or even alluded to) in this puzzling poem. The lyric, in
other words, has taken another one of its strange, unpredictable, yet
fascinatingly labyrinthine twists.

It then, immediately, takes yet another such turn as the speaker
quickly abandons any further talk of war; the subject is brought up
only to be quickly dropped. The possibility of war briefly adds dark
and ominous shadows to the lyric, but then the topic is discarded
just as suddenly and inexplicably as it was introduced. Instead the
speaker now returns once again to imagery from earlier in the work:
Once more he mentions the "dome of pleasure" (l. 32), and once
more he mentions the "fountain and the caves" (l. 35). And then,
for good measure, he combines the two, referring (in typically paradoxical phrasing) to "A sunny pleasure-dome with caves of ice!" (l.
36). Hypnotically, yet unpredictably, the poem will veer off in an
unexpected direction and then, just as mysteriously, circle back upon
itself. Its movement is anything but logical, straightforward, or linear,
and the process of reading it is indeed like being in a maze: A reader
can never quite predict what will happen next or what new detail will
suddenly emerge, and yet the phrasing seems hauntingly repetitious.
In moving from line to line while making one's way through this
poem, a reader never knows whether to expect something utterly new
or something strangely familiar. The poem moves in circles, yet its
unfolding is never regular or predictable. It not only introduces us to
a mysterious place, but it is also structured in mysterious ways.

Perhaps no shift in the poem's development is less predictable
than the sudden introduction of the "damsel with a dulcimer" in Line
37. Her abrupt appearance coincides with a newly explicit emphasis
on the speaker himself, as the poem unexpectedly shifts from its
earlier external focus on Kubla and his apparently Asian estate to a
new focus on an "Abyssinian [i.e., African or Ethiopian] maid" and
especially on the speaker's own desires and aspirations. The movement
of the poem, in other words, has involved an elaborate, unpredictable,
and indeed typically labyrinthine movement *inward*; no longer is the

speaker much concerned with Kubla or Xanadu per se; now his main interest is in his own, personal yearning to be able to re-create, within himself, the imaginative, creative power that Kubla and Xanadu have come to symbolize. It is in these closing lines of the poem, in fact, that the work becomes in some ways most explicitly labyrinthine in its imagery: Not only does the phrasing of the poem once again circle back upon itself (ll. 46–47), but it also now emphasizes repetition even within lines ("Beware! Beware!" [l. 49]). In addition, overtly circular imagery is now introduced in conjunction with the idea that something both sacred and frightening must be surrounded and enclosed; the potentially transformed speaker will seem so extraordinary that people are advised to "Weave a circle round him thrice, / And close your eyes with holy dread" (ll. 51–52). In the poem's final lines, just before the work breaks off abruptly into silence, we are left with a vision that is at once exciting and alarming, and it is in these lines that Coleridge's poem most clearly resembles a labyrinth: Something that is simultaneously holy and dreadful is discovered at the very end of our imaginative journey, and this final vision is at once so intoxicating, mystifying, and terrifying that its source must be enclosed in a kind of magical force field.

And then the poem suddenly stops. There is no slow, gradual emergence from *this* maze; there is no steady, reassuring retracing of steps, no calming return to an outside world that seems comforting because it is familiar. Instead, the poem ends just as abruptly and mysteriously as it began.

Works Cited or Consulted

Becker, Udo. *The Continuum Encyclopedia of Symbols.* Trans. Lance W. Garner. New York: Continuum, 1994.

Biedermann, Hans. *Dictionary of Symbolism.* Trans. James Hulbert. New York: Facts on File, 1992.

Chevalier, Jean, and Alain Gheerbrant. *The Penguin Dictionary of Symbols.* Trans. John Buchanan-Brown. New York: Penguin, 1996.

Cipolla, Gaetano. *Labyrinth: Studies on an Archetype.* New York: Lagas, 1987.

Cirlot, J.E. *A Dictionary of Symbols.* 2nd ed. Trans. Jack Sage. New York: Philosophical Library, 1971.

Cooper, J.C. *An Illustrated Encyclopedia of Traditional Symbols*. New York: Thames and Hudson, 1978.

Faris, Wendy B. "Labyrinth." *Dictionary of Literary Themes and Motifs*. Ed. Jean-Charles Seigneuret, et al. 2 vols. New York: Greenwood, 1988. 2: 691–96.

Ferber, Michael. *A Dictionary of Literary Symbols*. Cambridge: Cambridge UP, 1999.

Jaskolski, Helmut. *The Labyrinth: Symbol of Fear, Rebirth, and Liberation*. Boston: Shambhala, 1997.

Moon, Beverly. Ed. *An Encyclopedia of Archetypal Symbolism*. Boston: Shambhala, 1991.

THE LABYRINTH OF SOLITUDE
(OCTAVIO PAZ)

"The Labyrinth of Solitude,"
by Jose Quiroga,
in *Understanding Octavio Paz* (1999)

INTRODUCTION

Jose Quiroga focuses on the dual nature of Octavio Paz's writing—specifically, the intersection of its aesthetic and political dimensions. Written in a time of upheaval and transition, as Mexico struggled with its cultural identity and nationhood in the face of modernity, *The Labyrinth of Solitude* is envisioned by Jose Quiroga as Paz's attempt at "purgation, as medicine and cure to vacuous nationalism." Both a "psychoanalysis of Mexico" and a narration of its complicated history as a colonized culture, Paz's collection of essays chronicles and thoughtfully analyzes the forms of solitude experienced by those navigating the labyrinthine path toward self-understanding.

One of Octavio Paz's most ambitious and widely read works, *The Labyrinth of Solitude* was his most sustained meditation on Mexico—on its

---

Quiroga, Jose. *"The Labyrinth of Solitude." Understanding Octavio Paz.* Columbia, S.C.: University of South Carolina Press, 1999. 57-87.

history, society, internal structures of power, particular, paradoxical modernity, and relationship to Latin America and to the European and modern world. *The Labyrinth of Solitude* culminates Paz's attempts throughout the 1930s and 1940s to blend aesthetics and politics, commitment and solitude, Marxist thought with surrealism, by focusing on a critique on Mexico and nationalism. It represents Paz's most succinct combination of poetry, aesthetics, and politics; it fashions once and for all Paz's image as an intellectual engaged in a critique of the state and of its power.

Paz works from within the cultural crisis brought about by the progressive institutionalization of the Mexican Revolution, which fossilized a revolutionary language that had become, in the late 1940s, pamphleteering, sloganistic, debased. Language as the means of social exchange is immensely important to Paz. He complains, for example, that the only poetry left to Mexicans is found in the obscene verb *chingar*; that the linguistic world of the Mexican-American *pachuco* is a melange of Spanish and English, and so on. *The Labyrinth of Solitude* is fundamentally the work of a poet who reexamines the meaning of such words as *nation, love, society, poetry*. At times, its heightened emotion and despair (particularly in the rhetorical endings of chapters) signify Paz's attempt to communicate to his readers the state of crisis that the poet himself feels. In this sense, more than to persuade, as in a rhetorical tract, Paz wants the reader to *feel* the extent of the crisis that has provoked his discourse. Paz's constant appeals to emotion are, then, appeals that intend to involve readers' empathy. For Paz, Mexico is a neurotic patient, and the poet fashions himself into a hero—if not a healer, at least the one who makes others aware of the patient's status. If the society is ill, language is both index and cure. One should insist then, on the therapeutic effects of Paz's poetic journey through this labyrinth: the Mexican crisis is *named* in order to find a Mexican cure.

As Paz's first sustained meditation on politics and nationalism, *The Labyrinth of Solitude* presents an *other* Paz. But one must resist the temptation of critics who divide Paz's work into two different modes. If in his poetry since *Entre la piedra y la flor*, he had been trying to give an account of modern man's exploitation of Man, in *The Labyrinth of Solitude* Paz brings his concerns to touch upon a hidden cultural anthropology for Mexico, one that is poetic and moral, attentive to the outer as well as to the inner history of the nation. A historical as well as a semiotic treatise, this work will be the model upon which Paz will fashion his intellectual role in Mexican political discourse after 1950, by presenting himself as the one who defines Mexico as a particular geographical entity torn by the conflicting voices of the nation and the state. This other Paz is, as he says in his poetry, also the same. In *The Labyrinth of Solitude* Paz creates a sociology and an anthropology that are based on a poetics, and poetics itself rescues his interpretation from mere pamphleteering. In other words, Paz's political critique is based on a system internal to it and that spreads out toward his poetic texts.

As poetry and politics become more interrelated, particularly during the 1960s, Paz tries to explain his own dialectical categories. For example, in an essay from *El ogro filantrópico* (The Philanthropic Ogre) he focuses on the interplay among poetry, science, and history. If repetition entails degradation in poetry, in science repetition signals a regularity that confirms a hypothesis. The historian is situated at some midpoint between the scientist and the poet. His kingdom is like that of the poet, the realm of exception and uniqueness—but also like the scientist's, operating with natural phenomena that he intends to reproduce in terms of currents and tendencies. In this sense, "Los hechos históricos no están gobernados por leyes o, al menos, esas leyes no han sido descubiertas" (*OF* 38). (Historical events are not governed by laws, or at least those laws have not been discovered.) In these later words of Paz, he gives a holistic reading to his cultural work. The words remind us that Paz is attempting to fuse disparate realms of an activity grounded in poetry, seen as part and parcel of one and the same work.

It is important to understand *The Labyrinth of Solitude* as growing out of Paz's growing disaffection with the political developments of his time. He returned from Spain in 1938 full of political conviction that he expressed in a series of articles written for *El popular*, the pro-Communist paper of the Confederación de Trabajadores Mexicanos. After the Hitler–Stalin pact of 1939 and Trotsky's assassination in Mexico, Paz stopped writing for *El popular* and two years later, in 1941, entered into a dispute with Pablo Neruda over politics. In these shifts we can see Paz more vocally expressing his disaffection with the nationalist interpretation of Mexican reality. Paz, who had started to write about Mexico and its reality in 1938, undertakes his first journey to the United States in 1943, and it is during this trip that he will start consolidating many of the themes found in his work.

Paz repeatedly mentioned the year 1943 and his absence from Mexico for nine years as marking an epochal change for him. During those nine years, Paz lived in the United States and, later, in France, India, Japan, and Switzerland as a member of the Mexican diplomatic corps. But the most pertinent experiences for *The Labyrinth of Solitude*'s creation take place in the United States, which is where Paz encounters the Mexican-American *pachucos* that he portrays in the first chapter. It is his encounter with the Mexican reality in the United States that gives this series of meditations their sense of urgency. As Paz himself states in his book, he was able to see and to read the fate of Mexico implicitly and explicitly described in the body of the Pachuco. However, if the United States was important for the origin of the book, the bulk of its writing took place in Paris, and this situation of exile accounts for the essay's distance from the popular currents of Mexican thought at the time.

Paris represented the beginning of a fruitful decade for Paz. It was in Paris, in 1949, where Paz consolidated the first edition of *Libertad bajo palabra*, in 1949, as well as of *The Labyrinth of Solitude*, which was published the following year. In Europe during the decade of the 1950s Paz published such seminal books of poetry as *Semillas para un himno* (1954) and *La estación violenta* (1957), and *Sunstone* (1957), the essays *The Bow and the Lyre* (1956), and his collection *Las peras del olmo* (1957). In 1959, he published a second, revised edition of *The Labyrinth of Solitude*, underscoring the closed character of colonial society, amplifying the historical narration on the period of independence and the Mexican Revolution, and recasting chapter 8 into a much more critical assessment of the revolution itself. It is at this point that he also revised the book's psychoanalysis of Mexico.

The recastings of *The Labyrinth of Solitude* would have not changed the overall thrust of the book, had it not been for the addendum written after the events that occurred on 2 October 1968, in the Plaza de las Tres Culturas, or Tlatelolco, where the police fired on protesters who demanded a more open and democratic system of government. At that time, Paz was already a well-known writer, the author of essayistic and poetic works such as *Cuadrivio* (1964), *Claude*

Lévi-Strauss o el nuevo festín de Esopo (1965), *Alternating Current* (1967), *Blanco* (1967), *Conjunciones y disyunciones* (1969), and *East Slope* (1969). Paz's immediate reaction to the brutal police action was to resign from his diplomatic post in India. It was at this time, surely one of the most prolific in Paz's life, that he wrote "México: la última década" (1969), a critical assessment of the events known as "the massacre of Tlatelolco." This lecture has been published, in later editions, in *Postdata* (*The Other Mexico: Critique of the Pyramid*) and included as a sort of appendix or continuation of the theses that Paz had initially developed in his book. Both *Labyrinth* and its continuation in *Postdata* reflect the development of Paz's thoughts on Mexico over the course of twenty years. In this way, *Labyrinth* has become a kind of diary on twentieth-century Mexican politics. Remarkably, it is a book that remains immensely consistent over time. As we shall see, Paz has refined or nuanced his points of view, but he has never recanted the core basis of these ideas.

Like Paz's *Libertad bajo palabra*, *The Labyrinth of Solitude* is also a book that has grown and been revised over time. Paz wrote what we may now call the core of the book principally in Paris, between 1948 and 1949 (a period roughly contemporaneous to the poems of ¿*Aguila o sol?*), although the text originates out of meditations that precede it at least for a decade. Thus, it can be seen as the logical conclusion to experiences that begin after Paz's journey to Mérida and his encounters with the Mexican Indian milieu of Yucatán, and after his trip to Spain, in July 1937, to the Segundo Congreso Internacional de Escritores en Defensa de la Cultura. These two experiences are important to the development of Paz's political ideas; they beckon him to search for a language free of immediately partisan concerns. Paz's indebtedness in this regard spans a wide array of figures: from the national search for a Mexican philosophy undertaken by Leopoldo Zea, to the work of Alfonso Reyes, to the essayistic model of Samuel Ramos in his *Perfil del hombre y la cultura en Mexico* (1934) or Paz's search for a poetic discourse that was Mexican without the external trappings of nationalism. But the core thinkers in Paz's pantheon at the time of his writing are two dissenting members of the surrealist enterprise whose anthropological work was nevertheless steeped in surrealist responses to alienation. One was Roger Caillois, whose fundamental

Man and the Sacred illuminated the sacred importance of the fiesta; the other was Georges Bataille, who shed light on Mexican customs via his ideas of ritual sacrifice and expenditure in society. These two, of course, are added to a philosophical stratum that already included Friedrich Nietzsche and the Spanish Generation of '98.

The Labyrinth of Solitude then, is not so much a book on politics, as a political book. The distinction is as subtle as it is important; Paz's epic sweep, spanning centuries of Mexican history, is not meant to take sides on the petty and partisan political squabbles of the moment. Its sense of crisis is not, as in the later *Postdata*, the product of a concrete situation, but of a general sense of malaise, coupled with an awareness of changing historical times felt by a new generation of Mexican intellectuals that came of age after the revolutionary struggle had ended. The book's rhetorical "family" can be seen in its use of the work of the Spanish Generation of '98, particularly Miguel de Unamuno and José Ortega y Gasset. Unamuno sought to explain not only the visible, but also the invisible threads to Spanish culture; Ortega was the foremost Spanish philosopher of his time, as well as the editor of *Revista de Occidente*, where much of German philosophical thought was translated into Spanish. For Unamuno and Ortega, one had to search history's meaning far beyond the transparent details of a chronological narration. Unamuno, for example, read the nation as a living text. As such, the nation possessed a hidden center that the historian had to decipher, in order to read history from that hidden axis.

Unamuno's own indebtedness to German philosophy and to Nietzsche is clear, and these are also important precursors to Paz. But we should also clarify that what Paz does not take from Nietzsche is as important as what he does. Paz, for example, does not participate in the Nietzschean (and Emersonian) cult of "representative men," even if Paz defines eras according to the work of particular thinkers that define those eras. His debt to Nietzsche is found, rather, in the sweeping historical panoramas constructed by the German thinker. Counterbalanced by Nietzsche and later on by Lévi-Strauss, whose thought Paz discovers while in Paris, the Spanish "intrahistoria" can be seen to have a wide-ranging effect on Paz, from *The Labyrinth of Solitude* on.

Paz created in *The Labyrinth of Solitude* a mode of historical research that led to a method. In his writings on Mexico and the United States, as well as in his other essays on contemporary political or cultural situations, like *Los signos en rotación*, Paz used grand historical sweeping narratives. Few dates, and some individuals, incarnate given ideas that move and define particular centuries. The ideas that Paz wants to examine are not specifically or particularly conscious ones; rather, they are submerged in deeper strata of consciousness, and come up to the surface at particular historical junctures. All purely historical explanations are insufficient for Paz, because history should not be merely the accounting of facts. Historical events, he argues, are also full of humanity, by which we may understand "problematicity," and attitudes on life are not necessarily conditioned by historical events. In the introduction to the essays collected in *The Philanthropic Ogre*, Paz argues that the nation in itself is a product of not one, but of multiple pasts, and that historical narrations serve a therapeutic purpose for the nation (*OF* 11). For example, in chapter 4 of *The Labyrinth of Solitude*, "Los hijos de la Malinche" (The Sons of La Malinche), he explains how insufficient history is in accounting for the particular character of the Mexican; he pursues this idea by examining language along with history. This particular notion of a historical and philosophical critique of culture that is Paz's more immediate model was initiated in Mexico by Samuel Ramos in his *El perfil del hombre y la cultura en México*. But Paz's project was more revisionary and at the same time more ambitious.

In many ways, *The Labyrinth of Solitude* is a strange book, not only in terms of its style, but also because Mexico is looked at from a philosophical and geographical distance that is nevertheless psychologically near. Re-reading the book, one notices the particular absences that account for the fact that this is a book written by an exile. To use one example, there are many references to traditional culture, but few from popular culture, from cinema, radio, mass culture. Literature spans the space of exile; it crosses borders—but incompletely.

The Labyrinth of Solitude is divided into eight chapters and an appendix. The first, and perhaps the core essay of the book, is "El Pachuco y otros extremos" (El Pachuco and other extremes), and it opens with the figure of the Mexican-American immigrant to California that Paz encountered on his first visit to the United States in the 1940s. In the next three chapters, Paz analyzes what he considers particularly Mexican myths: "Mascaras mexicanas" (Mexican Masks), "Todos santos, dia de muertos" (The Day of the Dead), and "Los hijos de la Malinche" (The Sons of La Malinche). After this mythical coda, Paz devotes the next two chapters—"Conquista y colonia" (The Conquest and Colonialism) and "De la independencia a la Revolución" (From Independence to the Revolution)—to an analysis of Mexican history. The final two chapters in the book—"La inteligencia mexicana" (The Mexican Intelligentsia) and "Nuestros días" (The Present Day)—examine contemporary Mexico, with an appendix, added in the second edition of the book (1959) titled "La dialéctica de la soledad" (The Dialectic of Solitude). As Santí points out in the introduction to his edition, what seems like a basically straightforward account nevertheless does not give a clue as to the book's mode of structuration, its interrelated construction in terms of giant blocks of myth, history, and diagnosis of contemporary reality. As he sees it, *The Labyrinth of Solitude* obeys a sense of inductive reasoning, from particulars to generalities—from myth, to Mexican history, and finally, to what Paz himself terms a kind of vital and historic rhythm. The book proceeds, then, from the immediate experience, centered on the *pachuco*, to the mythical present of Mexico, and it is only after the mythical route has been completed that he moves on to history. What gives the book a certain flexibility as an essay, is precisely its discontinuous and even disarticulate, nature. Even the relationship between the mythical and the historical part of the book is neither explicit nor emphatic. The interplay between them both is insinuated, and not necessarily stated.

The Labyrinth of Solitude can be divided into two major blocks, composed of Myth and History, but there are other possible readings, particularly in relation to the first three sections on masks, feasts, and language. The first chapter posits an implicit essence for the Mexican, one that proceeds from the particular illegibility that Paz sees in the *pachuco*. The *pachuco* is seen as a reticent being, a kind of chiaroscuro subject. He inhabits a tenuous system of checks and balances. There is an implicit analogy between the *pachuco* and the collective sense of the Mexican *fiesta*, which Paz explores in the second chapter. Death and rebirth, inscribed and celebrated within the Mexican nation, are not unlike the cultural dislocation felt between North and South as it is written on the very body of the *pachuco*—a being who exaggeratedly mimics the North American in a rebellious gesture of excess. The fourth chapter, "The Sons of La Malinche," grounded on language and on the verb *chingar* inaugurates (by means of its filial metaphor—mother to sons) the historical section of the book. The procedure that Paz follows in the initial chapters of *The Labyrinth of Solitude* is thus aesthetic: it is grounded on poetic procedure, in that it establishes a tenuous equation between two realms, and it allows that equation (that relationship) to explode by means of metaphor. These relationships, or analogies, are then replicated in the equation between Myth and History in the two parts of the book.

The Labyrinth of Solitude is based on a series of analogies for modernity, seen as the most complex problem facing Mexico. Paz's analogy, borrowed from his experiences in the United States, as well as from the Parisian debate on Camus's and Sartre's notion of engagement, centers on the interplay between the individual and the collective life of Man. The book begins by trying to give us insight into the uniqueness of singularity, of individual life. This awareness of singularity, for Paz, is equivalent to an awareness of self: "El descubrimiento de nosotros mismos se manifiesta como un sabernos solos; entre el mundo y nosotros se abre una impalpable, transparente muralla: la de nuestra conciencia" (*LS* 143). ("Self-discovery is above all the realization that we are alone: it is the opening of an impalpable, transparent wall—that of our consciousness—between the world and ourselves" [*LSol* 9].) Children and adults, says Paz, may transcend their own solitude by immersing themselves in play or work. But the adolescent, the subject who vacillates between infancy and adulthood, remains "suspenso un instante ante la infinita riqueza del mundo" (*LS* 143). ("halting for a moment before the infinite richness of the world" [*LSol* 9].) It is precisely at the end of *The Labyrinth of Solitude*—in the ninth chapter—that Paz returns to that same vision of adolescence: "La adolescencia es ruptura con el mundo infantil y momento de pausa ante el universo de los adultos. . . . Narciso, el solitario, es la imagen misma del adolescente. En este período el hombre adquiere por primera vez conciencia de su singularidad" (*LS* 351). ("Adolescence is a break with the world of childhood and a pause on the threshold of the adult world. . . . Narcissus, the solitary, is the very image of the adolescent. It is during this period that we become aware of our singularity for the first time" [*LSol* 203].)

The central concept that underlies Paz's book is solitude and its relation to modernity. In order to introduce the reader to this

concept, from the onset of *The Labyrinth*, Paz equates individual to
national life—adolescence to adulthood. The adolescent's encounter
with his own singularity and with his own being is equivalent to the
nation's encounter with its own history. It is upon this grid, one that
equates the life of Man to the life of Nations, that the particular
disjunction of modernity is to be found: maturity is not the time for
solitude but the time for work, for reconciling ourselves with time.
Modernity, however, gives us the image of a Man permanently out of
touch with time, unable to lose himself in what he does. Modernity
is a disjunction, a kind of monstrous asynchronicity manifested in the
chronological fabric displayed between national and individual life;
ancient traditions have been submitted to a discontinuous growth that
has resulted in their being ill-prepared for the historical avalanche
of progress, while the individual is left pondering the state of his
own solitary endeavours upon reaching maturity. Paz seems to ask,
If adolescence is equated with solitude, and maturity with collective
endeavor, how can Mexicans, who have already fought a revolution,
still be questioning their identity? Shouldn't these questions seem
superfluous, now that the country has come out of its revolutionary
years? Identity is one of the enigmas that provokes Paz's historical
recounting of Mexican history, but this time from the particular
distance of one who seeks out the monster that lurks within the labyrinth. Paz will revise the nationalistic reading of the revolution as chief
guarantor of Mexico's singularity; at the same time he will diagnose
his contemporaries' nationalist preoccupations with Mexico as a sign
of self-defensive immaturity. As a modern nation, Mexico's adult
subjects are still immersed in their own solitude; they are ill-equipped
to deal with the modern world. In historical terms, the condition of
alienated Man is, by definition, modernity, since modernity is, in a
sense, the expression in time of Man's alienation. But alienation is
also a state that demands a resolution in utopia, seen and read as its
necessary end. Labyrinths are products of a mind that sees and examines the world in its own particular terms. Paz enters the labyrinth as
a modern Perseus; but in Paz's book the hero is not only Perseus but
also Narcissus, and at the same time Tantalus.

The labyrinth evolves out of, and tries to resolve, the dialectics
between myth and history. The prize at the end of the labyrinth, as
Paz explains in the appendix to the book, is the utopia of the fulfilled

human being. *The Labyrinth of Solitude* is conceived as a purgation, as medicine and cure to vacuous nationalism. The labyrinth is the imagistic link that allows Paz to narrate a series of ruptures that mark the book itself: from the disjunction of modernity and of the solitary individual, to that of a country ruptured within itself. The book seduces readers into the same labyrinth that Paz has constructed for himself, by creating and not resolving the dialectics that underlie its construction. Paz lives within this fragmented multiplicity, for history's fragmentation places the essayist within the labyrinth. These ruptures, which Paz reads as the "tradition of rupture" in *Children of the Mire* (1974) nevertheless contain within their movement a moment of precarious equilibrium; it is at this moment when the form itself can be apprehended and the figure read. If the labyrinth provides both a metaphor for Paz and his and the reader's act of textual seduction, it is only as a figure that the metaphor itself may be apprehended. In this case, however, the fragmentation of the labyrinth has once again consolidated itself (has petrified itself, to use Paz's vocabulary) into a pyramid, one that allows Paz to read, once again, a series of analogies—although in this case the analogies concern the nation as well as its geography.

METAMORPHOSES
(OVID)

"Daedalus in the Labyrinth
of Ovid's *Metamorphoses*,"
by Barbara Pavlock,
in *Classical World* (1998)

INTRODUCTION

In her analysis of Ovid, the source of the labyrinth myth in Western literature, Barbara Pavlock not only analyzes the myth in Book 8 of the *Metamorphoses* but also demonstrates how the myth has been used in other poetic works, namely Virgil's *Aeneid* and Ovid's *Ars Amatoria*. According to Pavlock, "While Ovid indicates 'an affinity with Daedalus in the labyrinthine intricacy of his poem [*Metamorphoses*], as a poet he reveals his superiority to the archetypal artisan in the nature of his own material. His numerous forms of repetition in the *Metamorphoses*, unlike the windings of the Cretan labyrinth, are inherently linked to a concept of play. Their aim is ultimately not to confuse the reader but to take him through an experience that will make him perceive the manifold paradoxes of the human condition more fully."

Pavlock, Barbara. "Daedalus in the Labyrinth of Ovid's *Metamorphoses*." *Classical World* 92.2 (1998) 141–57.

At the center of the *Metamorphoses*, Book 8 assumes a pivotal function, moving the poem into more overtly epic material, including the Calydonian boar hunt and the reception of Theseus and company by the river god Achelous. In the book's first section, on the Cretan legends, Ovid gives special prominence to the archetypal artisan Daedalus. The extended narrative of Daedalus' flight from Crete with his son Icarus culminates this section, after which the poet backtracks to the story of Daedalus' murder of his nephew Perdix and then concludes with the inventor's arrival in Sicily at the court of King Cocalus. As one of the most powerful artist figures in the *Metamorphoses*, Daedalus uses his inventive powers both for constraint, by constructing the labyrinth to contain the Minotaur, and for release, by fashioning wings to escape from Crete.

Ovid's Daedalus is a complex figure, whose brilliance is marred most glaringly by his failure to control his jealousy of his talented nephew. Recent critical studies have elaborated on Daedalus' limitations in his lack of real self-awareness and failure to sustain his Epicurean-style detachment in the face of his son's tragic death.[1] Although literary accounts of Daedalus prior to the Augustan age, including tragedies by Sophocles and Euripides, have not survived,[2] contemporary Roman poets provided complex, sometimes negative, perspectives on Daedalus' creativity. Horace in the *Odes* uses the flight of Daedalus and Icarus as an image of artistic hubris, in particular aspiring to the high genre of epic (1.3) or extending beyond the proper bounds of lyric (2.20 and 4.2).[3] As a major antecedent for Ovid, Vergil in *Aeneid* 6 summarizes Daedalus' associations with Crete in his *ekphrasis* of the temple doors of Apollo. Like Ovid, Vergil incorporates his story of Daedalus in the middle of his poem. This position, mediating between old and new, past and future,[4] lends itself to reflection not only on the heroic ethic but also on the poetics of the *Aeneid*. In a gesture that privileges Daedalus' achievement, Vergil makes the labyrinth emblematic: it anticipates both the hero's encounter with his past in his journey through the twisted paths of the underworld and the poet's review of Rome's own history, including its troubled recent past, through the Sibyl's intricate account of Tartarus and Anchises' roll call of heroes.

Ovid, I believe, responds to Vergil's *ekphrasis* by enlarging on the significance of the labyrinth for his own poem and by perceiving a more problematic aspect in Daedalus' invention of wings as a violation of boundaries. This study will consider Ovid's vision of the labyrinth as a metaphor for the design of the *Metamorphoses* in contrast to Vergil's maze, first by examining his poetic analogue for this structure. It will then analyze the strategies, including literary allusions, by which the poet implies a critical view of the archetypal artisan in contrast to the cultural values informing Vergil's ekphrastic portrait.

DAEDALUS AND THE LABYRINTH

The most elaborate of the descriptions of Daedalus' signal invention in Book 8 takes the form of an extended simile. The poet illustrates the windings of the labyrinth through an analogy with the river Maeander:

> non secus ac liquidis Phrygius Maeandrus in undis
> ludit et ambiguo lapsu refluitque fluitque
> occurrensque sibi venturas adspicit undas
> et nunc ad fontes, nunc ad mare versus apertum
> incertas exercet aquas, ita Daedalus inplet
> innumeras errore vias vixque ipse reverti
> ad limen potuit: tanta est fallacia tecti. (162–68)

> Just so the Phrygian Maeander sports in his clear waters and flows back and forth in an ambivalent course; rushing on, he sees the waves coming at him, and directs his uncertain waters now to the source, now to the open sea. Thus Daedalus fills the countless paths with windings and could himself barely return to the threshold: so great is the deceptiveness of the structure.

The use of an epic simile to compare the labyrinth with the river Maeander may be original with Ovid. But a virtuoso poetic description of the Maeander itself seems to have had a programmatic significance by the Augustan period. As W.S. Hollis notes, Seneca the Younger refers to the Maeander as the *poetarum omnium exercitatio et Indus* (*Ep.* 104.15).[5] This form of "practice" and "play" seems to have involved literary competition, if one can judge by Seneca's own version, which imitates the *Metamorphoses*.[6] The simile of the Maeander in Propertius

2.34 may well have been Ovid's model in Book 8: *atque etiam ut Phrygio fallax Maeandria campo / errat et ipsa suas decipit unda vias* (35–36), "and even How the deceptive river Maeander wanders over the Phrygian plain and its very waters confound its own course."

The elegist sets his own version of the tortuous river in a context of poetics, for he advises his addressee Lynceus to follow the example of Philetas and Callimachus. In place of the buskin of Aeschylus, Propertius urges Lynceus to relax his limbs *ad molles choros* (42): the reference to *mollis* privileges the lower style of elegy over the grander—and, by implication, more pompous—mode of tragedy. The image of the Maeander here seems to symbolize expansive forms of literature, especially epic, the high genre that Propertius dismisses along with tragedy in favor of elegy.[7] Yet at the same time the poet's description illustrates his own Callimachean principles. The chiasmus of *Phrygio fallax Maeandria campo* neatly conveys the sense of a winding course, and the elisions of the first two words of the hexameter lend a sense of abruptness analogous to the uncertain flow of the river. In the pentameter, the personification implied as the *unda* "confounds" (*decipit*) the river's course and adds a playfully humorous note to the impression of nature's power.

In the Maeander simile here in the *Metamorphoses*, Ovid may have Propertius' passage in the background in order to show his relation to the elegist's poetics. Ovid's description wittily collapses the distinction between Maeander as river and as river god. By the clever shifting of point of view or focus, his Maeander simile conveys the repetitiveness of the labyrinth's twistings without being repetitive itself. The poet provides three different ways of envisioning the Maeander's errant course. The first, containing prominent liquid "l" sound and employing the compound verb *refluo* and its root form joined with a double connective *-que*, mimics the sense of a back-and-forth flowing movement. The second personifies the river as the tutelary god and projects the divinity's surprise over the waves coming at him even as he rushes on. The river as anthropomorphic being plays (*ludit*) and watches (*adspicit*). The heavily spondaic meter in these lines nicely counters the predominantly dactylic pattern in the first part of the simile. The third contrasts direction as movement towards the source versus the open sea and, while giving control to the god (*exercet*, "drives"), personifies the waters as *incertas* ("uncertain"). The simile encapsulates Ovid's skill, on the level of poetic imagination, at blurring the boundaries between natural phenomena and the anthropomorphic in the *Metamorphoses*. In his epic, Ovid thus surpasses the elegist through his mimetic devices and more expanded personification of this natural force.

Ovid further calls attention to his own poetics by differentiating himself from Vergil in this simile. The phrase *ambiguo lapsu* succinctly captures the essence of the river with its circuitous flow. By using the word *lapsus* in the Maeander simile, his analogue for the labyrinth, Ovid associates the winding structure closely with the verb *labor*, "to glide" or "to flow." Ovid shows, I believe, that he was aware of Vergil's wordplay with the labyrinth sculpted by Daedalus on the doors of Apollo's temple in *Aeneid* 6. The *ekphrasis* of the temple doors is a kind of emblem of Vergil's epic, for the poet had prophesied in the *Georgics* that he would in the future construct a temple to honor the achievements of Augustus (3.10–39).[8] Here, the poet refers to the labyrinth periphrastically: *hic labor ille domus et inextricabilis error* (6.27). It is well known that Vergil makes a striking etymological play by deriving the word "labyrinth" from the noun *labor* and thus associates the structure with toil and struggle, concepts closely linked with his hero and the ultimate foundation of Rome.[9] Vergil's etymology for Daedalus' supreme creation is especially appropriate at this point in Book 6. The hero himself views this representation of the labyrinth while on his way to consult the Sibyl about descending to the underworld to reunite with his father. Illuminating Vergil's extensive wordplay in the *ekphrasis*, Frederick Ahl has commented on his punning with the word *pater*, which reinforces the thematic significance of paternity in this section of the *Aeneid*.[10] Furthermore, as the hero embarks on his arduous journey through the winding paths of Hades, Vergil's etymology for the labyrinth points up Aeneas's relation to Theseus, another hero of many labors, who not only re-emerged from the labyrinth after defeating the Minotaur but also penetrated the underworld.[11]

The *Aeneid* in its entirety has strong structural and motival links to the labyrinth. Because of Brooks Otis' work, readers of Vergil can appreciate more fully the complex patterning of the *Aeneid* through temporal shifts, both in narrative sequence and in the repetition of historical prophecies and of past events, ring composition, and the

interlacement of images and motifs.[12] In her recent study of labyrinths in ancient and medieval literature, Penelope Doob elaborates
on the specifically labyrinthine design of Vergil's epic, achieved
through the pronounced *labores* and *errores* in the first half of the
poem and through individual episodes with intricate patterning,
such as the fate of Laocoon, the wooden horse penetrating Troy,
and Aeneas's return to Troy for Creusa in Book 2; the ship race and
Trojan games in Book 5; the temple doors and the whole complex
of Apollo's temple, the Sibyl's cave, and the hero's journey through
Hades in Book 6; the cave of Cacus and the shield of Aeneas in Book
8; the flight of Nisus and Euryalus into the woods in Book 9; the
forest where Turnus plans to ambush the Trojans in Book 11; and
the final combat between Aeneas and Turnus in Book 12.[13] Even the
quintessentially labyrinthine Book 3, with its highly circuitous plot,
focuses on the hero's effort to fulfill divine prophecy by searching for
a new homeland for the survivors of Troy.

Ovid dissociates his labyrinth from the grueling labors of the
Vergilian hero. His etymological play connecting the verb *labor* with
the labyrinth perfectly characterizes the form of his own poem, its
fluid movement from tale to tale and the clever, if tenuous, transitions
from one book to another. The adjective *ambiguus* furthermore points
to the unexpected twists and turns in this poem. Like the Maeander
as labyrinth, Ovid's poem is ever-changing, shifting in direction. This
labyrinthine movement derives in part from the interlacement created
by the interruption of a tale with an intervening story and from the
recollection of a myth already recounted through similarities of theme
or plot line. But *ambiguus* also suggests the shifts in appearance that
take place so frequently within Ovid's poem, not least by the shape
changing of divinities as well as by the metamorphoses inflicted
upon so many of its characters.[14] While Vergil's epic has a maze-like
symmetry, Ovid's poem is labyrinthine in its emphasis on fluid process
rather than intricate structure.

Ovid further defines his poetics by contrast to Vergil in his
description of the playfulness of the Maeander (*liquidis . . . in undis
/ Judit*). *Lusus* is an important Augustan literary concept, which
characterizes Ovid's elegiac poetry.[15] Here, Ovid extends this poetic
"play," to epic, as he incorporates light subjects not normally included
in traditional epic and often parodies more serious subject matter.[16]

The adjective *liquidus* describing the waves of the Maeander further connects the simile to poetics, for the word occurs among Roman writers to characterize a fluid, smooth style.[17] Here, *liquidus* may be a Latin equivalent of the Greek καθαρός, used by Callimachus at the end of the "Hymn to Apollo" (2.111) to contrast the clear stream from a sacred fountain with the garbage-laden Euphrates, a symbol of the antithesis between the elegance of his own small-scale poems and the lack of polish of the more traditional longer works preferred by his detractors.[18] Later in Book 8, Ovid represents the river Achelous as both a swollen stream and a divinity, who boasts of sweeping away trees and boulders, riverside stables with their flocks, cattle and horses, and even strong men in his torrent (552–57). As the narrator of the tale of Erysichton and in Book 9 of his own contest with Hercules, Achelous is a long-winded, overly dramatic speaker whose tumid style matches his swollen flood (*imbre tumens*, 250). The allusions to the *Aeneid* in both stories suggest the speaker's preference for Vergilian high style.[19] In a playfully parodic manner, Ovid exposes the potentially ludicrous consequences of trying to re-create Vergilian epic. Ovid's *liquidus lusus,* characterized by an easy flow and light wit, is the antithesis of Achelous' pompous "Vergilian" style.

THE FLIGHT OF DAEDALUS AND ICARUS

The remainder of Ovid's narrative on Daedalus illuminates the contrast with Vergil's etymology for the labyrinth with its emphasis on difficult labors contained within the maze-like structure of his epic. The center of the Daedalus episode is the inventor's flight from Crete with his son Icarus (183–235). Ovid picks up where the *ekphrasis* in the *Aeneid* leaves off, for Vergil concludes his account of Daedalus' sculptures by noting what is absent: *tu quoque magnam / partem opere in tanto, sineret dolor, Icare, haberes* (30–31). Whereas Vergil stresses that the artist's pain over his son's death was too great to enable him to portray the flight with Icarus, Ovid elaborates on that adventure. He begins by providing a picture of Daedalus at work:[20]

> . . . nam ponit in ordine pennas,
> a minima coeptas, longam breviore sequenti,

ut clivo crevisse putes. sic rustica quondam
fistula disparibus paulatim surgit avenis. (189–92)

> For he arranged the feathers in order, beginning with the
> smallest, short following upon long, so that you would think
> it had acquired a sloping shape naturally. Thus the rustic Pan
> pipes sometimes gradually rise with unequal reeds.

By comparing the carefully gradated arrangement of the feathers
to the Pan pipes, Ovid seems to associate Daedalus' work with the
activity of a poet. But the literary background for this reference to
the rustic pipes may qualify the analogy. Marjorie Hoefmans has
recently suggested that Ovid alludes to Lucretius' account of the
invention of music, where nature provides the model for humans
to produce music technically (5.1379–83).[21] From that perspective,
Daedalus wisely follows Epicurean precepts. But in his discussion of
technology, Lucretius views the role of nature as a suggestive model:
the chirping of birds first gave men melodies to imitate, and the sound
of wind blowing upon reeds gave rise to the idea of constructing
musical instruments. By contrast, although they may look real, the
wings constructed by Daedalus are only a close copy of an anatomical
feature, belonging to another species.[22] As a mere imitation of nature,
they deceive the eye and create the appearance, but not the reality, of
a metamorphosis.

The Epicurean poet furthermore elaborates on the useful-
ness of the rustic instruments by providing delight and alleviating
cares (1384–411). Ovid himself has already made the reader aware
of the function of Pan pipes in a narrative that exemplifies his
light, witty style. His aetiology of the *syrinx* (1.689–712), interlaced with the story of Jupiter and Io, illustrates the benefit of
this instrument in the form of consolation and pleasure: Pan loses
his object of sexual desire but gains the reeds that produce delightful
music. In this narrative example of the light poetic mode characteristic
of the Pan pipes, Ovid humorously makes the story itself, as deftly told
by Mercury, a sleep-inducing narcotic for its uncouth audience.[23]

In contrast to Vergil's apostrophe explaining Icarus' absence from
the temple doors, Ovid gives considerable attention to the young boy
in this episode. As Daedalus concentrates on constructing the wings,

Icarus plays with the materials. The poet offers a highly visual description of the boy's amusement:

> puer Icarus una
> stabat et, ignarus sua se tractare pericla,
> ore renidenti modo quas vaga moverat aura
> captabat plumas, flavam modo pollice ceram
> mollibat, lusuque suo mirabile patris
> impediebat opus. (195–200)

> The boy Icarus stood around, and unaware that he was handling a source of danger to himself, now snatched at the feathers which the wandering breeze had wafted, with his face beaming, now softened the yellow wax with his thumb, and he hindered his father's marvelous work with his play.

By juxtaposing the *lusus* of Icarus with the *labor* of Daedalus, Ovid includes a quotidian vignette in a typically Alexandrian manner, yet adds a somber foreshadowing of death to this seemingly frivolous detail. The narrator's remark about the boy's ignorance of the danger in his playthings highlights the irony of Icarus softening the wax. The wax, of course, will soon be softened naturally by proximity to the sun, at the cost of Icarus' life. Ovid's ostensibly positive comment here that Daedalus "changes nature" (*naturamque novat*, 189) takes on added meaning that the inventor would not have assumed: his alteration of nature will at best be only temporary and will turn his son into a ludicrous sight, something "strange" rather than "new," as Icarus desperately flails his bare arms (*nudos quatit ille lacertos*, 227).

Whereas Vergil ends his *ekphrasis* by mentioning Daedalus' inability to portray Icarus on the temple doors, Ovid elaborates on Icarus' participation in the flight, as the two progress over the Aegean and the boy, eagerly flying too high, meets his doom. Ovid's account echoes Vergil's *ekphrasis* at the crucial moment of departure. When Daedalus finishes his warnings to Icarus, the phrase *et patriae tremuere manus* (211), as Hollis notes, recalls Vergil's description of Daedalus' inability to complete his pictures: *bis patriae cecidere manus* (6.33).[24] Vergil achieves an effect of pathos in part through metrics, for this expression of the artist's inability to proceed follows a heavily spondaic line, and the caesura of this verse falls emphatically after three tripping dactyls on the final syllable of *manus*. The anaphora of *bis* at the beginning of the two consecutive lines (33–34) suggests Daedalus' effort as well as his inability to complete his work. By his apostrophe to Icarus, whose pitiful death caused his father so much grief, Vergil seems to share the father's pain and calls attention to the father–son bond, which is not only a defining value for the hero of the *Aeneid* but also informs Vergil's narrative of the young men such as Pallas and Lausus, whose fathers are unable to protect them from death in the war in Latium.[25]

Ovid, on the other hand, resists an empathetic identification with the artist. As the father and son set out, he compares them to a mother bird teaching her fledgling how to fly: *velut ales, ab alto / quae teneram prolem produxit in aera nido* (213–14). Yet he immediately follows this description with a negative phrase that foreshadows Icarus' tragedy: *damnosasque erudit artes* (215). The poet's critical detachment from the inventor here is evident in the strong adjective *damnosus* ("destructive") applied to his skill. The negative implications of that word are reinforced immediately after Icarus' fall, when Daedalus, failing to get a response to his calls for Icarus, sees the feathers floating on the water. The father then curses his own skill: *devovitque suas artes* (234). As Hoefmans observes, the verb *devoveo* here alludes to Vergil's *ekphrasis* in *Aeneid* 6.[26] In an act of piety, Daedalus there, by contrast, "consecrated the oarage of his wings" (*sacravit / remigium alarum*, 18–19) to Apollo even though it was the sun, Apollo's divine image, that caused Icarus' wings to decompose. The irony is increased as the two verbs, *devovqo* and *sacro*, can be synonyms for "devote," but their antithetical meanings in these two accounts reflect the wide gap between Ovid's artist and Vergil's.

THE FLIGHT OF DAEDALUS AND ICARUS
IN THE *ARS AMATORIA*

Ovid not only alludes to Vergil and Lucretius but even turns to his own earlier version of the flight at *Ars Amatoria* 2.22–98. In a highly self-referential gesture, the poet even repeats several lines verbatim from the *Ars* passage.[27] Although scholars in general have not considered this repetition problematic, Alison Sharrock has recently argued that Ovid in the Daedalus episode alludes to the *Ars* as the cause of Augustus' anger and the poet's exile.[28] While it is tempting to consider that Ovid may have inserted this episode, or revised it, after receiving the notice of his *relegatio*, the echoes of the *Ars* bear more on the nature of Ovid's poem than on his autobiography. Much as the Maeander looks back at his own course, so Ovid returns to his earlier work and reveals the complex turns of his poem as a literary labyrinth.

As an indication of the difference in perspective with his earlier version, Ovid changes his description of the island Calymne over which Daedalus and Icarus fly from *silvisque umbrosa* (2.81) to *fecundaque melle* (222). Sharrock notes the etymological play on the meaning of Calymne (from the Greek κάλυμμα, "veil") with the description "shaded by trees" in the *Ars*.[29] But the phrase "fertile with honey" in the *Metamorphoses* is likewise a significant etymological gloss, which "corrects" the *Ars*, for the word κάλυμμα also refers to the cover of a honeycomb.[30] The image of honey suggests the transformative nature of the bees' activity, highly appropriate to the complex art of this epic. As if to point up its importance, Ovid recalls this image later in Book 8. The centerpiece of the humble, yet amusingly varied, banquet that Baucis and Philemon provide for Jupiter and Mercury is a honeycomb (*candidus in medio favus est*, 677). There, the playful irony throughout Laelex's narrative of the simple couple who entertain the two divinities is fitting to Ovid's variation on a Callimachean theme, in contrast to Achelous' inflated, "high" epic version of the story of Erysichthon.[31]

In several references to his earlier version of Daedalus' flight, Ovid reflects negatively on the artisan's relation to the gods. The *praeceptor* of the *Ars* depicts Daedalus in a positive light, even as an exemplar of piety. When the artisan contemplates his daring flight, he piously prays to Jupiter for pardon and assures the god that he does not seek to challenge the heavenly abodes:

> "da veniam coepto, Iuppiter alte, meo.
>   non ego sidereas adfecto tangere sedes;
>   qua fugiam dominum, nulla nisi ista via est." (2.38–40)

"Pardon my enterprise, lofty Jupiter. I do not attempt to touch
the abodes of the stars. There is no way except that one for me
to escape my master."

The poet emphasizes Daedalus' piety here, as he himself makes a point
of seeking divine favor in the *Ars*.[32] In Book 8, Daedalus shows hubris
by failing to invoke the gods at all before beginning his bold flight or
at any time in the episode.

In contrast to his earlier version, Ovid here suggests that Daedalus'
invention of wings is a hubristic violation of the realm belonging to
the gods and to birds. In the *Ars*, the *praeceptor* shows a simple fish-
erman responding to the sight of the two winged creatures on high:
*has aliquis tremula dum captat harundine pisces / vidit, et inceptum dextra
relinquit opus* (77–78). In the *Metamorphoses*, Ovid incorporates the
first line of this description and then expands upon it:

> hos aliquis tremula dum captat harundine pisces,
> aut pastor baculo stivave innixus arator
> vidit et obstipuit, quique aethera carpere possent
> credidit esse deos. (217–20)

> Someone while he was catching fish with his quivering pole
> or a shepherd leaning on his staff or a plowman on his plow
> handle saw them and was stunned, and he believed that they
> who could occupy the skies were gods.

By adding the examples of the shepherd and the plowman, Ovid goes
beyond the sense of astonishment in the *Ars* passage, for he reveals
that to ordinary people such anthropomorphic beings in flight could
be nothing other than divinities.[33] Their traditional beliefs are put in
strong antithesis to Daedalus' apparent indifference to the gods. Yet
the poet goes even further here by describing Icarus ascending higher:
caelique cupidine tactus (224). Although Daedalus in the *Ars* may not
have wished to "touch" (*tangere*, 2.39) the heavenly realms, his son
does here, with a passion (*cupido*). Daedalus' invention, it would seem,
has an inevitably transgressive effect on Icarus. The language suggests
a kind of challenge to the divine realm similar to the Giants' attempt
to scale Olympus.

Ovid's incorporation of the concept of the "middle way" is more complex in the epic than in the didactic poem as it contrasts Daedalus with divine powers. Daedalus' lecture to Icarus on flying a middle course repeats the artisan's general strictures about the dangers of flying too low or too high in the *Ars*. In both versions, Daedalus explains that the wings will be damaged by the sun's heat if they fly too high or by dampness from the sea if they fly too low (203–5; *Ars* 2.59–62). Ovid even repeats verbatim the essential injunction: *inter utrumque vola* (206; *Ars* 2.63), along with the emphasis on Daedalus' own leadership (*me duce*, 208; *Ars* 2.58). But the poet compounds the allusion to the middle way by looking back to the flight myth of Phaethon in *Metamorphoses* 2. There, the god Phoebus is unable to persuade the youth to reconsider his request to drive the chariot of the sun.[34] To make the best of a bad situation, Phoebus warns his son that flying too high will burn the heavenly abodes and too low, the earth; a middle path is therefore the safest: *medio tutissimus ibis* (2.137). Daedalus similarly admonishes his own son: *"Medio" que "ut limite curras"* (204).

If Ovid makes Daedalus a kind of Phoebus figure, he shows the artisan falling far short of the divine model. Phoebus is much more detailed in his advice and gives his son guidelines about navigating past the constellations. Initially hoping to discourage Phaethon's foolhardy desire, the sun god explains that the awesome appearance of the heavenly bodies may cause him to lose control of the chariot. He reinforces the substance of his warnings, for instance, with alliterative cacophony to impress upon the boy the menacing aspect of Scorpio: *saevaque circuitu curvantem bracchia longo* (2.82). But after failing to dissuade his son from undertaking the journey, the god advises him to stay between the twisting Serpent on the right and the oppressive Altars on the left (2.138–40). Daedalus assumes that Icarus should pay no attention whatsoever to the constellations: *nec te spectare Booten / aut Helicen iubeo strictumque Orionis ensem* (206–7). Instead, he instructs the boy to proceed simply by following him (*me duce carpe viam!* 208). Phoebus' point that Phaethon seeks what even the other gods cannot perform (60–61) is lost on his eager son. Daedalus does not even contemplate such limitations on mortals.

Ovid also puts Daedalus' relation to higher powers in a negative light by echoing the *Ars* when he advises Icarus not to fly with the aid of the constellations. In the earlier poem, the artisan dismisses the same three prominent constellations as guides for the boy: *sed tibi non virgo Tegeaea comesque Boolae, / ensiger Orion, aspiciendus erit* (55–56), "but you should not look at the maiden of Tegea and the companion of Bootes, sword-bearing Orion." The archetype for both Ovidian passages is important background, for the poet has Daedalus contradict a classic literary passage on navigation in *Odyssey* 5, Odysseus' departure from Calypso's island on a boat that he himself built. As J.E. Sharwood Smith points out, Odysseus wisely chooses to watch the Pleiades, Bootes, Arctus, and Orion (272–77) as the means of maintaining an easterly course towards Ithaca, since such a grouping would be easier to follow than one star.[35] Perhaps, as Sharwood Smith believes, Ovid has Daedalus imply that Icarus knows Homer's text but should not follow it because, unlike Odysseus, they are proceeding in a northwest direction. Yet the brightness of these particular constellations in itself made them the most useful source of guidance for navigators sailing the seas in antiquity.

The text of the *Odyssey* furthermore provides information about these constellations that is relevant to the issue of divine influence. The third one mentioned by Homer, "Arktos, which they also call by name Amaksa" (273), is the same constellation which Ovid calls Helice. While using the name most common in extant Hellenistic literature,[36] Ovid may wish to tease the reader into recalling the variety of names given to the most familiar of constellations, since he himself recounted in Book 2 the etiological tale of the nymph known as Callisto, who was metamorphosed into Ursa Major, the Great Bear. Although he narrates the tale at considerable length (400–568), the poet never actually names the young object of Jupiter's desire, who is driven out of Diana's circle when she is discovered to be pregnant. After giving birth to a son named Areas, the nymph is transformed into a bear by a jealous Juno and later narrowly misses being killed by her own son in a hunting expedition. Although Jupiter intervenes by metamorphosing both mother and son into constellations, Juno further seeks revenge by prevailing upon the sea goddess Tethys to prevent the Bears from ever setting in the ocean. Homer refers to this specific prohibition by describing Arctos as the one that "alone has no portion of the baths of the ocean" (5.275). This constellation furthermore is threatened by the neighboring Orion, the hunter who was killed by Artemis for his hubris and then catasterized, as Homer indicates that it "watches Orion" (274). Ovid alludes to this etiological myth about Helice and Orion when Daedalus mentions "*strictumque Orionis ensem*" (207). Although Daedalus appears uninterested in the interaction between humans and mortals in the background to these constellations, Ovid subtly reminds his reader of the power of divine influence on human life, especially in the form of punishment. He also implies the irony of the reference to Helice vis-a-vis Icarus: while the constellation is permanently kept from the ocean waters, Daedalus' son will forfeit his life in the deep and give his name to the sea.

Ovid's allusion to Homer, furthermore, recalls the Greek hero's rescue by divine help. Although his craft is shattered by Poseidon, Odysseus is able to redeem himself and is not, like Icarus, fatally immersed in the sea. He is saved by his characteristic ability to adapt to unforeseen circumstances: although hesitant, he puts on the magic veil given to him by the sea goddess Leucothea and is then able to swim to land (351–463). Odysseus understands that skill alone is not enough; divine assistance is sometimes essential. Ovid makes Daedalus' desire to control events and to rely on his own authority highly problematic. Even with his most impressive invention, the artisan almost destroyed himself when he nearly failed to get out of the labyrinth (167–68). In the flight from Crete, Daedalus does not perceive the deeper significance to the constellations that he dismisses. He himself is not able to rescue his son, and no god intervenes to save him.

DAEDALUS AND PERDIX

In the narrative following the death of Icarus, Ovid adds to the labyrinthine nature of his poem as a process of unexpectedly turning back and exposes Daedalus' negative repetitions. For he relates the story of Perdix, which is not found in the other extant literary accounts of Daedalus, out of chronological sequence. As a partridge, seeing Daedalus place his son's body in a tomb, applauds vigorously with its wings and sings joyfully (236–38), the poet provides the reason for Daedalus' *longum exilium* (183–84): the artisan pushed his nephew off the Acropolis but then lied about the boy's fall (*lapsum mentitus*, 251). Ovid here sustains the etymology for his labyrinth from the verb *labor* with his use of the word *lapsus*. As the term here denotes a "falling" rather than the "gliding" of the Maeander, Daedalus is now clearly associated with a moral flaw.

With the Perdix story, Ovid emphasizes that the artisan repeats himself with destructive results. The poet makes the relationship between Daedalus and Perdix virtually that of father and son, since the artisan's sister, called not by her name but only as *germana* ("twin," 242), had handed her child over to her brother as his ward so that Daedalus could serve as his mentor. Daedalus became envious of (*invidit*, 250) the boy when he produced two very significant inventions, the saw and the draftsman's compass. Ovid implies Daedalus' obsession with his own role as supreme artisan since these inventions, essential tools for the work of architects and artisans, in effect reversed the relation of master and pupil.

The poet's account of Perdix's inventions evokes the true genius of the boy. Recalling his earlier description of Daedalus in the phrase *naturamque novat* (189), Ovid suggests that Perdix is the one who truly transformed nature. The young boy saw patterns in nature from which he was able to extract designs; the creations completely superseded the originals and became something entirely new. Thus, he invented the saw by using the backbone of a fish as a model. In the construction of his verse, Ovid captures some of the essential qualities of these inventions. He conveys the bound arms of the compass, for instance, by a framing technique that encloses the words for the two iron arms within the phrase for the single knot: *ex uno duo ferrea bracchia nodo* (247). Similarly, he gives the impression of the way by which one arm always remains stable as the other moves by intricate word patterning: *altera pars staret, pars altera duceret orbem* (249). The anaphora in a chiastic pattern here neatly suggests the opposite, but complementary, functions of the scribe and point of the compass. By giving the reader a sense of the great ingenuity of Perdix's inventions, Ovid places Daedalus in an even more negative light for his inability to tolerate any competition from the boy.

Ovid reveals the negative nature of Daedalus' labyrinthine repetitions more fully as the story of Perdix unfolds, for his actions with his nephew have disturbing parallels with the flight from Crete, so disastrous for Icarus.[37] Perdix was only twelve years old when sent to live with Daedalus (242–43). His age approximates Icarus' at the time of the flight, since the poet describes the boy interfering with his father's work of constructing the wings by snatching at the feathers blowing in the breeze and by pressing the soft wax with his thumb (197–200). When Daedalus thrust his nephew off the Acropolis, he intended to murder the boy. But Pallas, the protector of genius, saved him from utter extinction by transforming him into a bird while still in the air (252–53). Daedalus is thus indirectly responsible for the metamorphosis of Perdix into a bird. He is, of course, the actual cause of his own son's attempt to fly, which Ovid describes in the simile comparing the two to real birds as they begin their flight: *velut ales, ab alto / quae teneram prolem produxit in aera nido* (213–14). Ovid leaves implicit in the *Metamorphoses* what he expresses directly in the *Ars*, that Daedalus and Icarus took off by leaping from a cliff (2.71–72), much as the mother bird pushes her fledgling out of the nest to teach it to fly. Here, moreover, the poet calls attention to the special nature of the place from which Daedalus thrust the boy, *sacraque ex arce Minervae* (250). The artisan thus violated the sacred precinct of the very goddess to whom he should have shown the utmost piety.

In associating Perdix with Icarus through the concept of the "middle way," Ovid sustains a negative view of Daedalus. By hurling his nephew off the Acropolis, Daedalus causes the boy in his metamorphosed state to be forever afraid of high places. Ovid elaborates on the partridge's fear of heights as he concludes the story of Daedalus and Perdix:

> non lamen haec alte volucris sua corpora tollit
> nec facit in ramis altoque cacumine nidos;
> propter humum volitat ponitque in saepibus ova
> antiquique memor metuit sublimia casus. (256–59)

> Nevertheless, this bird does not raise its body on high,
> nor does it make its nests on the branches of the very top.
> It flits near the ground and places its eggs in hedges, and
> mindful of its prior fall, it fears the heights.

The hendiadys of the phrase *in ramis altoque cacumine*, which makes the words *alto cacumine* grammatically equivalent to *ramis* instead of subordinate to it, calls attention to the problem of height.

By his murderous act, Daedalus keeps his nephew from ever flying too high (*non tamen haec alte volucris sua corpora tollit*, 256). The *perdix* does not remain too close to the ground, either, for at the beginning of this story, the poet locates the bird on an *ilex* tree: *Hunc miseri tumulo ponentem corpora nati /garrula ramosa prospexit ab ilice perdix* (236–37).[38] Thus, the *perdix* perches on the branches of trees, though not on the highest ones. While flitting above the ground (*propter humum volitat*), it builds its nests in hedges to protect its young (*ponitque in saepibus ova*, 258). The *perdix* would therefore seem instinctively to represent the principle of *mediocritas*. Ironically, Daedalus tried unsuccessfully to enforce a middle path for Icarus so as to avoid dampening the wings in the sea or melting the wax by proximity to the sun. As Perdix is now compelled to follow Daedalus' prescriptive "middle way" in a manner that heightens the discrepancy between his present limitation as a bird and his earlier brilliance as a youth, Ovid implies that the middle way is not inherently ideal.

According to Sharrock, Daedalus in the *Ars* and the *Metamorphoses* is a figure for the Callimachean poet, who like Ovid, maintains a stylistic middle ground, whereas Icarus represents the type of poet who aspires to the high genre of Homeric-style epic.[39] In the *Metamorphoses*, however, Ovid incorporates multiple levels of style, reflecting a deliberate break with traditional stylistic boundaries. Although he achieves this variety in part through characters such as Achelous, who temporarily assume the narrative voice, Ovid's epic narrator himself rises to more elevated levels of style in a number of sustained passages. The account of Phaethon's flight, for instance, contains a topographical survey of the universe scorched by the young boy's mishandling of the sun god's chariot. The poet includes two examples of the catalogue, a hallmark of high epic, in this passage, one for mountains and the other for rivers. If Daedalus symbolizes a stylistic middle ground, Ovid rejects such consistency.

While Ovid indicates an affinity with Daedalus in the labyrinthine intricacy of his poem, as a poet he reveals his superiority to the archetypal artisan in the nature of his own material. His numerous forms of repetition in the *Metamorphoses*, unlike the windings of the Cretan labyrinth, are inherently linked to a concept of play. Their aim is ultimately not to confuse the reader but to take him through an experience that will make him perceive the manifold paradoxes of the human condition more fully. That process in the *Metamorphoses* requires a different design from the maze-like structure of the *Aeneid*, with its emphasis on the constructive, if painful, labor necessary to achieve a lasting goal. Ovid's contrast with Vergil in the artisan's indifference to traditional piety and in his problematic paternal role challenges the very core of his predecessor's epic. With his own version of the Maeander simile as an analogue for the labyrinth, Ovid has truly done Propertius one better: his use of that seminal image illustrates his ability to incorporate into the *Metamorphoses* the light, playful mode that the elegist could only contrast with the works of "Lynceus" or even the *Aeneid* of Vergil without losing the power and grandeur of epic itself.

NOTES

1. M.H.T. Davisson, "The Observers of Daedalus and Icarus in Ovid," *CW* 90 (1997) 263–78, comparing the versions of the Daedalus myth in the *Ars Amatoria* and the *Metamorphoses*, considers the points of view of the rustics who view the flight and of the bird Perdix vis-a-vis Daedalus. She includes Daedalus among the artistic failures of the poem, in part because "his art can neither produce foolproof inventions nor control his son's impulses," and compares him to Orpheus, who reveals a similar pattern as he penetrates a sphere normally unavailable to humans, almost saves his wife, but finally fails in his effort. I am grateful to the author for permitting me to read a pre-publication copy of her article. M. Hoefmans, "Myth into Reality: The Metamorphosis of Daedalus and Icarus (Ovid, *Metamorphoses*, VIII, 183–235)," *AC* 63 (1994) 137–60, viewing Daedalus against the background of the *homo faber* and hubris theme, finds that traditional moral criticism referring to Daedalus' boldness is counterbalanced by Lucretian resonances which suggest a more positive view of the artist, especially in the absence of divine elements in the episode and in the artist's imitation of nature, though ultimately Daedalus loses his Epicurean *ataraxia* by his anxiety and grief over his son.

2. S.P. Morris, *Daidalos and the Origins of Greek Art* (Princeton 1992) 215–16, refers to dramas by Sophocles, Euripides,

Aristophanes, Plato, and Euboulus, with Daedalus as the title
character, as well as other plays related to Daedalus's adventures
in Sicily and Crete.

3. See A. Sharrock, *Seduction and Repetition in Ovid's Ars Amatoria
II* (Oxford 1994) 112–26, on the lyric poet's use of the Daedalus
and Icarus myth in all three *Odes* as a reflection of the necessity
for breaking boundaries in artistic creativity. Whereas Icarus is
at issue in 2.20 and 4.2, Daedalus is specifically named in 1.3,
on which see especially D.A. Kidd, "Virgil's Voyage," *Prudentia*
9 (1977) 91–103, and R. Basto, "Horace's Propempticon to
Vergil: A Re-examination," *Vergilius* 28 (1982) 30–43.

4. See R.D. Williams, "The Sixth Book of the *Aeneid*," *G & R*, n.s.
11 (1964) 48–63, on aspects of the hero's education in Book 6
for moving away from the Trojan and Homeric past and into a
world reflecting the idealized values of Augustan Rome.

5. A.S. Hollis, ed., *Ovid's Metamorphoses, Book VIII* (Oxford 1970)
ad 162, cites Propertius 2.34.35–36, Silius 7.139, and Seneca,
Hercules Furens 683–85, as examples of literary practice with
descriptions of the Maeander.

6. Hollis also notes ad 162 that Seneca imitates Ovid by having
the river god play in his stream: "qualis incertis vagus /
Maeander undis ludit et cedit sibi, / instatque dubius litus an
fontem petat." Like Ovid, Seneca extends the personification, as
the god here ponders whether his stream should flow towards
the coast or back to the source.

7. H.E. Butler and E.A. Barber, eds., *The Elegies of Propertius*
(Oxford 1933) ad 29, note that, while it is clear that Lynceus
wrote tragedy, details in lines 33–40 suggest epic, as does the
mention in 45 of Homer and Antimachus, who were associated
with epics on Thebes. W.A. Camps, ed., *Propertius, Elegies, Book
II* (rpt. Bristol 1985), in postscript notes ad 25–54, also assumes
epic as part of the poetic output of Lynceus.

8. See R.F. Thomas, ed., *Virgil: Georgics. Vol. 2, Books III and
IV* (Cambridge 1988) ad 3.1–48, for a concise discussion of
the temple as a metaphor for the epic poem that Vergil is
considering.

9. On Vergil's etymology for the labyrinth, W. Fitzgerald, "Aeneas,
Daedalus, and the Labyrinth," *Arethusa* 17 (1984) 55 and n. 13,

citing Norden's edition of *Aeneid* 6, also connects 1.27 with the underworld as a maze from which it is difficult to return and notes the Sibyl's comment on the journey: "Hoc opus, hic labor est" (6.29). The noun *labor*, of course, is not related etymologically to the verb *labor*, the quantity of the stem vowel "a" constituting a primary difference in each case. But, I believe, as Vergil had created a fanciful etymological pun, so Ovid responded with an analogous wordplay.

10. F. Ahl, *Metaformations: Wordplay in Ovid and Other Latin Poets* (Ithaca 1986) 253–54. In his study of the numerous forms of wordplay that Ovid exploits throughout the *Metamorphoses*, Ahl shows that a keen interest in etymologizing puns was part of a longstanding Roman tradition, documented by Varro in his *Lingua Latino*. The prevalence of such punning would suggest that Ovid might well respond to a pun on a single word that Vergil had etymologized, as a variation on a literary allusion or echo.

11. J.W. Zarker, "Aeneas and Theseus in *Aeneid* 6," *CJ* 62 (1972) 220–26, discusses Theseus as a potential model for Aeneas in the *ekphrasis*, but one who is ultimately rejected because of his failure of *pietas*.

12. B. Otis, *Virgil: A Study in Civilized Poetry* (Oxford 1963), analyzed some of the most essential forms of symmetrical design in both the "Odyssean" and "Iliadic" halves of the *Aeneid*; see esp. 217, 228, 247, and 242 for useful schematic charts.

13. P.R. Doob, *The Idea of the Labyrinth from Classical Antiquity through the Middle Ages* (Ithaca 1990) 229–45, provides sound analyses of the primary passages that contribute to the labyrinthine nature of Vergil's narrative, both structurally and thematically, especially on the interrelation of *labores* and *errores*.

14. See, for example. *Metamorphoses* 2.9, where *ambiguus* is applied to the sea god Proteus as represented on the doors of the palace of the Sun; 4.280, where it describes Sithon's sex change from female to male; and 7.271, where it refers to a werewolf whose innards Medea mixes into her potion to rejuvenate Aeson, prior to deceiving the daughters of Pelias about the same drug. This adjective thus describes much of the content of the

Metamorphoses itself, from the marvelous and bizarre to the tragic.

15. See G. Williams, *Banished Voices: Headings in Ovid's Exile Poetry* (Cambridge 1994) 204–5, on Ovid's own retrospective views in the *Tristia* on his poetic *lusus* in the *Ars Amatoria*.

16. On Ovid's relation to Hellenistic poetics, see recently R.O.A.M. Lyne, "Ovid's *Metamorphoses*, Callimachus, and L'Art Pour L'Art," *MD* 12 (1984) 9–34; P.E. Knox, "Ovid's *Metamorphoses* and the Traditions of Augustan Poetry," *C.Ph.S.*, suppl. 11 (Cambridge 1986) 55–98; and H. Hofmann, "Ovid's *Metamorphoses: Carmen Perpetuum, Carmen Deductum*," in *Papers of the Liverpool Latin Seminar V* (Liverpool 1986) 223–41.

17. The word *liquidus* as a stylistic term is used, for example, by Cicero, *Brutus* 274, to describe the smooth and charming oratorical style of Marcus Callidius: "quae primum ita pura erat ut nihil liquidius, ita libere fluebat ut nusquam adhaeresceret"; cf. Horace, *Ep.* 2.2.120.

18. Callimachus emphasizes the purity of his stream by combining with καθαρή the adjective ἀχράαντος. F. Williams, ed. *Callimachus, Hymn to Apollo: A Commentary* (Oxford 1978) ad 2.111, comments on the cleverness of the latter word, conveying the meaning "unsullied," since it is a neologism formed on the model of the Homeric ἀχράαντος: it thus simultaneously reflects the poet's originality and his facility with Homeric scholarship.

19. See especially F. Bomer, *P. Ovidius Naso: Metamorphosen, Buch VII–IX* (Heidelberg 1977), for echoes of Vergil in the Erysichthon episode, e.g., on 8.743–44, 758, 762, 774.

20. Hollis (above, n. 5), who deletes the problematic 1.190 because of the confusion of perspective created by *longam*, interprets *clivo* (usually a "hill") to mean that the feathers grow "in order of ascending length," since the image of the Pan pipes follows immediately after. My translation reflects Hollis' interpretation.

21. Hoefmans (above, n. 1) 152–53.

22. L. Barkan, *The Gods Made Flesh: Metamorphosis and the Pursuit of Paganism* (New Haven 1986) 75, comments that Daedalus' "creations tend to embrace all the flaws of proteanism without achieving its glories" and that Daedalus "attains neither the

accurate imitation of nature nor the artistic transcendence of nature."

23. On Ovid's wit in Mercury's tale of Syrinx to "charm" Argus to sleep, see D. Konstan, "The Death of Argus, Or What Stories Do: Audience Response in Ancient Fiction and Theory," *Helios* 18 (1991) 15–30.

24. Hollis (above, n. 5) ad 211 observes that Ovid echoes Vergil's "poignant line" but does not elaborate on the effect of the borrowing.

25. M.C.J. Putnam, "Daedalus, Virgil, and the End of Art," *AJP* 108 (1987) 182, observes that in his empathetic expression of grief for Icarus, the narrator substitutes for Daedalus and assumes a Daedalian nature, as he eternalizes the father's grief in his own artwork. Putnam applies this notion to Vergil's effort in the *Aeneid* more generally by discerning Daedalian qualities in the deceit of the wooden horse, in such "hybrid" creatures as Polyphemus in the hero's adventures, and in the illicit love of Dido, pitied by the poet.

26. Hoefmans (above, n. 1) 147.

27. M. Janan, "The Labyrinth and the Mirror: Incest and Influence in *Metamorphoses* 9," *Arethusa* 24 (1991) 240–48, discusses the problem of self-reference in the Byblis and Caunis episode. She finds that Maeander, grandfather of Byblis, is the paradigm for the young woman's erotic and poetic self-referentiality, for Byblis "turns back" to her own brother as the object of desire and, as a skewed version of the poet, repeats Ovid's own earlier works, the *Amores*, *Ars Amatoria*, and *Heroides*.

28. Sharrock (above, n. 3) 168–73 points to a number of references to the Daedalus and Icarus myth in Ovid's exile poetry that associate it closely with the *Ars* as a source of the poet's downfall; Ovid's insistence on the incompleteness of the *Metamorphoses* at the time of his exile would then allow for the possibility that he revised the Daedalus and Icarus story there (or added it later) and gave it self-referential significance.

29. Sharrock (above, n. 3) 176.

30. See *LSJ*, s.v. κάλυμμα 6: "covering of a honeycomb."

31. M.K. Gamel, "Baucis and Philemon: Paradigm or Paradox?" *Helios* 11 (1984) 117–31, comments on the narrator Laelex's

inability to appreciate the rustic simplicity of Philemon and Baucis because of his "social superiority." Thus, his language reflects ambiguity and even sarcasm, as when Laelex refers to the wine bowl "engraved with the same silver" as the plates, which are in fact earthenware (668).

32. See C.F. Ahern, Jr., "Daedalus and Icarus in the *Ars Amatoria*" *HSCP* 92 (1989) 279.

33. Sharrock (above, n. 3) 180–81 observes that this type of expansion itself and the attribution of a marvelous event to the gods can be explained as typical of epic.

34. V.M. Wise, "Flight Myths in Ovid's *Metamorphoses*," *Ramus* 6 (1977) 44–59, discusses the episodes of Phaethon and Daedalus and Icarus as parallel myths involving flight as a metaphor for the creative process. In her view, Phaethon is destroyed by his obsession with a material vision of reality in contrast to the metamorphic imagination implied by the designs on doors of Phoebus' palace. With Daedalus and Icarus, she finds that the wings compared to Pan pipes suggest the ambiguity of art imitating art and that, while Icarus lacks the self-discipline to attain a higher vision, Daedalus' murder of Perdix implies an inability of the artist to accept anyone else's inventiveness.

35. J.E. Sharwood Smith, "Icarus's Astral Navigation," *G & R* 21 (1974) 19–20.

36. See Aratus, *Phaemonema* 37–41, on Helice as the constellation by which Greek sailors guide their ships because of its brightness and appearance early in the evening. In setting the scene to Medea's sleeplessness over Jason's plight, Apollonius, *Argonautica* 3.744–46, mentions Helice along with Orion as the constellation sailors watch at night.

37. A. Crabbe, "Structure and Content in Ovid's *Metamorphoses*," *ANRW* 11.31.4 (1981) 2277–84, cites various motival links among the Scylla, Daedalus and Icarus, and Perdix episodes in an analysis of the larger structure of Book 8. She notes the similarity of age between Icarus and Perdix, but mainly finds differences between the two, such as the boldness of the former in his flight and the latter's fear of high places. On the other hand, she sees several close points of contact between Scylla and Perdix, such as the transformation into a bird in mid-air and the

fall from a tower, which Scylla fantasizes as a way into Minos' camp and which the unfortunate Perdix actually experiences.

38. This line has continued to vex scholars. I accept the manuscript reading, which Hollis (above, n. 5) prints, though admittedly after some reluctance. But he sensibly notes that Ovid implies only that this bird does not nest in the topmost branches (I. 257). He also dismisses the objection that the partridge generally does not perch, by noting that Ovid may have in mind the red-legged partridge and was probably influenced by the Hellenistic *topos* of a watching bird speaking from a tree. And he considers aesthetically unacceptable the image represented by the common emendation, "garrula limoso prospexit ab elice perdix," which W.S. Anderson, *P. Ovidii Nasonis Metamorphoses* (Leipzig 1993), prints.

39. Sharrock (above, n. 3) 133–46 and 155–68.

A MIDSUMMER NIGHT'S DREAM
(WILLIAM SHAKESPEARE)

"*A Midsummer Night's Dream,*"
by G.K. Chesterton,
in *The Common Man* (1950)

INTRODUCTION

Calling *A Midsummer Night's Dream* the greatest of Shake-speare's comedies and, "from a certain point of view, the greatest of his plays," G.K. Chesterton analyzes how the play corresponds to the labyrinthine nature of dreams, finding that "The chase and tangle and frustration of the incidents and personalities are well known to everyone who has dreamt of perpetually falling over precipices or perpetually missing trains." Such commentary is the hallmark of Chesterton's exploration of the psychological elements of the play. Vacil-lating between historical, thematic, poetical, and psycho-logical approaches, Chesterton pulls together Shakespeare's complicated plot and forest imagery and considers how the characters negotiate the labyrinth of images.

Chesterton, G.K. "*A Midsummer Night's Dream.*" *The Common Man.* New York: Sheed and Ward, 1950. 10-21. (first published in *Good Words*, Vol. 45 [1904]: 621–9)

The greatest of Shakespeare's comedies is also, from a certain point of view, the greatest of his plays. No one would maintain that it occupied this position in the matter of psychological study, if by psychological study we mean the study of individual characters in a play: No one would maintain that Puck was a character in the sense that Falstaff is a character, or that the critic stood awed before the psychology of Peaseblossom. But there is a sense in which the play is perhaps a greater triumph of psychology than *Hamlet* itself. It may well be questioned whether in any other literary work in the world is so vividly rendered a social and spiritual atmosphere. There is an atmosphere in *Hamlet*, for instance, a somewhat murky and even melodramatic one, but it is subordinate to the great character, and morally inferior to him; the darkness is only a background for the isolated star of intellect. But *A Midsummer Night's Dream* is a psychological study, not of a solitary man, but of a spirit that unites mankind. The six men may sit talking in an inn; they may not know each other's names or see each other's faces before or after, but night or wine or great stories, or some rich and branching discussion may make them all at one, if not absolutely with each other, at least with that invisible seventh man who is the harmony of all of them. That seventh man is the hero of *A Midsummer Night's Dream*.

A study of the play from a literary or philosophical point of view must therefore be founded upon some serious realization of what this atmosphere is. In a lecture upon *As You Like It*, Mr. Bernard Shaw made a suggestion which is an admirable example of his amazing ingenuity and of his one most interesting limitation. In maintaining that the light sentiment and optimism of the comedy were regarded by Shakespeare merely as the characteristics of a more or less cynical pot-boiler, he actually suggested that the title "As You Like It" was a taunting address to the public in disparagement of their taste and the dramatist's own work. If Mr. Bernard Shaw had conceived of Shakespeare as insisting that Ben Jonson should wear Jaeger underclothing or join the Blue Ribbon Army, or distribute little pamphlets for the non-payment of rates, he could scarcely have conceived anything more violently opposed to the whole spirit of Elizabethan comedy than the spiteful and priggish modernism of such a taunt. Shakespeare might make the fastidious and cultivated Hamlet, moving in his own melancholy and purely mental world, warn players against an overindulgence towards the rabble. But the very soul and meaning of the great comedies is that of an uproarious communion, between the public and the play, a communion so chaotic that whole scenes of silliness and violence lead us almost to think that some of the "rowdies" from the pit have climbed over the footlights. The title "As You Like It" is, of course, an expression of utter carelessness, but it is not the bitter carelessness which Mr. Bernard Shaw fantastically reads into it; it is the godlike and inexhaustible carelessness of a happy man. And the simple proof of this is that there are scores of these genially taunting titles scattered through the whole of Elizabethan comedy. Is "As You Like It" a title demanding a dark and ironic explanation in a school of comedy which called its plays, "What You Will", "A Mad World, My Masters", "If It Be Not Good, the Devil Is In It", "The Devil is an Ass", "An Humorous Day's Mirth", and "A Midsummer Night's Dream"? Every one of these titles is flung at the head of the public as a drunken lord might fling a purse at his footman. Would Mr. Shaw maintain that "If It Be Not Good, the Devil Is In It", was the opposite of "As You Like It", and was a solemn invocation of the supernatural powers to testify to the care and perfection of the literary workmanship? The one explanation is as Elizabethan as the other.

Now in the reason for this modern and pedantic error lies the whole secret and difficulty of such plays as *A Midsummer Night's Dream*. The sentiment of such a play, so far as it can be summed up at all, can be summed up in one sentence. It is the mysticism of happiness. That is to say, it is the conception that as man lives upon a borderland he may find himself in the spiritual or supernatural atmosphere, not only through being profoundly sad or meditative, but by being extravagantly happy. The soul might be rapt out of the body in an agony of sorrow, or a trance of ecstasy; but it might also be rapt out of the body in a paroxysm of laughter. Sorrow we know can go beyond itself; so, according to Shakespeare, can pleasure go beyond itself and become something dangerous and unknown. And the reason that the logical and destructive modern school, of which Mr. Bernard Shaw is an example, does not grasp this purely exuberant nature of the comedies is simply that their logical and destructive attitude have rendered impossible the very experience of this preternatural exuberance. We cannot realize *As You Like It* if we are always considering it as we understand it. We cannot have *A Midsummer Night's Dream* if our one object in life is to keep ourselves awake with the black coffee of criticism. The whole question which is balanced, and balanced nobly and fairly, in *A Midsummer Night's Dream*, is whether the life of waking, or the life of the vision, is the real life, the *sine quâ non* of man. But it is difficult to see what superiority for the purpose of judging is possessed by people whose pride it is not to live the life of vision at all. At least it is questionable whether the Elizabethan did not know more about both worlds than the modern intellectual; it is not altogether improbable that Shakespeare would not only have had a clearer vision of the fairies, but would have shot very much straighter at a deer and netted much more money for his performances than a member of the Stage Society.

In pure poetry and the intoxication of words, Shakespeare never rose higher than he rises in this play. But in spite of this fact the supreme literary merit of *A Midsummer Night's Dream* is a merit of design. The amazing symmetry, the amazing artistic and moral beauty of that design, can be stated very briefly. The story opens in the sane and common world with the pleasant seriousness of very young lovers and very young friends. Then, as the figures advance into the tangled wood of young troubles and stolen happiness, a change and bewilderment begins to fall on them. They lose their way and their wits for they are in the heart of fairyland. Their words, their hungers, their very figures grow more and more dim and fantastic, like dreams within dreams, in the supernatural mist of Puck. Then the dream-fumes begin to clear, and characters and spectators begin to awaken together to the noise of horns and dogs and the clean and bracing morning. Theseus, the incarnation of a happy and generous rationalism, expounds in hackneyed and superb lines the sane view of such psychic experiences, pointing out with a reverent and sympathetic scepticism that all these fairies and spells are themselves but the emanations, the unconscious masterpieces, of man himself. The whole company falls back into a splendid human laughter. There is a rush for banqueting and private theatricals, and over all these things ripples one of those frivolous and inspired conversations in which every good saying seems to die in giving birth to another. If ever the son of man in his wanderings was at home and drinking by the fireside, he is at home in the house of Theseus. All the dreams have been forgotten, as a melancholy dream remembered throughout the morning might be forgotten in the human certainty of any other triumphant evening party; and so the play seems naturally ended. It began on the earth and it ends on the earth. Thus to round off the whole midsummer night's dream in an eclipse of daylight is an effect of genius. But of this comedy, as I have said, the mark is that genius goes beyond itself; and one touch is added which makes the play colossal. Theseus and his train retire with a crashing finale, full of Humour and wisdom and things set right, and silence falls on the house. Then there comes a faint sound of little feet, and for a moment, as it were, the elves look into the house, asking which is the reality. "Suppose we are the realities and they the shadows." If that ending were acted properly any modern man would feel shaken to his marrow if he had to walk home from the theatre through a country lane.

It is a trite matter, of course, though in a general criticism a more or less indispensable one to comment upon another point of artistic perfection, the extraordinarily human and accurate manner in which the play catches the atmosphere of a dream. The chase and tangle and frustration of the incidents and personalities are well known to everyone who has dreamt of perpetually falling over precipices or perpetually missing trains. While following out clearly and legally the necessary narrative of the drama, the author contrives to include every one of the main peculiarities of the exasperating dream. Here is the pursuit of the man we cannot catch, the flight from the man we cannot see; here is the perpetual returning to the same place, here is the crazy alteration in the very objects of our desire, the substitution of one face for another face, the putting of the wrong souls in the wrong bodies, the fantastic disloyalties of the night, all this is as obvious as it is important. It is perhaps somewhat more worth remarking that there is about this confusion of comedy yet another essential characteristic of dreams. A dream can commonly be described as possessing an utter discordance of incident combined with a curious unity of mood; everything changes but the dreamer. It may begin with anything and end with anything, but if the dreamer is sad at the end he will be sad as if by prescience at the beginning; if he is cheerful at the beginning he will be cheerful if the stars fail. *A Midsummer Night's Dream* has in a most singular degree effected this difficult, this almost desperate subtlety. The events in the wandering wood are in themselves, and regarded as in broad daylight, not merely melancholy but bitterly cruel and ignominious. But yet by the spreading of an atmosphere as magic as the fog of Puck, Shakespeare contrives to make the whole matter mysteriously hilarious while it is palpably tragic, and mysteriously charitable, while it is in itself cynical. He contrives somehow to rob tragedy and treachery of their full sharpness, just as a toothache or a deadly danger from a tiger, or a precipice, is robbed of its sharpness in a pleasant dream. The creation of a brooding sentiment like this, a sentiment not merely independent of but actually opposed to the events, is a much greater triumph of art than the creation of the character of Othello.

It is difficult to approach critically so great a figure as that of Bottom the Weaver. He is greater and more mysterious than Hamlet, because the interest of such men as Bottom consists of a rich subconsciousness, and that of Hamlet in the comparatively superficial matter of a rich consciousness. And it is especially difficult in the present age which has become hag-ridden with the mere intellect. We are the victims of a curious confusion whereby being great is supposed to have something to do with being clever, as if there were the smallest reason to suppose that Achilles was clever, as if there were not on the contrary a great deal of internal evidence to indicate that he was next door to a fool. Greatness is a certain indescribable but perfectly familiar and palpable quality of size in the personality, of steadfastness, of strong flavour, of easy and natural self-expression. Such a man is as firm as a tree and as unique as a rhinoceros, and he might quite easily be as stupid as either of them. Fully as much as the great poet towers above the small poet the great fool towers above the small fool. We have all of us known rustics like Bottom the Weaver, men whose faces would be blank with idiocy if we tried for ten days to explain the meaning of the National Debt, but who are yet great men, akin to Sigurd and Hercules, heroes of the morning of the earth, because their words were their own words, their memories their own memories, and their vanity as large and simple as a great hill. We have all of us known friends in our own circle, men whom the intellectuals might justly describe as brainless, but whose presence in a room was like a fire roaring in the grate changing everything, lights and shadows and the air, whose entrances and exits were in some strange fashion events, whose point of view once expressed haunts and persuades the mind and almost intimidates it, whose manifest absurdity clings to the fancy like the beauty of first love, and whose follies are recounted like the legends of a paladin. These are great men, there are millions of them in the world, though very few perhaps in the House of Commons. It is not in the cold halls of cleverness where celebrities seem to be important that we should look for the great. An intellectual salon is merely a training-ground for one faculty, and is akin to a fencing class or a rifle corps. It is in our own homes and environments, from Croydon to St. John's Wood, in old nurses, and gentlemen with hobbies, and talkative spinsters and vast incomparable butlers, that we may feel the presence of that blood of the gods. And this creature so hard to describe, so easy to remember, the august and memorable fool, has never been so sumptuously painted as in the Bottom of *A Midsummer Night's Dream.*

Bottom has the supreme mark of this real greatness in that like the true saint or the true hero he only differs from humanity in being as it were more human than humanity. It is not true, as the idle materialists of today suggest, that compared to the majority of men the hero appears cold and dehumanized; it is the majority who appear cold and dehumanized in the presence of greatness. Bottom, like Don Quixote and Uncle Toby and Mr. Richard Swiveller and the rest of the Titans, has a huge and unfathomable weakness, his silliness is on a great scale, and when he blows his own trumpet it is like the trumpet of the Resurrection. The other rustics in the play accept his leadership not merely naturally but exuberantly; they have to the full that primary and savage unselfishness, that uproarious abnegation which makes simple men take pleasure in falling short of a hero, that unquestionable element of basic human nature which has never been expressed, outside this play, so perfectly as in the incomparable chapter at the beginning of *Evan Harrington* in which the praises of The Great Mel are sung with a lyric energy by the tradesmen whom he has cheated. Twopenny sceptics write of the egoism of primal human nature; it is reserved for great men like Shakespeare and Meredith to detect and make vivid this rude and subconscious unselfishness which is older than self. They alone with their insatiable tolerance can perceive all the spiritual devotion in the soul of a snob. And it is this natural play between the rich simplicity of Bottom and the simple simplicity of his comrades which constitutes the unapproachable excellence of the farcical scenes in this play. Bottom's sensibility to literature is perfectly fiery and genuine, a great deal more genuine than that of a great many cultivated critics of literature—"the raging rocks and shivering shocks shall break the locks of prison gates, and Phibbus' car shall shine from far, and make and mar the foolish fates", is exceedingly good poetical diction with a real throb and swell in it, and if it is slightly and almost imperceptibly deficient in the matter of sense, it is certainly every bit as sensible as a good many other rhetorical speeches in Shakespeare put into the mouths of kings and lovers and even the spirits of the dead. If Bottom liked cant for its own sake the fact only constitutes another point of sympathy between him and his literary creator. But the style of the thing, though deliberately bombastic and ludicrous, is quite literary, the alliteration falls like wave upon wave, and the whole verse, like a billow mounts higher and higher before it crashes. There is nothing mean about this folly; nor is there in the whole realm of literature a figure so free from vulgarity. The man vitally base and foolish sings "The Honeysuckle and the Bee"; he does not rant about "raging rocks" and "the car of Phibbus". Dickens, who more perhaps than any modern man had the mental hospitality and the thoughtless wisdom of Shakespeare, perceived and expressed admirably the same truth. He perceived, that is to say, that quite indefensible idiots have very often a real sense of, and enthusiasm for letters. Mr. Micawber loved eloquence and poetry with his whole immortal soul; words and visionary pictures kept him alive in the absence of food and money, as they might have kept a saint fasting in a desert. Dick Swiveller did not make his inimitable quotations from Moore and Byron merely as flippant digressions. He made them because he loved a great school of poetry. The sincere love of books has nothing to do with cleverness or stupidity any more than any other sincere love. It is a quality of character, a freshness, a power of pleasure, a power of faith. A silly person may delight in reading masterpieces just as a silly person may delight in picking flowers. A fool may be in love with a poet as he may be in love with a woman. And the triumph of Bottom is that he loves rhetoric and his own taste in the arts, and this is all that can be achieved by Theseus, or for the matter of that by Cosimo di Medici. It is worth remarking as an extremely fine touch in the picture of

Bottom that his literary taste is almost everywhere concerned with sound rather than sense. He begins the rehearsal with a boisterous readiness, "Thisby, the flowers of odious savours sweete." "Odours, odours," says Quince, in remonstrance, and the word is accepted in accordance with the cold and heavy rules which require an element of meaning in a poetical passage. But "Thisby, the flowers of odious savours sweete", Bottom's version, is an immeasurably finer and more resonant line. The "i" which he inserts is an inspiration of metricism.

There is another aspect of this great play which ought to be kept familiarly in the mind. Extravagant as is the masquerade of the story, it is a very perfect aesthetic harmony down to such *coup-de-maître* as the name of Bottom, or the flower called Love-in-Idleness. In the whole matter it may be said that there is one accidental discord; that is in the name of Theseus, and the whole city of Athens in which the events take place. Shakespeare's description of Athens in *A Midsummer Night's Dream* is the best description of England that he or any one else ever wrote. Theseus is quite obviously only an English squire, fond of hunting, kindly to his tenants, hospitable with a certain flamboyant vanity. The mechanics are English mechanics, talking to each other with the queer formality of the poor. Above all, the fairies are English; to compare them with the beautiful patrician spirits of Irish legend, for instance, is suddenly to discover that we have, after all, a folklore and a mythology, or had it at least in Shakespeare's day. Robin Goodfellow, upsetting the old women's ale, or pulling the stool from under them, has nothing of the poignant Celtic beauty; his is the horseplay of the invisible world. Perhaps it is some debased inheritance of English life which makes American ghosts so fond of quite undignified practical jokes. But this union of mystery with farce is a note of the medieval English. The play is the last glimpse of Merrie England, that distant but shining and quite indubitable country. It would be difficult indeed to define wherein lay the peculiar truth of the phrase "merrie England", though some conception of it is quite necessary to the comprehension of *A Midsummer Night's Dream*. In some cases at least, it may be said to lie in this, that the English of the Middle Ages and the Renaissance, unlike the England of today, could conceive of the idea of a merry supernaturalism. Amid all the great work of Puritanism the damning indictment of it consists in one fact, that there was one only of the fables of Christendom that it retained and renewed, and that was the belief in witchcraft. It cast away the generous and wholesome superstition, it approved only of the morbid and the dangerous. In their treatment of the great national fairy-tale of good and evil, the Puritans killed St. George but carefully preserved the Dragon. And this seventeenth-century tradition of dealing with the psychic life still lies like a great shadow over England and America, so that if we glance at a novel about occultism we may be perfectly certain that it deals with sad or evil destiny. Whatever else we expect we certainly should never expect to find in it spirits such as those in *Aylwin* as inspirers of a tale of tomfoolery like the *Wrong Box* or *The Londoners*. That impossibility is the disappearance of "merrie England" and Robin Goodfellow. It was a land to us incredible, the land of a jolly occultism where the peasant cracked jokes with his patron saint, and only cursed the fairies good-humouredly, as he might curse a lazy servant. Shakespeare is English in everything, above all in his weaknesses. Just as London, one of the greatest cities in the world, shows more slums and hides more beauties than any other, so Shakespeare alone among the four giants of poetry is a careless writer, and lets us come upon his splendours by accident, as we come upon an old City church in the twist of a city street. He is English in nothing so much as in that noble cosmopolitan unconsciousness which makes him look eastward with the eyes of a child towards Athens or Verona. He loved to talk of the glory of foreign lands, but he talked of them with the tongue and unquenchable spirit of England. It is too much the custom of a later patriotism to reverse this method and talk of England from morning till night, but to talk of her in a manner totally un-English. Casualness, incongruities, and a certain fine absence of mind are in the temper of England; the unconscious man with the ass's head is no bad type of the people. Materialistic philosophers and mechanical politicians have certainly succeeded in some cases in giving him a greater unity. The only question is, to which animal has he been thus successfully conformed?

THE NAME OF THE ROSE
(UMBERTO ECO)

"The Name of the Rose and the Labyrinths of Reading"
by Rossitsa Terzieva-Artemis,
Intercollege, Cyprus

Over the past four decades, the career of Umberto Eco as a writer, critic, and scholar has crossed the fields of literature, journalism, semiotics, and philosophy. Eco's lifelong dedication to the world of books and texts is probably best embodied in his novel *The Name of the Rose* (1980). The book has been variously described as a historical detective story, a medieval discussion on morals and aesthetics, and a postmodern novel. Despite the difficulty in classifying the novel's genre, one thing is certain: Some twenty-seven years after its first publication, *The Name of the Rose* still stirs its readers' imaginations and challenges them to find meaning through signs that seem unrelated at times. Eco invites his readers into a labyrinth built by words, of which his own writing is only a part. The rest of the labyrinth is built from the words of philosophers, clergy, and even modern novelists, forcing the reader to consider all of these words and signs when trying to decipher the text's meaning. None of these approaches alone will deliver the reader from the labyrinth. Rather, only after walking alongside William of Baskerville and reading through the labyrinth's various halls will the reader decipher the novel's true meaning: That meaning lies not in any one word or worldview but in the complex interplay of them all.

If we accept Eco's argument that any text is "a machine for generating interpretations," we can easily see how a rich novel like *The Name of the Rose* can be interpreted on several levels (Eco, "Postscript" 2). As detective fiction, the novel entangles the reader from its very first pages. Not just an entertaining yarn, the text can also be unraveled as an intellectual approach to the pursuit of knowledge and meaning. The story of conjecture, as Cannon claims, "is closely related to a question central to the discourse of our culture, the question of legitimation of knowledge" (Eco, *NR* 80). By "our culture" in this sense we can understand the human need in general for reaching *the* truth and finding explanations of the dubious and the problematic and sometimes even the apparent in our lives. Such a need is not restricted to a postmodern questioning of the world around us, but it is an intrinsic feature of the human mind and world perception.

From the very ambiguous motto of the novel ("naturally, a manuscript") to the curious foreword by the author to the completely fascinating story of deceit and death in a medieval abbey, we are surely engaged by Eco and the protagonist of the novel, William of Baskerville, in an exercise of detection and, just as much, in an exercise in hypothetical, or abductive, reasoning. Yet both detection and abduction do not exclude fallibility or misdirection. As Eco points out, *The Name of the Rose* "[. . .] is a detective novel where precious little is discovered and where the detective is beaten in the end" (Rosso, 6). If the detective is beaten in the end, then what is the point of his work? one might ask. The answer, in Eco's terms, is not the final discovery itself but the actual process of discovery, of decoding the signs that, when read together, lead to meaning.

Sir Arthur Conan Doyle's character Sherlock Holmes and Maurice Leblanc's Arsène Lupin are undoubtedly the inspirations for the character of William of Baskerville, as are a number of philosophers like Aristotle, William of Occam, and Roger Bacon—all detectives of knowledge, metaphorically speaking. The intellectual superiority of Holmes and Lupin in reasoning proves invaluable in their encounters with the darker, criminal aspects in the minds of their fellow human beings. The philosophers' attitudes toward the eternal questions of truth and knowledge, on the other hand, are equally important in the interpretation of *The Name of the Rose*.

As a detective, William of Baskerville displays the finesse of reasoning found in the models of Holmes and Lupin yet with a significant twist: By using the method of abduction, he tries to penetrate not simply the riddles of nature but also of the human psyche with all its deviations. In abductive reasoning, one chooses the hypothesis that, if proved true, will explain in the best way the given fact. For example, in the episode with the abbot's horse, Brunellus, William demonstrates to his young student Adso and to the abbot's men the superiority of his thinking after a series of simple but brilliant inferences.

William is far from infallible, as the numerous complications and plot twists of the novel demonstrate, and very often he relies on guesswork. Though his young pupil eagerly accepts his master's words as a pure exercise in superior reasoning, William reminds Adso of the importance of an educated guess: "There is no secret writing that cannot be deciphered without a bit of patience; the first rule of deciphering a message is to guess what it means" (Eco, *NR* 166). Yet William is only too human in interpreting what the great book of the universe and the people in it have to offer, and the people in this book seem to be the most treacherous variables. Despite being exposed to numerous instances of sidetracking and misdirection, he claims almost as a modern semiotician: "I have never doubted the truth of signs, Adso; they are the only things man has with which to orient himself in the world. What I did not understand was the relation among signs" (492).

Ultimately, William fails to understand the relation among these signs. In investigating the murders, William often finds explanations leading not to the truth but to a desired answer. As a philosopher, though, he surely follows in the steps of the giants of fourteenth-century scholarship, William of Occam and Roger Bacon, who introduced Aristotle to the Western world after centuries of Platonic and neo-Platonic philosophy, which the church strongly supported. In the tradition of these scholars, William is a skeptic who does not trust the senses as a source of knowledge, instead choosing to observe nature as the basis of empirical knowledge. Thus, in his conversation with Nicholas, the master glazier, William refers to the "veiled truths" in life that could be equally dangerous if unveiled by an unsuitable hand and dangerous if kept veiled for a long time. William reinforces the

importance of sight as a means of obtaining knowledge to Adso. He
says to his young student, with a trace of unholy but understandable
pride:

> [...] I have been teaching you to recognize the evidence
> through which the world speaks to us like a great book [... ,]
> of the endless array of symbols with which God, through His
> creatures, speaks to us of the eternal life. But the universe is
> even more talkative [...] and it speaks not only of the ultimate
> things (which it does always in an obscure fashion) but also of
> closer things, and then it speaks quite clearly. (Eco, *NR* 24)

If we interpret the abbey's *aedificium* as a universe in its man-made
plan, then the signs dispersed in it prompt further investigation,
which leads to the clues that the great book offers "quite clearly,"
though not quite easily, to William for interpretation.

In this manner Eco works into the novel the underlying issue
of doubting, of asking questions even after the message seems to
be decoded. Eco very skillfully introduces the motif of doubt and
doubting that runs conspicuously through the detective, the medieval,
and the postmodern readings of *The Name of the Rose*. This becomes
evident in the very foreword, where the author claims:

> In short, I am full of doubts. I really don't know why I have
> decided to pluck my courage and present, as if it were authentic,
> the manuscript of Adso of Melk. Let us say it is an act of love.
> Or, if you like, a way of ridding myself of numerous, persistent
> obsessions. (Eco, *NR* 5)

Thus the author passes onto the reader some of these obsessions: In
the search for a meaning or, rather, in the search for *meanings*, and
in the insecurity of interpretation, we give in to what Eco refers to
as the "drift or sliding of meaning" (*Interpretation and Overinterpretation* 1992). The text he offers to translate has a doubtful origin in
the first place ("an Italian version of an obscure, neo-Gothic French
version of a seventeenth-century Latin edition of a work written in
Latin by a German monk toward the end of the fourteenth century"),
and the doubts are not easily dispensed with in Adso's text itself

(Eco, *NR* 4). In this way, Eco subverts the traditional claim for authenticity of the text that many authors cherish. He puts into question not simply his own endeavor as a "translator" but also the very originality of the primary or, rather, the "tertiary" source of this translation. Adso, the original author, expresses similar doubts when starting his manuscript at the end of his "poor sinner's life":

> I did not then know what Brother William was seeking, and to tell the truth, I still do not know today, and I presume he himself did not know, moved as he was solely by the desire for truth, and by the suspicion—which I could see he always harbored—that the truth was not what was appearing to him at any given moment. (Eco, *NR* 14)

The theme of doubt directly contrasts the world of dogma and uniformed knowledge prescribed by the church and its Benedictine and Franciscan orders. For William the detective, however, doubt is the instrument that oddly leads into interpretation and decoding of messages in a universe of signs. For William the Franciscan monk, doubt is an orientation in a pseudo-holy, well-protected world of evil that the abbey unexpectedly turns out to be. For William the skeptic, doubt is a method of thinking in the tradition of Occam and Bacon that illuminates knowledge in dark, medieval times.

The ideas of order in the universe and a grand design behind human existence obviously support the church dogma of a creator and, by extension, his divine plan for man. Doubting any of these ideas inevitably leads to questioning of authority and power and dangerous secularization—something the church, for obvious reasons, cannot accept. Doubt seems to be the crux of the debate about Christ's poverty between the Franciscan representatives and the papal legation, a discussion that ominously cuts through the plot of *The Name of the Rose*. Doubt, however, is also embedded in the personal debates that William of Baskerville has with Abbot Abo and Jorge of Burgos. Thus, the epistemological search for knowledge arises on several occasions, each time a "dangerous" knowledge akin to heresy.

Both this approach to knowledge and the issue of authority center on the idea of doubt. If freedom is based on questioning the obvious and the accepted, then the interpretation of holy texts and doctrines inevitably leads to the corruption of established dogma. William, for example, clearly considers the Gospels open texts in the tradition of interpretation and, for that matter, in the tradition of the great book of the universe. This is how he answers Adso's question about Christ's poverty: "But the question is not whether Christ was poor: it is whether the church must be poor. And 'poor' does not so much mean owning a palace or not; it means rather keeping or renouncing the right to legislate on earthly matters" (Eco, *NR* 345).

The obvious danger the abbot perceives in such an interpretation concerns the church's authority, as when he warns Adso:

> And who decides what is the level of interpretation and what is the proper context? [...] It is authority, the most reliable commentator of all and the most invested with prestige, and therefore with sanctity. Otherwise how to interpret the multiple signs that the world sets before our sinner's eyes, how to avoid the misunderstandings into which the Devil lures us? (448)

The controversy between Abbo's words and William's earlier statement ("But the universe is even more talkative" [. . .]) clearly illustrates the clash between the dogmatic and scholastic worldviews. For William, doubt and interpretation lead one from knowledge to certainty and truth. For Abbo, the path instead runs from established truth to the controlled knowledge of the church.

Even more than Abbot Abbo, Jorge of Burgos is the abbey's staunch keeper of secrets and ultimate source of authority. Through his strict distribution of knowledge and control over the aedificium's books, Jorge represents the truth and certainty in the church's dogma. Jorge sees himself as the gatekeeper of the library, where secrets are preserved ("veiled") and "proper" distribution of knowledge is administered. That is how he defines his role in the universe of the aedificum:

> Preservation of, I say, and not search, because the property of knowledge, as a divine thing, is that it is complete and has been

defined since the beginning, in the perfection of the Word
which expresses itself to itself. (Eco, *NR* 399)

The issue of authority and the right to knowledge is exemplified
in William's debates with Jorge over the sinfulness of laughter and
Aristotle's book on comedy. William cannot accept Jorge's self-
referentiality of the Word despite its holiness, for it is just one sign
among the universe's many. He believes mankind should view all
signs together and that the library should be the place in which to
do so.

Of all human fallibilities, Jorge considers laughter a most
dangerous exercise of liberty that easily leads to doubt and, therefore,
to questioning of authority. Such a view well exaggerates the medieval
sternness and call for austerity of expression. We might interpret it
from the point of view that in *The Name of the Rose*, Aristotle's book
on comedy is the one that permits questioning of dogma and traditions that have regulated knowledge for centuries. William, however,
eloquently argues that there is a liberating and self-knowing aspect of
laughter that is beneficial to the growth of the individual: "Perhaps
the mission of those who love mankind is to make people laugh at
the truth, *to make truth laugh*, because the only truth lies in learning
to free ourselves from insane passion for the truth" (491).

This insane passion for *the* truth is what ultimately makes Jorge
a monster in a holy disguise: Deprived of ethical discrimination
between right and wrong, between the evil and the good in life, he is
easily transformed into an evil protector of truth for truth's sake. As
William makes clear at the end of the novel, truth is only commensu-
rate with the ethical and the good in our lives. Beyond the medieval
reading of *The Name of the Rose*, then, lies the ethical issue of pursuing
truth and knowledge: blindly and by all means, as Jorge seeks it, or
with the wholehearted human investment that recognizes the limits
of good and evil, as William finds it.

Eco also offers fascinating postmodern nuances in *The Name of the
Rose*. The questions of postmodern chaos, rules, and unpredictability
are incorporated in a text filled with references to other iconic literary
works. The already mentioned sources in detective literature, namely
Conan Doyle and Maurice Leblanc, but also Edgar Allan Poe and
Jorge Luis Borges, make the novel a treasure of intertextuality and,

at the same time, a challenging text for interpretation. This, however, follows once again Eco's ultimate belief in the power of interpreting signs through the labyrinthine aspects of the text. As he points out, *The Name of the Rose* is "a tale of books, not of everyday worries," and that is why it demands of the reader total absorption in hard intertextual work (5).

The labyrinthine dimension of the text is visually doubled in the labyrinth of the aedificium. On the surface, the chaos of doors, corridors, and mirrors that dominate the building have a deep, well-structured plan behind them. The man-made labyrinth also represents the labyrinth of language and referentiality Eco posits as the heart of communication. The layering of meaning—like the layering of corridors in the aedificium—is at the same time such a challenge and necessity for William that he admits, "It's hard to accept the idea that there cannot be an order in the universe because it would offend the free will of God and His omnipotence. So the freedom of God is our condemnation, or at least the condemnation of our pride" (492–3).

The universe of the labyrinth that Eco calls "an abstract model of conjecturality" (Eco, "Postscript" 57) is a challenge, yet a challenge that requires intellect and human understanding to make sense of it. Beyond William's skills in detection, his greatest skill lies in interpreting human nature and the universe it inhabits. In doing so, William often interprets the universe of language as the meanings it creates. If we accept that *The Name of the Rose* is a labyrinthine text, Eco will once again remind us of the multiple interpretations many excellent literary texts pose: Where do we stand as readers? From what perspective do we interpret? Is this *the* correct, ultimate meaning of the text? Or, at the end of the manuscript, do we prescribe to the tired Adso's opinion: "The more I reread this list the more I am convinced it is the result of chance and contains no message" (Eco, *NR* 501). Instead of offering a single message or no message at all, Eco, it seems, prefers to involve his readers in a game of interpretation. Readers can discover meaning in the many words and signs that fill Eco's labyrinth, and they have only to read them as they pass.

WORKS CITED

Cannon, J. *Postmodern Italian Fiction*. Rutherford: Farleigh Dickinson
    University Press, 1989.

Eco, U. *The Name of the Rose*. Trans. William Weaver. London: Vintage, 1998.

————. *Interpretation and Overinterpretation*. Ed. Stefan Collini. Cambridge:
    Cambridge University Press, 1992.

————. "Postscript to *The Name of the Rose*." Trans. William Weaver. New
    York: Harcourt Brace Jovanovich, 1983.

Rosso, St. "Correspondence with Umberto Eco," *Boundary 2*, 12 (Fall 1983):
    6–7.

PARADISE LOST
(JOHN MILTON)

"The Art of the Maze in Book IX
of *Paradise Lost*,"
by Kathleen M. Swaim,
Studies in English Literature, 1500-1900 (1972)

INTRODUCTION

In her study of the words *labyrinth* and *maze* in *Paradise Lost*, Swain focuses on Milton's "manipulations of the maze design within Book IX ... and other instances of *maze* words throughout *Paradise Lost* that prove to carry the same kind of implications with regard to the Fall and to Reason." Thus, Swaim addresses the labyrinthine language and the thematic and symbolic significance of the maze/labyrinth in Milton's epic poem. Accord to Swaim's introduction to this essay: "*Maze* is first concretely offered as Satan's physical and spatial form in the serpent. Descriptions shift from the adjectival 'mazy folds' to the static 'labyrinth' to the numinous vitality of 'surging maze.' Thereafter *maze* comes to describe abstractly and with poetic richness through incrementation, the verbal, psychological, and spiritual processes Satan employs to controvert the reason and death of Eve and thus

---

Swaim, Kathleen M. "The Art of the Maze in Book IX of *Paradise Lost*." *Studies in English Literature, 1500-1900* Vol. 12, No. 1, The English Renaissance (Winter 1972), 129–140.

of Adam. Satan creates a labyrinth of language and logic in
which, imitating him, Eve draws herself into loss."

⟨~⟩

A review of the uses of the word and image *maze* through Book
IX of Milton's *Paradise Lost* is an exercise in tracing the rich varied
complexity of one small but significant element in what is agreed to
be one of the greatest and most artful of poems. It is thus a glimpse
at some of the kinds of devices and effects a great poet can command.
Among these this review concerns itself with the focusing within a
tiny word of such pervasive and wide-ranging concepts and themes of
the whole poem as Evil, Reason, and the Fall, and with such artistic
matters as characterization, psychology, action, setting, and style
within the same small unit.

Maze has caught the attention of several earlier students of
Milton's imagery and poetics. Although the title of G.W. Knight's
essay on Milton, "The Frozen Labyrinth," suggests that it may explore
the materials under consideration here, in fact Knight undertakes a
much more generalized review of Milton's imagery and devotes only
a page or so to glancing at mazes. He observes that Milton's labyrinthine music ("the linked sweetness" of *L'Allegro*) often counteracts the
severity of the mechanical images and tone he explicates throughout
the poetry, and he distinguishes between positively and negatively
weighted mazes, the negative linking *mazes* with the Serpent, with
"distress and confusion" and "Life's difficulties" and frustrations, and
the positive as a symbol of harmony. He describes the verse and structure of *Paradise Lost* as "melodic, serpentine, rather than symphonic."[1]
In considering Milton's imagery and the myth of the quest, Isabel
MacCaffrey glances also at *mazes*. The labyrinth she equates with
"the difficulties of the dark voyage, the stage where the monster is
encountered and the deceitful sorcerer appears with 'baits and seeming
pleasures,'" "the dangerous crookedness of earth," and "the wayward
and misleading powers of error" in the human soul and embodied in
Satan as serpent. In a different connection she points out that the
intellectual maze of the fallen angels in Book II, 562–565, shifts into a
maze of action with "th' adventrous Bands" roving "in confused mark"
to first explore Hell.[2]

Although my concern is primarily with Milton's manipulations of the maze design within Book IX, we may glance at the other instances of *maze* words throughout *Paradise Lost* that prove to carry the same kind of implications with regard to the Fall and to Reason. Recalling Ovid's use of a river simile to describe Daedalus's maze (*Metamorphoses*, viii), Milton links *maze* words with rivers in *Paradise Lost*, II, 583–586; VII, 303; and IV, 237–240. Arnold Stein finds in the last mentioned of these instances a compression of the whole rhetorical argument of *Paradise Lost*.[3] The Falls of Satan and the Rebel Host offer instances of *amazement*: I, 278–282 and 311–313; II, 758–760; and VI, 198–200. In Book II some of the Fallen Angels beguile the time of Satan's absence philosophically "in wand'ring mazes lost" (561),[4] that is, in labyrinthine argument and verbiage. As in the instance cited below from Book IX, the rhetorical movement here coils back on itself in "Foreknowledge, Will, and Fate, / Fixt Fate, Free will, Foreknowledge absolute" (559–560). After questioning God's justice, Adam also invokes the *maze* image to describe intricate argument (X, 828–834), but what remains of Adam's Right Reason enables him to perceive the pattern of truth, despite delusive experience, and selfish twisting rationalizing. Clearly, here as elsewhere in *Paradise Lost*, Right Reason is the Ariadne's thread. In the description of the movement of the heavenly spheres in Book V as

> mazes intricate,
> Eccentric, intervolv'd, yet regular
> Then most, when most irregular they seem
> And in thir motions harmony Divine . . . (622–625)

the emphasis is upon the magnificent complexity of God's patterned universe, His ability to perceive and execute pattern beyond man's perceptive capacity, and the consequent human duty of faith. Thus, wrong reasoning may lead to "wand'ring mazes lost" but Right Reason or faith may prevent *amazement*, that is, becoming lost in the maze of delusive experience. Once fallen, spirits are amazed by manifestations of divine power (VI, 646–649) and Satanic power (X, 452–453), and Satan's resumption of his own shape at the "Touch of Celestial temper" "half amaz'd" (IV, 820) Ithuriel and Zephon. In his peroration Michael speaks of men's spiritual Armor and its capacity to "amaze / Thir proudest persecutors" (XII, 496–497). One should note also the "moon-loved Maze" of Nativity *Hymn*, l. 236.

In concentrating upon *maze* in Book IX of *Paradise Lost*, my purposes are at once narrower and (I believe) wider than those of the critics mentioned above. When narrating the Serpent's successful temptation of Eve, Milton manipulates the rich word and image *maze* to structure the concept of the Fall. Milton describes the serpentine form Satan takes as labyrinthine and the effects on Eve as amazement; moreover, Satan captures Eve in a maze of rhetoric and logic. Since *maze* words mark the stages of the sequence of the Fall at intervals throughout Book IX—lines 161, 183, 499, 552, 614, 640, and 889—it seems safe to assume Milton's conscious manipulation of this verbal design, the more so since the sequence of meanings moves steadily from the more concrete to the more abstract. *Maze* may be seen as capturing in miniature the concept of the Fall and the artistry of the epic.

The English word *maze* as used today refers primarily to what the Greeks and Romans knew as a labyrinth, that is, a constructed network of winding and intercommunicating paths and passages arranged in bewildering complexity, a usage recorded in and since Chaucer. Once entered, such a structure is virtually impossible to extricate oneself from without the assistance of a guide. Behind the English *maze* lies a more abstract and psychological conception, however. Skeat traces the etymology of *maze* to Scandinavian roots and suggests that the original sense was to be lost in thought. The *OED* records uses of *maze* in Middle English, dating to the fifteenth century, signifying vanity, a delusive fancy, and a trick or deception, and in Modern English, dating 1430–1819, signifying a state of bewilderment. As a noun *maze* seems to refer more to a design than a construction, and notably in uses dating from 1610–1742 signifies a winding movement or dance and even a floor modelled on the labyrinth whose mosaics guided ancient dancers through complicated figures.[5] In considering Milton's use of the maze concept, it is valuable to keep in mind what encyclopedias remind us of, that for Greeks, Romans, and Egyptians a maze was regularly a building of many rooms, especially one entirely or partly subterranean; while for the English a maze is generally a garden structure built of thick hedges, as at Hampton Court. As a verb the primary meaning of *maze*, with uses recorded from 1300–1870, is to stupefy, daze, or put out of one's wits, with secondary meanings of to be stupefied or delirious, to wander in mind (1350–1568); to bewilder, perplex, confuse (1482–1868); to move in a mazy track (1591–1865); and to involve in a maze or in intricate windings (1606–1654). The *OED* records uses of *labyrinth* as a structure from 1387 on and as "a tortuous, entangled, or inextricable condition of things, events, ideas, etc.," dating from 1548. Clearly, from well before Milton's time both *maze* and *labyrinth* carried abstract or psychological as well as concrete meanings.

The story of the labyrinth which the fabulous artificer Daedalus constructed for King Minos of Crete to house the Minotaur is recorded in Ovid's *Metamorphoses*, viii, and hence continuously available to European culture, not given a rebirth by Renaissance classical studies. This monster, half-bull and half-man—whose conception on Pasiphae Daedalus's invention made possible—required the sacrifice of seven Athenian youths and seven maidens until bested by Theseus who then escaped the maze with the help of Ariadne's ball of thread. Daedalus, too, in some versions of the story escaped his own punishment within the labyrinth in the famous ill-fated flight with his son Icarus.

It may at first seem curious that Milton should make virtually no uses of the myth of the labyrinth or of the principals involved in the myth, especially in *Paradise Lost*. The Columbia Index records only an oblique reference to Lawes's setting of William Cartwright's poem *The Complaint of Ariadne* in Milton's Sonnet XIII and one use of the "clue that winds out this labyrinth of servitude" in the notes to *Doctrine and Discipline of Divorce*. With flight and falling and the fate of pride such important images and ideas in *Paradise Lost* (as Jackson I. Cope has abundantly shown),[6] Icarus at least might be expected to provide some parallels to the Satanic host. The Renaissance viewed Daedalus as a mechanical genius, but also as a man of depraved character, jealous, deceitful, and guilty of betrayals, murders, and pandering to perverse lusts. Although his scientific interests make him something of a special case, Francis Bacon labels the labyrinth "opus fine et destinatione nefarium."[7] Ariadne's love for Theseus, too, is lustful, shameful, and quickly betrayed before her marriage to Dionysus. Although the maze itself may safely image the tangled passages of this world, obviously the precedents for escapes from the maze cannot image a Christian message. It is beyond question that Milton knew the myth thoroughly, but he uses only the generalized construction and the aura of evil surrounding the design and affecting all associated with it.

As this review of the word and image makes clear, a *maze* is thus a physical and spatial form and a process imposed upon or received by the intellectual faculty. Its opposite is straightforward form and movement and clear and secure reasoning. From its mythological origin as a place of physical and psychological punishment and certain danger, inhabited by a monstrous and unnatural embodiment of evil that feeds especially on the innocent, a place provoking loss of what is most valuable, life and reason and community, the term *maze* carries with it an aura of destruction, evil, and grim death. This dark aura attends *maze* throughout *Paradise Lost*. Since Milton's epic operates most richly by internalizing and rendering psychologically, spiritually, and poetically external facts of place, character, and consciousness, we are right in expecting the main threat of the *maze* to be against the life of the spirit or Christianized Right Reason. In *Paradise Lost*, IX, *maze* is at first concretely offered as the physical and spatial form assumed by Satan in the serpent. As the sequence of uses proceeds, *maze* comes to describe more abstractly and with a poetic richness that comes from incrementation, the verbal, logical, and spiritual processes Satan employs to controvert the reason and faith of Eve and thus of Adam.

The first and most concrete maze in *Paradise Lost*, Book IX, refers to the serpent's shape, and Milton's three descriptions of Satan in this form are incremental. At first there is only an adjectival suggestion of complexity. When searching out the serpent early in Book IX, Satan says

> in whose mazy folds
> To hide me, and the dark intent I bring. (161–162)

The labyrinth image is invoked more largely when Satan discovers the serpent:

> him fast sleeping soon he found
> In labyrinth of many a round self-roll'd,
> His head the midst, well stor'd with subtle wiles. (182–184)

Here are evoked the ideas of circularity, selfishness, and the subtle intellect as generating center. In this second description we become conscious of the labyrinth as a device by which or in which one becomes lost. In the third description of the Satanic the emphasis is on energy and magnificence

> So spake the Enemy of Mankind, enclos'd
> In Serpent, Inmate bad, and toward *Eve*
> Address'd his way, not with indented wave,
> Prone on the ground, as since, but on his rear,
> Circular base of rising folds, that tow'r'd
> Fold above fold a surging Maze, his Head
> Crested aloft, and Carbuncle his Eyes;
> With burnisht Neck of verdant Gold, erect
> Amidst his circling Spires, that on the grass
> Floated redundant: pleasing was his shape,
> And lovely.... (494–504)

In addition to the sense of mystery conveyed here, an image of pride emerges. "Rising," "Tow'r'd / Fold above fold," "aloft," and "erect" offer the aspiration upward of pride founded on the "circular base" of the self. The ambiguity and mystery characteristic of many of Milton's descriptions of what is experientially unknowable are present in the doubly-envisioned, even contradictory movement of "not with indented wave, / Prone on the ground" and "on the grass / Floated redundant." As before complexity, circularity, and intellectual energy and prominence are apparent. The sequence moves from the generalized adjectival of "mazy folds," to the substantive of static design in "labyrinth," to the numinous substantive vitality of "surging maze."

That *maze* is a spatial form or even a dance form as well as a physical form is shown as Satan winds his way into Eve's presence and recognition. In "tract oblique" (510) and "sidelong" (512), Satan veers and steers and shifts (515):

> So varied hee, and of his tortuous Train
> Curl'd many a wanton wreath in sight of *Eve*,
> To lure her Eye. (516–518)

This spatial movement is complemented by a rhetorical "tract oblique" in one of the richest instances of Milton's use of imitative poetics, as Satan approaches Eve:

> He sought them both, but wish'd his hap might find
> *Eve* separate, he wish'd, but not with hope
> Of what so seldom chanc'd, when to his wish
> Beyond his hope, *Eve* separate he spies,
> Veil'd in a Cloud of Fragrance, where she stood,
> Half spi'd, so thick the Roses bushing round
> About her glow'd, oft stooping to support
> Each Flow'r of slender stalk, whose head though gay
> Carnation, Purple, Azure, or speckt with Gold,
> Hung drooping unsustain'd, them she upstays
> Gently with Myrtle band, mindless the while,
> Herself, though fairest unsupported Flow'r,
> From her best prop so far, and storm so nigh. (421–443)

The language "floats redundant" (503) in "mazy folds" (161). Repetitions twist into and among each other: *he sought* (417 and 421); *wish'd* (421 and 422) and *wish* (423); *hap* (421) and *hope* (422 and 424); *Eve separate* (422 and 424); and *spies* (424) and *half spi'd* (426). The repetitions imitatively convey the serpentine and labyrinthine winding of Satan's approach, "now hid, now seen" (436). The action and delicate life of Eve and the flowers vacillate in complement: *stood* (425), *stooping to support* (427), *hung drooping unsustained* (430), *upstays* (430), *unsupported* (432), and *prop* (433). Clearly, with Satan's movement as with his form Milton's language invokes and combines the snake and the maze.

Shape conveys character and externals convey internals characteristically throughout *Paradise Lost*. As Satan himself is equated with a maze or trap, so Eve is amazed, that is, caught in a trap.[8] The *OED* records that *amaze* and *a maze* were often identified, and that the *a-* prefix may serve to intensify *maze* as well as render *maze* a verb. Eve's temptation is regularly punctuated with *maze* words, four in all. The first three of these we can glimpse quickly in a review of the narrative; the fourth shifts to Adam and marks the conclusion of the Fall. The "fawning" Serpent approaches Eve with elaborate circular rhetoric, flattering her "Celestial Beauty" (50). Eve is surprised at his speech—"Not unamaz'd" (552)—but not submiss. Satan continues with appeals not just to her personal vanity, but to her pride (with emphasis on potential godlikeness and aspiration) and appetite (especially through the senses of smell and taste) and profit or avarice (here in Eden the increase of reason). This long speech, lines 568–612, concludes again with elaborate personal flattery. Eve finds herself "yet more amaz'd" and "unwary" (614). But Eve is safe and reasonable in her response to the flattery of her person; she instantly labels Satan's peroration "over-praising" (615). Eve's conversation with the "wily Adder, blithe and glad" (625) draws her consent to approach the fateful tree.

> Lead then, said *Eve*. Hee leading swiftly roll'd
> In tangles, and made intricate seem straight,
> To mischief swift. (631–633)

This reminder of the spatial *maze* (recalling Isaiah 40:4, 42:16, and 45:2, and Luke 3:5, and in contrast with Ecclesiastes 1:15 and 7:13) amidst the rhetorical efforts at bewilderment is enlarged through the descriptive simile of "a wand'ring Fire" that "with delusive Light, / Misleads th' amaz'd Night-wanderer from his way" (634–640). But again Eve rightly apprehends the tree and has no hesitation remembering and retreating to God's commandment and the Law of Reason (652–654).

As above we saw the three descriptions of Satan moving from the generalized and adjectival to the vital and powerful, and then saw the physical maze shift into the spatial maze and that spatial maze rendered syntactically, so now we watch the psychological process of amazement poetically rendered, that is, rendered through the rhetoric and logic as Satan proceeds, rather than tagged for us by the poet in descriptive participles or simile. In his next ploy, Satan

> New parts puts on, and as to passion mov'd,
> Fluctuates disturb'd, yet comely. (667–668)

And after idolatrizing the tree, he builds the verbal and logical labyrinth which succeeds in amazing Eve. His argument is elaborately rhetorical, and consists of a barrage of quick rhetorical questions which he persuasively answers. He offers himself as example and pointedly interprets and displays his being. He uses loaded words [*petty* (693) and *dauntless* (695)], and condescendingly discredits the alternate case ["whatever thing Death be" (695) and "if what is evil / Be real" (698–699)]. The most dazzling display of his rhetoric and reasoning occurs in the cryptic syllogisms of lines 698–702:

> Of good, how just? of evil, if what is evil
> Be real, why not known, since easier shunn'd?
> God therefore cannot hurt ye, and be just;
> Not just, not God; not fear'd then, nor obey'd:
> Your fear itself of Death removes the fear.

The reasoning is amazingly tight, even for us who may pore over the text, yet to the listener apparently simple and sympathetic. Satan approaches the words *death* and *evil* tentatively, but exploits the terms *fear* and *just*, concepts equally unfamiliar to Eve. Many commentators on the temptation of Eve seem not to notice the precise nature of the flattery at work in this passage, and thus also the precise bait of Satan's toil. Satan treats Eve's limited reasoning powers as unlimited. When the words are so simple and apparently familiar, and the logical relationships so apparently inevitable, who can resist acquiescence? We are all more vulnerably vain in the areas of our weakness than in the areas of our strength. Eve is safe, reasonable, and self-possessed when her great beauty is flattered, but at a loss when her weaker reason is approached.

The tortuous path of Satan's labyrinthine persuasion is constructed skillfully out of the blank walls of Eve's linguistic naiveté. Even if Eve were on the brink of requesting a slower, simpler, fuller explanation of the argument, Satan shifts the grounds of his persuasion to admit and blame the limitations of mind that might prompt such querying. In this process, too, he confidently and falsely redefines the dangerous word *death*:

> he knows that in the day
> Ye Eat thereof, your Eyes that seem so clear,
> Yet are but dim, shall perfectly be then

> Op'n'd and clear'd, and ye shall be as Gods,
> Knowing both Good and Evil as they know,
> That ye should be as Gods, since I as Man,
> Internal Man, is but proportion meet,
> I of brute human, yee of human Gods.
> So ye shall die perhaps, by putting off
> Human, to put on Gods, death to be wisht,
> Though threat'n'd, which no worse than this
>   can bring. (705–715)

By building his argument upon proportion and hierarchy of being, matters that Raphael has explained to Eve as well as to Adam in Book V, lines 469 and following, and by recalling and distorting the promised future elevation of mankind, Satan again flatters Eve's intellectual powers and exploits her simplicity.

There is one additional and very significant stage in the process of Eve's Fall. She does not act merely upon Satan's persuasive instigation. Eve's nature is sensual, vain, and submissive, but also imitative. The latter tendency she exercises in her meditation, lines 745–779, and the model she imitates is what of Satan we have just seen: careful syllogisms based on words apparently simple but not understood and rhetorical questions with resounding, simplified answers:

> For good unknown, sure is not had, or had
> And yet unknown, is as not had at all.
> In plain then, what forbids he but to know,
> Forbids us good, forbids us to be wise?
> Such prohibitions bind not. (756–760)

The point is that in the persuasion to eat the fruit, Eve brings about her own downfall. After the Fall her imitation of Satan becomes even more obvious in her echoing idolatry of the tree. Whereas Satan had said: "O Sacred, Wise, and Wisdom-giving Plant, / Mother of Science . . ." (680–681), Eve begins: "O Sovran, virtuous, precious of all Trees / In Paradise, of operation blest / To sapience . . ." (795–797). A maze is a created structure, physical or otherwise, but although another may present one with a maze or force one over the threshold of a maze, in fact to become lost in a maze requires the expenditure of one's own energies. In a labyrinth of patterned logic, walled in by blanks and dead-ends of language, the effects of her innocence, Eve imitatively amazes herself, and paradise becomes lost. Further, when Eve returns to Adam after eating the fruit, she presents him with a maze into which he too draws himself:

> On th' other side, *Adam*, soon as he heard
> The fatal Trespass done by *Eve*, amaz'd,
> Astonied stood and Blank, while horror chill
> Ran through his veins, and all his joints relax'd. (888–891)

Unreason in Eve is negatively offered as a lack of judgment; unreason in Adam results from excess of passion. Even the word *amaze* builds upon the balances of reason and emotion that distinguish the sexes of our first parents.

On her own with the Serpent, far from her "best prop" and without the clue of Right Reason, the imitative Eve is caught in the mazy folds of Satanic design, circularity, dark complexity, and subtly self-centered and self-generating thought and energy. The story of the "paradise without" may end thus, and the verbal design I have been speaking of is contained by Book IX, but the final books of *Paradise Lost*, as we know, clarify suggestively the larger context of the fact of evil and Christianity working through time and show that "one just man" through labor and faith may achieve a higher destiny or through divine love and grace may escape the mazy error of this world, after defeating the monstrous enemy it contains, and gain a paradise within. *Maze* itself is a tiny fragment in the total design of *Paradise Lost*, but within Book IX I think it is clear that *maze* is a very skillfully manipulated physical, spatial, verbal, intellectual, and spiritual pattern in which Milton richly embodies the internal and external action of the Fall and an extended and suggestive commentary on the import of that action.

Notes

1. G.W. Knight, *The Burning Oracle: Studies in the Poetry of Action* (Oxford, 1939), pp. 62, 98, and 99.

2. Isabel MacCaffrey, *Paradise Lost as Myth* (Cambridge, 1959), pp. 188, 189, and 183–184. In *The Earthly Paradise and the Renaissance Epic* (Princeton, 1966), A. Bartlett Giamatti's regular placement of *maze* and *amaze* words in quotation marks (*passim*) suggests more than does the discussion of *maze*, pp. 303–306, the views developed throughout the present essay.

3. Arnold Stein, *Answerable Style: Essays on Paradise Lost* (Minneapolis, 1953), pp. 66–67 and 72.

4. The text used for all Milton quotations in this essay is *John Milton: Complete Poems and Major Prose*, ed. Merritt Y. Hughes (New York, 1957).

5. See Plutarch, *Theseus*, 21.

6. Jackson I. Cope, *The Metaphoric Structure of Paradise Lost* (Baltimore, 1962).

7. *De Sapientia Veterum*, in *Works*, ed. James Spedding et al. (Boston, 1860), XIII, 29. Bacon's interpretation of the labyrinth ("the general nature of mechanics") shows moral ambiguity. The clue for him is experiment, and he comments: "the same man who devised the mazes of the labyrinth disclosed likewise the use of the clue. For the mechanical arts may be turned either way, and serve as well for the cure as for the hurt and have power for the most part to dissolve their own spell" (p. 131).

8. Milton's treatment of *a-muse* in *Paradise Lost*, Book VI, 581 and 623, is analogous.

"The Second Coming"
(William Butler Yeats)

"The Secrets of the Sphinx:
The Labyrinth in 'The Second Coming'"
by Josephine A. McQuail,
Tennessee Technological University

William Butler Yeats's "The Second Coming," published in his collection *Michael Robartes and the Dancer* after appearing in *The Nation* and *The Dial*, is one of his best-known works and one of the best-known short poems of the twentieth century. The concept of the labyrinth is introduced in the poem by an obscure allusion to Dante Gabriel Rossetti's poem "The Burden of Nineveh." Harold Bloom has explored in depth the poets who influenced Yeats in his book of 1970 titled simply *Yeats*, but Bloom's attention to Rossetti is confined mainly to the chapter "Late Victorian Poetry and Pater," while William Blake and Percy Shelley are given entire chapters in which Bloom explores their influence on Yeats. Bloom concedes, though, that Yeats declared that Rossetti was probably a subconscious influence on himself and his contemporaries at the end of the nineteenth century and probably the most powerful influence (Bloom 28), even though Walter Pater, influential critic and Oxford professor, would seem the predominant contemporary influence on Yeats. One of the most powerful symbols of Yeats's poem is, of course, the "rough beast"—its "lion body" with "the head of a man" and "gaze blank and pitiless as the sun" (l. 21; l. 14; l. 15). The usual interpretation of this beast in the "sands of the desert" (1.13) is the Sphinx. However, as Nathan Carvo points out,

Yeats could be alluding to Rossetti's "The Burden of Ninevah"; Carvo even asserts that Yeats's poem is a "pendant" to the Rossetti poem.

Rossetti's poem describes the installing of "A winged beast from Nineveh" in the British Museum and records his thoughts as he observes the statue. It is useful to keep Rossetti's poem—and the similar "Ozymandias" by Shelley—in mind when reading Yeats's poem. Rossetti's "The Burden of Ninevah" explicitly identifies the statue it describes as "mitred Minotaur" (l. 13), a symbol of pre-Christian religion. In Greek mythology, the beast is imprisoned in a labyrinth created by Daedalus to confine it. Rossetti makes a change in the myth, however, apparently to suit the actual statue he sees: In the myth, the Minotaur has a human body and the head of a bull. Rossetti describes it: "A human face the creature wore, and hoofs behind and hoofs before" (l. 11–12). Yeats's symbol is well known as a description of the Sphinx, the mammoth statue of the lion's body topped by a human head. For Yeats, the Sphinx becomes the apex of his theory of human history oscillating in cycles. History, according to Yeats, spins out in cycles of colliding opposites, recurring every 2,000 years. Each millennium, history swings on its axis to its contrary tendency. Yeats conceptualized the cycle by envisioning two intersecting "gyres," like tornadoes or cyclones, spinning in opposite directions, the apex of which is in the center of its opposed gyre (the "rocking cradle" of Yeat's poem signifies the shift to the other pole). William Blake was the source of a part of this image, for he had the image of the "vortex."

There may be a connection between the imagery of the falcon and the falconer that form the symbolic center of the gyre of Yeats's own time, which is spinning out of control ("the falcon cannot hear the falconer") and other manifestations of the sphinx—there were various styles of sphinxes in Egypt, including one with the body of a falcon, the *Hieraco*-sphinx. The gyre, too, has other correspondences in Yeats's poetry: "Winding Stair" (a title, even, of one of Yeats's volumes of poetry), or spiral staircase, also is a symbol of the gyre, maze, or labyrinth. The year of the beginning time of the gyre spinning out of control in Yeats's poem would be the year of Christ's birth; the ending year would be 2000 A.D. (or C.E.)—in other words, the beginning of the twenty-first century. The originary date of the old gyre that intersected and superseded Yeats's own age was 2000 B.C.

(B.C.E.) In the early twentieth century the Sphinx was thought to have been made around this date. The image of the falcon unable to find the falconer in the middle of the circle, which it inscribes, is also reminiscent of the image of the maze, in the middle of which, according to the Daedalus myth, was the Minotaur. The Sphinx, like the Minotaur, then, is generally taken as a negative symbol in Yeats's poem. However, at least one critic, John R. Harrison in "'What Rough Beast'? Yeats, Nietzsche and Historical Rhetoric in 'The Second Coming'" argues that Yeats's poem actually "has been taken to mean the opposite of what he intended." Bloom agrees, pointing out that the first drafts of the poem refer not to a "second coming" but to a second birth—of the sphinx (Bloom 318–9).

"Turning and turning in the widening gyre"—the falcon is in a sense in the middle of an uninscribed maze, not able to find the "center," from which the falconer calls. The two central images of the poem are opposites: The Sphinx is the center of the second gyre, circled by the "indignant desert birds." The falconer is often associated with Christ. The Sphinx, on the contrary, is compared to the Beast of biblical Revelation. Apocalypic beliefs were widespread at this time, indeed, as they are at the turn of any century. The Sphinx, as a combination of animal and human, is reminiscent of the Minotaur. The Minotaur was the child of the Queen of Crete, Pasiphaë, and a magnificent snow-white bull that was sent to King Minos to be sacrificed. The king refused to sacrifice the beautiful bull, and to punish him, his wife, under an enchantment from Poseidon, fell in love with the bull and bore the child that was half-bull and half-human, the Minotaur. The Minotaur was monstrous, yet also, as the popular commentator on myth and the hero, Joseph Campbell, points out in *The Hero with a Thousand Faces*, the bull was a positive symbol, since Zeus himself had seduced Europa, Minos's mother, and Minos himself was the product of that union. Minos had prayed to the god Poseidon to send him a bull from the sea as a sign that he was the rightful ruler of Crete (Campbell 13). Minos thought the bull was too beautiful to sacrifice, and so he substituted an ordinary bull from his own herd to be sacrificed, angering Poseidon, who made Pasiphaë fall in love with the beautiful bull he had sent. In mythology, after the beast was confined to Daedalus' labyrinth, specially constructed to house the Minotaur, human sacrifices were made to him. Yeats's "rough beast" is not explicitly associated with human sacrifice, unless its gaze, "blank and pitiless as the sun," is a reference to the sun gods to whom human sacrifice was often made (Frazer 326). The Sphinx, in Egyptian culture, was also a positive symbol: The lion's body symbolized the strength of the ruler whose likeness was inscribed in the human head of the Sphinx. Nonetheless, the lines "everywhere / The ceremony of innocence is drowned" perhaps refer to child sacrifice, a theme in *Macbeth*, when Macbeth orders the murder of his rival Duncan's wife and children. The "blood-dimmed tide" of the first verse also is implicitly linked to the "rough beast" of the last lines.

The falconer of the first half of the poem could represent the destructive war that had just ended at the time Yeats drafted "The Second Coming." "The falcon cannot hear the falconer" implies that the bird, or tool of the human who calls it, has stopped responding to the human voice that calls it back, perhaps symbolizing the weapons of war that were used to such destructive purpose in World War I.

If the Russian Revolution is taken to be the referent of the poem, a similar interpretation can be made: The tool (revolution) meant to do the revolutionaries' bidding, to right historical wrong and oppression, escapes the control of its wielders and disintegrates into "Mere anarchy." Of course, also in Yeats's mind would have been the fight for Irish independence that was being waged at this time, to a large extent with the help of one of the most important people in his life, Maude Gonne. Famously, Maude Gonne—for whom Yeats created roles in his plays and with whom he was so obsessed that he would later court her daughter Iseult—was the great love of Yeats's life. In his poems, after she refused his proposals of marriage and vows of love, she is often portrayed as a destructive figure—a difficult woman who causes problems because of her beauty and her power.

Thus, we come to another tangential connection between Yeats and Rossetti, involving Rossetti's poem "Troy Town." Just as in several of Rossetti's poems Helen of Troy was an important symbol for Yeats, Helen herself was a product of a strange union of animal and human: Zeus, disguised as a swan, raped Leda, as another famous poem by Yeats, "Leda and the Swan," famously immortalizes. The phrase "Troy Town" or "Troy Fair" was synonymous with the notion of the labyrinth or scene of confusion (McGann, notes to "Troy

Town," 379; "Troy" *OED*). "Troy Town" is another poem about chaos and cultural extinction. For Yeats, the conception of Helen of Troy marked another crucial turning point in history.

When Yeats was drafting "Leda and the Swan," in fact, Lady Gregory—his friend and patron and a popularizer of Irish folklore— wrote of the poem:

> Yeats talked of his long belief that the reign of democracy is over for the present, and in reaction there will be violent government from above, as now in Russia, and is beginning here. It is the thought of this force coming into the world that he is expressing in his Leda poem, not yet quite complete. He sat up till 3 o'c this morning working over it, and read it to me as complete at midday, and then half an hour later I heard him at it again. (qtd in Foster II 243)

Indeed, in Yeats's "Leda and the Swan" note the lines describing the impregnation of Leda by Zeus: "A shudder in the loins engenders there / The broken wall, the burning roof and tower / And Agamemnon dead" (l. 9–11).

In "The Double Vision of Michael Robartes" there is another sphinx: "A Sphinx with woman breast and lion paw" (l. 18) "who "lashed her tail; her eyes lit by the moon/Gazed upon all things known, all things unknown" (1.29–30). This female sphinx is flanked by a Buddha, while in the middle dances a girl. It is from this poem that the volume containing "The Second Coming" gets its name: *Michael Robartes and the Dancer*. Yeats said that this poem and "The Phases of the Moon" were written in "'an attempt to get subjective hardness'" (Yeats, qtd in Foster II 126) to his philosophy. In mythology, a female Sphinx guarded Thebes, killing anyone who could not answer her riddle, a story Sophocles features in his play *Oedipus Rex*.

Another connection with "The Second Coming" is this line from "Leda and the Swan": "How can those terrified vague fingers push/ The feathered glory from her loosening thighs!"—those lines echo the "slow thighs" of the moving sphinx in the earlier poem, and the bestial mingling of human woman and the ravishing swan echoes the uncanny combination of animal body and human head of the sphinx. Yeats does seem preoccupied with pregnancy and conception in both "The Second Coming" and "Leda and the Swan": In *A Vision* he contrasts the virgin birth of Mary announced by the dove as told in the Bible to the rape of Leda in a section called "Dove or Swan," commenting, "I imagine the annunciation that founded Greece as made to Leda, remembering that they showed in a Spartan Temple, strung up to the roof as a holy relic, an unhatched egg of hers; and that from one of her eggs, came Love and from the other War" (Yeats qtd in Foster II 244).

The poem by Blake called "The Mental Traveller" was also an influence on this poem. Blake describes a recurring cycle where an old woman nails a male infant to a rock; he grows old and a female baby is born from "the fire on the hearth" (l. 43); she find her true love and drives the old man out; he wanders and finally wins a maiden. The old man pursues the woman "on the desert wild" (l. 75) "Till the wide desart (sic) planted oer / With Laybrinths of wayward Love" (l. 82–3). Once having captured the young woman, he grows younger and younger until he is once again a baby, and the cycle repeats. In his commentary on "The Mental Traveler" in *William Blake: His Philosophy and Symbols*, Yeats declares, "The Mental Traveller is at the same time a sun-myth and a story of the Incarnation. It is also a vision of Time and Space, Love and morality, Imagination and materialism" (II 34). Yeats's vision of human history as intersecting gyres also, in a sense, entraps humanity in its intertwined labyrinth. How close Blake's poem is to the substance of "The Second Coming" is shown in the reaction of the eventual inhabitants of the desert to the babe the old man becomes once again: "They cry the Babe the Babe is Born / And flee away on Every side" (l. 95–6). Even though Yeats's comments on "The Mental Traveller" were written almost 30 years before "The Second Coming," Blake's images seem to have gestated within him to express his own cyclical theory of history. As a comment on the miraculous birth of the woman from the old man's hearth or fireplace, Yeats declares: "From his mental fire a form of beauty springs that becomes another man's delight. He, like Tiriel, is driven out, having exhausted his masculine—that is to say, mental—potency" (Yeats & Ellis II 36).

Finally, Yeats's "The Second Coming" should not simply be taken as an indictment of Oriental, or Eastern, culture, as associations with the Sphinx might imply but as an indictment of Yeats's own culture and time. T.S. Eliot's work, particularly *The Waste Land* (1922), was a product of the same time period and may be seen as sharing themes with Yeats's poem—the living death of modernist or early-twentieth-century Western culture and the exploration of Eastern philosophies and traditions. As a final comment on "The Second Coming," the psychoanalytic critic Brenda Maddox contends that "The Second Coming" also expresses Yeats's fear of the impending birth of his first child. Though this interpretation may seem far-fetched, Yeats's philosophy, especially as evidenced in the poems discussed here, does seem to express itself in sexual terms. Yeats refers to the "geometry" of *A Vision* apparently without irony. The oscillation of the gyres works in an individual as well as macrocosmically. In his *Vision Papers* Yeats revealed, "The overlapping cones Man & Woman—Father & Mother being the two cones inverted into each other" (qtd in Maddox 84). It seems that his fellow Irishman James Joyce, in fact, lampoons Yeats's theory of gyres in the strange geometry of *Finnegans Wake* (see Joyce 293). Perhaps the aging Yeats is facing his own mortality in "The Second Coming" and is imagining the loss of his own individual identity collapsed in the new millennial swing to the gyre that will return forces more inimical to the individual personality than his present millennium, which he imagines dying out.

Bestiality, imagined rape, monsters and spirits—all of these things obsessed Yeats as themes in his poetry. Yet, from his beginnings as a poet in the late nineteenth century, Yeats found inspiration in myth and history, including the legendary labyrinth of Dedalus, "Troy Town," and the powerful images of the Sphinx. Indeed, Yeats's strength as a poet could be said to find its source in the "*Spiritus Mundi*" or collective unconscious, as Carl Jung termed it, or "dream associations" as Yeats himself put it in "A General Introduction for My Work" (*Essays and Introductions* 525)—the storehouse of images and ideas that darkly resonate with humanity's deepest impulses and preoccupations, from which he says in "The Second Coming," the image of the mysterious Sphinx itself arises. Yeats says in his "A General Introduction for My Plays": "I recall an Indian tale: certain men said to the greatest of the sages, 'Who are your Masters?' And he replied, 'The wind and the harlot, the virgin and the child, the lion and the eagle'" (*Essays and Introductions* 530). But this response is disingenuous: Yeats's ideas are not self-fashioned (perhaps what the spirit communication was meant unconsciously—and erroneously—to prove); he is, on the contrary, indebted to earlier artists and poets, like Blake and Rossetti, who also explored similar themes. The greatest of Yeats's symbols come from the creative center of the labyrinthine human mind, from which all great myths, and all great poetry, derive.

WORKS CITED

Blake, William. *The Complete Poetry and Prose of William Blake*. Ed. David Erdman. Commentary by Harold Bloom. New York: Anchor, 1982.

Bloom, Harold. *Yeats*. New York: Oxford UP, 1970.

Campbell, Joseph. *The Hero with a Thousand Faces*. 2nd ed. Princeton: Princeton UP, 1968.

Carvo, Nathan A. "Yeats's 'The Second Coming.'" *The Explicator* 59.2 (2001). Gale Expanded Academic ASAP. 7 Feb. 2008.

Damon, S. Foster. *A Blake Dictionary*. London: Thames and Hudson, 1973.

Foster, R.F. *W.B. Yeats: A Life*. 2 vols. Oxford: Oxford UP, 1997–2003.

Frazer, Sir James George. *The Golden Bough: A Study in Magic and Religion*. Abridged Version in 1 volume. New York: Macmillan, 1950.

Harrison, John R. "What Rough Beast? Yeats, Nietzsche and Historical Rhetoric in 'The Second Coming,'" *Papers on Language and Literature*. 31.4 (1995). Gale. 7 Feb. 2008.

Jeffares, A. Norman. *A Commentary on the Collected Poems of W.B. Yeats*. Stanford: Stanford UP, 1956.

Joyce, James. *Finnegans Wake*. New York: Viking, 1939.

Maddox, Brenda. *Yeats's Ghosts: The Secret Life of W.B. Yeats*. New York: Harper Collins, 1999.

Rossetti, Dante Gabriel. *Dante Gabriel Rossetti: Collected Poetry and Prose*. Jerome McGann, ed. New Haven and London: Yale UP, 2003.

Said, Edward W. *Orientalism*. New York: Vintage, 1979.

"Troy" Def. 1. *Oxford English Dictionary*, Compact Edition, 1982.

Yeats, W.B. *The Collected Poems of W.B. Yeats*. Richard J. Finneran, ed. 2nd ed. New York: Scribner, 1989.

———. *Essays and Introductions*. New York: Macmillan 1961.

———, and Edwin Ellis. *William Blake: His Philosophy and Symbols*. Vol. II. *The Meaning*. London: Bernard Quaritch, 1893.

ULYSSES
(JAMES JOYCE)

"James Joyce's *Ulysses*: Dedalus in the Labyrinth"
by Andrew J. Shipe,
Broward Community College

James Joyce's *Ulysses* is one of the most engaging and frustrating puzzles any author has constructed. Analyzing Joyce's tangles, we may wish for a badge of honor as reward for traversing the intricacy of its structure and following every narrow thread to its most trivial allusions. Or we may wish for an easy way out, a scheme or a skeleton key, a Daedalus to fashion wings, by which we can bypass the walls of actual reading. Before we look for the key, we must beware the fate of Icarus. The easy way out of the labyrinth has serious consequences. We must remember that the purpose of a labyrinth is not merely to hide something or to keep us from getting out, but also to force us to stop and ponder along the way. As Patrick McCarthy points out, "[W]e may begin *Ulysses* with the assumption that we will be spoon-fed information in an orderly fashion, but very soon we either abandon this assumption or abandon the book" (71). Thus reading the book is like entering the labyrinth, and so is navigating the book's intricate schema.

Joyce has given us two immediate references to the classical labyrinth: the name of Stephen Dedalus and the "schemata" that Joyce provided Carlo Linati and Stuart Gilbert as explanations (and promotions) of his work. The first correspondence, Stephen Dedalus and the mythological Daedalus, makes more sense in Joyce's preceding novel, *A Portrait of the Artist as a Young Man.* In that novel, we see Stephen's growth constantly through bird imagery:

> When the soul of a man is born in this country there are nets flung at it to hold it back from flight. You talk to me of nationality, language, religion. I shall try to fly by those nets. (203)

The escape of Dedalus is the promise of flying by those nets to create a new labyrinth: "I go to encounter for the millionth time the reality of experience and to forge in the smithy of my soul the uncreated conscience of my race" (252–53). Yet, at first glance, the Dedalus in *Ulysses* doesn't seem to fly very well. The Homeric parallels put Stephen in the position of a son, and we know what happens to the son in the labyrinth. Stephen in *Ulysses* compares more closely to Icarus: proud, unaccomplished, rumpled after a fall (15.4747–16.3). Forging a conscience is a complex endeavor. Conscience, initially defined as the knowledge of right and wrong, is an ever-changing entity. Perhaps forging a conscience in the smithy of one's soul means forging a labyrinth.

This leads to the more immediately fruitful second clue: Joyce's schemata for Linati and Gilbert both list "labyrinth" under "technic" for the tenth chapter, "Wandering Rocks." Joyce had provided these schemata—outlines of Homeric parallels, symbols, and narrative strategies—as *Ulysses* was near completion to close associates who were working on translations. "Wandering Rocks" is composed of nineteen vignettes of scenes in and around Dublin. Most sections contain references to other sections and sometimes even to other episodes in *Ulysses.* For example, "A onelegged sailor, swinging himself onward by lazy jerks of his crutches" (10.9–10), receives money from Father Conmee in the first section and reappears in the third section: "A onelegged sailor crutched himself round MacConnell's corner, skirting Rabaiotti's icecream car, and jerked himself up Eccles street" (10.228–29), where he would receive another coin from Molly Bloom.

The specificity of location Joyce provides invites us to trace characters' movements on a map: "Father Conmee crossed to Mountjoy square" (10.12), "Almidano Artifoni walked past Holles street, past Sewell's yard" (10.1101–02), "Opposite Ruggy O'Donohoe's Master Patrick Aloysius Dignam, pawing the pound and a half of Mangan's, late Fehrenbach's, porksteaks he had been sent for, went along warm Wicklow street dawdling" (10.1122–23). Some of the movements seem like characters stuck in a labyrinth: While Conmee reads from his breviary, he spots Lynch coming out of a hedge with a young woman—one way for the frustrated to attempt getting out of a labyrinth (10.199–202). Artifoni, Stephen's music teacher, misses his train while regimental band members pass with their instruments (10.363–67). Lenehan shows M'Coy where Tom Rochford had rescued a worker trapped in a sewage pipe (10.498–502), another promise of getting out of a trap. Ben Dollard assures Father Cowley, "We're on the right lay" (10.938)—that is, on the right path—and Simon Dedalus changes his route to go with them. These calculations would replicate Joyce's in putting together the episode. According to close friend Frank Budgen, "Joyce wrote the *Wandering Rocks* with a map of Dublin before him on which were traced in red ink the paths of the Earl of Dudly and Father Conmee. He calculated to a minute the time necessary for his characters to cover a given distance of the city" (124–25). Plotting the characters' meanderings on a map of 1904 Dublin shows the movements resemble a labyrinth, a maze that starts in one place and ends in another. Such a map reveals a more meaningful point: At the middle of the labyrinth, described in the middle section of the episode (the tenth of nineteen), reading a book, is Leopold Bloom.

The center of a labyrinth is significant. Penelope Reed Doob points out that the labyrinth often may harness an evil or contain a secret, the knowledge of which becomes a sort of epiphany. At the center of the labyrinth then is something important, meaningful. These theories make sense when we renew the Homeric parallel of a son's search for his father: Bloom is the father Stephen is searching for, providing the epiphany Stephen needs to continue his art. Before Bloom's central section, the last line of the ninth section is Lenehan's pronouncement: "There's a touch of the artist about old Bloom" (10.582–83). But we can take these conclusions even further. Bloom is at the center of *Ulysses* reading a book. A smutty book it may be ("*The beautiful woman threw off her sabletrimmed wrap, displaying her queenly shoulders and having embonpoint*" [10.615–16]), but—as the shopman points out—"*Sweets of Sin*. . . . That's a good one" (10.641). And it does lead Bloom, twice, to affirm, "Yes" (10.610, 613). Seeing Bloom at the center of "Wandering Rocks" reading a book that makes him say, "Yes," leads us to widen our scope to compare *Ulysses* itself to a labyrinth with "Scylla and Charybdis" and "Wandering Rocks" at its center (the ninth and tenth of eighteen episodes). Dermot Kelly claims that "Wandering Rocks" marks the end of a realistic interior monologue style that had slowly been called into question in previous episodes (20–23). If so, the center of the book is a significant place to investigate the novel's prominent stylistic features.

Contemporary reviews of *Ulysses* were split between praising the realism of Joyce's internal monologue and criticizing the artifice of Joyce's puzzles. Valery Larbaud, in his lecture on *Ulysses* at Adrienne Monnier's bookstore on December 7, 1921, said, "As far as we can judge, James Joyce presents an altogether impartial, historical portrait of the political situation of Ireland" (qtd. Manganiello 168–69). Edmund Wilson, in an early review of *Ulysses*, wrote, "It is, in short, perhaps the most faithful X-ray ever taken of the ordinary human consciousness" (qtd. Steinberg, *Ulysses* 3). Disparagement of *Ulysses* often invoked the argument that the book was too much a puzzle than a mimetic representation of experience. J.M. Murry was ambivalent, his praise tempered by what he saw as Joyce's hyperaesthetic disregard of truth: "*Ulysses* is a work of genius; but in spite of its objective moments, it is also a *reductio ad absurdum* of subjectivism. It is the triumph of the desire to discover the truth over the desire to communicate that which is felt as truth" (Steinberg, *Modern Novel* 104).

At times praise and scorn came from the same source. Virgina Woolf publicly praised the novel for the mimetic potential of Joyce's technique: "If we want life itself, here surely we have it" (123–24). However, by the time Woolf read the episodes in the second half of *Ulysses*, she was less laudatory, in the privacy of her journals. There she saw Joyce as ruined by "the damned egotistical self" (Steinberg, *Modern Novel* 70) and *Ulysses* as

> the book of a self taught working man, and we all know how
> distressing they are, how egotistic, insistent, raw, striking, and

ultimately nauseating. . . . I'm reminded all the time of some callow board school boy . . . one hopes he'll grow out of it; but as Joyce is 40 this scarcely seems likely. (Steinberg, *Modern Novel* 71)

To Stuart Gilbert, Joyce discounted the mimetic potential of his use of stream-of-consciousness techniques: "From my point of view, it hardly matters whether the technique is 'veracious' or not; it has served me as a bridge over which to march my eighteen episodes" (qtd. Steinberg, *Ulysses* 6). But as to the purpose of that march, Joyce was not altogether clear. In a letter to Harriet Shaw Weaver of June 24, 1921, Joyce expressed his own difficulty with the novel as a coherent whole:

> The task I set for myself technically in writing a book from eighteen different points of view and in as many styles, all apparently unknown or undiscovered by my fellow tradesman, that and the nature of the legend chosen would be enough to upset anyone's mental balance. I want to finish the book and try to settle my entangled material affairs definitely one way or the other . . . . After that I want a good long rest in which to forget *Ulysses* completely. (*Letters I* 167)

The tension between interior monologue and the artificial styles reaches its height in chapters nine and ten. What challenges the primacy of interior monologue in *Ulysses* is what we might call "exterior polylogue": the recognition that whatever language we use "within" our minds ultimately comes from the languages into which we are continuously socialized.

The transitional stage seems to be a point where Joyce acknowledged, to a point rare for a Modernist writer, the public side of discourse and the difficulty of replicating an internal monologue free from social, historical forms. If we look at the episode preceding "Wandering Rocks," we see this amalgamation of language as internal thought and social performance. Bernard Benstock observes that "Scylla and Charybdis" is "the most highly choreographic element of Ulysses. . . . On the small stage of the Head Librarian's office, the staff members are on their feet much of the time, moving about while Stephen—at times standing, at times sitting—holds forth on his Shakespeare's theory" (53). More so than previous episodes, the opening paragraphs of "Scylla and Charybdis" seem filled with stage directions: "the quaker librarian purred" (9.1), "Two left" (9.15), "Smile. Smile Cranly's smile" (9.21), "Stephen said superpolitely" (9.56), "He laughed again at the now smiling bearded face" (9.60), "Mr Best entered, tall, young, mild, light. He bore in his hand with grace a notebook, new, large, clean, bright" (9.74–75). The narrative pays particular attention to John Eglinton's extraverbal performance: "John Eglinton asked with elder's gall" (9.18–19), "John Eglinton sedately said" (9.58), "John Eglinton, frowning, said, waxing wroth" (9.79), "He [Best] repeated to John Eglinton's newgathered frown" (9.122), "John Eglinton laughed" (9.126). The theatrical emphasis of the narrative at times stretches the limits of standard English diction, forcing it to use archaisms and neologisms: "He came a step a sinka-pace forward on neatsleather creaking and a step backward a sinkapace on the solemn floor" (9.5–6), "Glittereyed his rufous skull close to his greencapped desklamp sought the face bearded amid darkgreener shadow, an ollav, holyeyed" (9.29–30). The performative aspects of this episode force the narrative strategy to digress into Gregorian chant, blank verse, and speech prefixes. In a way, the narrative is able to liberate itself from convention, but that liberation comes only with the appropriation of other conventions.

The abundance of the other conventions and the complexity of their appropriation continue to make *Ulysses* one of the most difficult novels readers have seen. But why is *Ulysses* so labyrinthine?

Let us remember that at the center of the labyrinth of *Ulysses* is "Scylla and Charybdis" and "Wandering Rocks." And let us remember that at the center of "Wandering Rocks" is Bloom, reading a book. McCarthy points out that, in complement to *Portrait*'s portrayal of the artist/writer Stephen as a hero, *Ulysses* presents Bloom as a hero (62–63). McCarthy argues, based on Marshall McLuhan's theories expressed in *The Gutenberg Galaxy*, that Bloom's literacy—like our own—launches his individuality and the breaking free from oral culture, which tends to be parochial and tribal (60–62).

Joyce seems to have enjoyed the difficulty of these writerly styles and allusions in *Ulysses*, as seen in his famous comment to French translator Jacques Benoît-Méchin: "If I gave it all up immediately, I'd lose my immortality. I've put in so many enigmas and puzzles that it will keep professors busy for centuries arguing over what I meant, and that's the only way of insuring one's immortality" (*Letters II* 521).

The difficulty of *Ulysses* fits into its historical context, as in the early twentieth century literary criticism moved from the public sphere of newspapers and journals to the bureaucratic sphere of academic institutions (Grady 28). This historical context provides a further opportunity to look at "Scylla and Charybdis," where Stephen discusses his Shakespeare theory in the National Library of Ireland. From today's perspective, Stephen's discussion may seem to take place in a rather austere, imposing setting, but in Joyce's time, the National Library was relatively new. The National Library was formed in 1876 with funds provided by the Royal Dublin Society as part of the British government's attempt to create scientific and artistic institutions open to the public, and the building in which Stephen holds his discussion did not open until 1891 (Casteleyn 92). Stephen's invocation "Coffined thoughts around me, in mummycases, embalmed in spice of words" (9.352–53) is not entirely accurate. The little "high culture" and scholarship available at the National Library were acquired secondhand (Casteleyn 93), while Old Irish manuscripts were more likely found at the Royal Irish Academy Library or the Trinity College Library, which held *The Book of Kells* and *The Book of Leinster* (Casteleyn 95, 123). The National Library was primarily a repository for popular books, acquired on subscription with other libraries (Casteleyn 93), as well as inexpensive acquisitions such as periodicals and newspapers.

The National Library was therefore by no means the most respected library in Dublin, but it was the most accessible (most of the others allowed only paid subscribers to borrow books), particularly to University College Dublin students, who had no suitable library of their own. Thus the library became not the book repository and meeting place for the elite but rather for working- and middle-class college students. So many discussions like the ones described in *Portrait* and *Ulysses* took place at the library that David Sheehy called it the "real Alma Mater" of U.C.D. students (qtd. Schutte 32n).

The first character who appears in "Scylla and Charybdis" is Thomas Lyster, the head librarian. During his tenure as director of the National Library from 1895 to 1920, Lyster, according to

Stephen Gwynn, "set himself to make every book in his library easily at command of any and every reader, but more especially of the young" (qtd. Schutte 31–32). His generous approach to the library's services meant Lyster "had no objection to hear it called jokingly 'the Library of University College'" (Fathers 235). The discussion in the library then is not a group of Dublin's elite discussing an academic discipline but a group of bright, young Dubliners discussing a popular playwright (even if that popularity was ultimately founded on two hundred years of criticism and the British educational project in the colonies).

Joyce recognized the popularity of studies of Shakespeare and used that popularity to "expound Shakespeare to docile Trieste" (*Giacomo* 10), thereby earning some much-needed money. Between his graduation from U.C.D. and his patronage from Harriet Shaw Weaver, Joyce made his living as the kind of independent lecturer and teacher that was becoming phased out in the twentieth century with the rise of professional, academic literary criticism. The newer criticism was different not only in its production but also in its emphasis. The criticism that the universities would develop would emphasize text, form, and language in order to produce skillful readers and writers capable of critical thought and nonviolent social transformation. This new criticism (and in its American manifestation in the 1930s, it would be called New Criticism) provided an antidote to the Romanticist author-as-hero notion. However, it is the older type of criticism that Stephen practices in "Scylla and Charybdis." Stephen combines the ideas of independent scholars like F.J. Furnivall and Sidney Lee with biographers George Brandes and Frank Harris.

If Stephen does not represent the cutting edge in academic criticism, neither do his listeners. Of Richard Best, Lyster's assistant, Schutte notes accurately, "Nothing that Best says in the scene indicates that he has more than the untrained enthusiast's appreciation of literature, and his enthusiasms clearly are confined to those deemed appropriate in a disciple of Pater and Wilde" (38). Lyster is the only one who responds positively to Stephen's theory, half of which he misses due to frequent interruptions calling him to his duties. But his comparison of Stephen's theory to the work of Frank Harris ("His articles on Shakespeare in the *Saturday Review* were surely brilliant") is not taken as the compliment he intends (9.438–41), and he disappoints Stephen by encouraging Buck Mulligan to contribute: "Mr

Mulligan, I'll be bound, has his theory too of the play and of Shakespeare. All sides of life should be represented" (9.503–05).

John Eglinton, Stephen's main addressee as editor of *Dana* and prospective publisher of the young artist's work, is the member of Stephen's audience most like Stephen (and Joyce), an independent man of letters who disapproved of the sentimentalizing aspects of the Revival: "The indefeasible right of humanity in this island to think and feel for itself on all matters has not so far been the inspiring dream of our writers" (qtd. Schutte 43). Stephen does flatter Eglinton by quoting from his book, *Pebbles from a Brook*: "[N]ature . . . abhors perfection" (9.870–71), but it is Eglinton who disputes Stephen's citation of *Pericles*, calls Stephen a "delusion," and asks if he believes his own theory. Stephen ultimately fails to convince his most important, and potentially his most empathetic, audience member.

Reading "Scylla and Charybdis" in the context of the shifting sites of late-nineteenth- and early-twentieth-century literary criticism provides a different perspective from how the episode has been traditionally read. Stephen's performance in the library is more than a prospective artist manipulating the English literary canon in order to make a place for himself in it. It is a play of the literary critical discourses prevalent in the late nineteenth and early twentieth centuries.

Despite the movement toward professionalized criticism that was anticipated and in some ways supported by *Ulysses*, reading the book is not an insulated, disengaged process. *Ulysses* forces us to investigate its classical references and seek interpretive apparatuses, while it also forces us to study maps of modern Dublin and the popular culture of the day. In sum, rather than a disengaged escape into an idealized past or a skeptical conquest over the present, *Ulysses* leads us to engage with other readers and attempt to refigure a common bond. In many ways, *Ulysses* presents a labyrinth not as a challenge from which we must escape but one with which we strive with others toward the center, toward the image of Bloom reading a book.

WORKS CITED

Benstock, Bernard. *Narrative Con/Texts in* Ulysses. Urbana and Chicago: U of
    Illinois P, 1991.

Budgen, Frank. *James Joyce and the Making of "Ulysses" and Other Writings*. London: Oxford UP, 1972.

Casteleyn, Mary. *A History of Literacy and Libraries in Ireland: The Long Traced Pedigree*. Brookfield, Vt.: Gower, 1984.

Doob, Penelope Reed. *The Idea of the Labyrinth: From Classical Antiquity through the Middle Ages*. Ithaca, NY: Cornell UP, 1992.

Fathers of the Society of Jesus. *A Page of Irish History: Story of University College, Dublin*. Dublin: The Talbot Press, 1930.

Grady, Hugh. *The Modernist Shakespeare: Critical Texts in a Material World*. New York: Oxford UP, 1991.

Joyce, James. *Giacomo Joyce*. Ed. Richard Ellmann. New York: Viking Press, 1968.

———. *Letters of James Joyce*. Vol. 1, ed. Stuart Gilbert. New York: Viking Press, 1966.

———. *Letters of James Joyce*. Vols. 2 and 3, ed. Richard Ellmann. New York: Viking Press, 1964.

———. *A Portrait of the Artist as a Young Man*. New York: Viking, 1968.

———. *Ulysses*. Ed. Hans Walter Gabler, et al. [Indicated with episode and line number.] New York: Random House, 1986.

Kelly, Dermot. *Narrative Strategies in Joyce's* Ulysses. Ann Arbor: UMI Research Press, 1988.

Manganiello, Dominic. *Joyce's Politics*. London: Routledge and Kegan Paul, 1980.

McCarthy, Patrick A. "*Ulysses* and the Printed Page." In *Joyce's* Ulysses: *The Larger Perspective*. Eds. Robert D. Newman and Weldon Thornton. Newark: U of Delaware P, 1987. 59–73.

Schutte, William H. *Joyce and Shakespeare*. New Haven: Yale UP, 1957.

Steinberg, Erwin R. *The Stream of Consciousness and Beyond in* Ulysses. Pittsburgh: U of Pittsburgh P, 1973.

———, ed. *The Stream of Consciousness Technique in the Modern Novel*. Port Washington, N.Y.: Kennikat Press, 1979.

Woolf, Virginia. "Modern Fiction." In *The Modern Tradition: Backgrounds of Modern Literature*. Eds. Richard Ellmann and Charles Feidelson. New York: Oxford UP, 1965. 121–26.

~~~ *Acknowledgments* ~~~

Chesterton, G.K. "*A Midsummer Night's Dream.*" *The Common Man.* New York: Sheed and Ward, 1950. 10–21. (first published in *Good Words*, Vol. 45 [1904]: 621–9).

Doob, Penelope Reed. "*Virgil's Aeneid.*" *The Idea of the Labyrinth: From Classical Antiquity through the Middle Ages.* Ithaca, NY: Cornell UP, 1990. 227–53. Copyright 1990 by Cornell University Press. Used by permission of the publisher.

Fletcher, Angus. "The Prophetic Moment." *The Prophetic Moment: An Essay on Spenser.* Chicago: University of Chicago Press, 1971. 11–56. Copyright 1971 by University of Chicago Press. Used by permission.

Hagan, John H. Jr. "The Poor Labyrinth: The Theme of Social Injustice in Dickens's *Great Expectations.*" *Nineteenth-Century Fiction*, Vol. 9, No. 3. (December 1954), 169–178.

Pavlock, Barbara. "Daedalus in the Labyrinth of Ovid's *Metamorphoses.*" *Classical World* 92.2 (1998) 141–57. Copyright 1998. Reprinted with permission of the editor of *Classical World.*

Quiroga, Jose. "*The Labyrinth of Solitude.*" *Understanding Octavio Paz.* Columbia, SC: University of South Carolina Press, 1999. 57–87. Copyright 1999 by University of South Carolina. Used by permission.

Swaim, Kathleen M. "The Art of the Maze in Book IX of *Paradise Lost.*" *Studies in English Literature, 1500-1900* Vol. 12, No. 1, The English Renaissance (Winter 1972), 129–140. Copyright 1972 by *Studies In English Literature, 1500-1900.* Reprinted by permission.

Vossler, Karl. "The Poetry of the *Divine Comedy.*" *Medieval Culture: An Introduction to Dante and his Times, Vol. II.* Trans. W.C. Lawton. New York: Harcourt Brace, 1929. 207–300.

215

Index